Praise for AGAINST THE WALL

"This courageous and compelling book by a Border Patrol agent-turned immigration-activist is essential reading to understand how today's heartless and abusive Border Patrol culture came into being and what needs to be done to transform immigration policy in America."

—Ruth Ben-Ghiat, author of *Strongmen: Mussolini to the Present*

"With painstaking honesty and the sharp eye of a natural storyteller, Jenn Budd chronicles her journey from oppressor to activist. She investigates and condemns the agency she once was proud to be a part of while simultaneously exploring her own complicity. As a woman in a heavily male-dominated law enforcement agency, a daughter of an alcoholic, a gay woman in a misogynistic, racist, and homophobic environment, she was determined to fit in, even at the expense of her own moral compass and mental health, ultimately numbed by the sexual violence and physical harm perpetrated on her by male colleagues. Jenn's story, so deftly told, is a powerful testament to the importance of confronting both our own personal demons and our country's corrupt systems of power. This beautifully written book at its heart is about atonement and the unwavering advocacy that can grow from self-forgiveness."

—Barbara Feinman Todd, author of *Pretend I'm Not Here* and founding journalism director at Georgetown University

"This book is a must-read for anyone who is interested in a first-hand account of how immigration enforcement plays out at the U.S.-Mexico border. Through this poignantly written book, Jenn succeeds in not only sharing and humanizing the face of childhood and adult trauma, but deftly connects these tragic incidents to the societal harms and trauma imposed on border and immigrant communities as the result of problematic national policies and politics. Jenn, who as a former Border Patrol agent witnessed corruption at our nation's largest law enforcement agency and who personally experienced sexism and abuse, illustrates why this agency, which regularly violates basic rights with impunity, needs to be brought under control."

—Vicki B. Gaubeca, a long-time human rights advocate and current director of the Southern Border Communities Coalition

"As Americans, we invest so much power and responsibility in our law enforcement officers. When that power is abused, it's our responsibility to stand up and speak out about it—and Jenn Budd does that so courageously in this compelling book. Please read it. Please internalize it. And please join Jenn in her incredible activism to make sure the abuses of power stop now and never happen again."

—Alyssa Milano, activist-actress-author of *Sorry Not Sorry*

AGAINST THE WALL

Jenn Budd

AGAINST THE WALL

Jenn Budd

My Journey from Border Patrol Agent to Immigrant Rights Activist

Heliotrope Books
New York

Heliotrope Books LLC
heliotropebooks@gmail.com

ISBN 978-1-942762-93-5
ISBN 978-1-942762-92-8 eBook

Cover photo by John Kurc
Interior photos courtesy of Jenn Budd and John Kurc
Typeset by Naomi Rosenblatt with AJ&J Design

For my wife, Sandi.

For all of those seeking safety.

CONTENTS

Foreword by Jose Antonio Vargas 13
Introduction 17

Part I

Game of Smiles 25
Honor First 32
Raped In 35
Getting By 47
Starting Anew 56
Journeymen 62
Honor First Is a Lie 82
Proving Myself 90
I was Running Away 103
Who Do You Love? 117
Coverup Central 120
Words Matter 123
Keep Your Mouth Shut 126
Who Needs Warrants 131
Indio 137
Coming Out 143
Who Am I? 148
Headquarters Intelligence 151
Quitter 170

Part II

Good for Nothing 181
Hiding 188
Untethered 192
Fifty-One Fifty 198

Part III

Listening 233
Speaking Up 242
We Deport Our Veterans 251
Missing 256
El Paso 259
Witnessing 265
The American Nightmare 274
Game of Smiles II 280
Pee Pee Tapes 284
Full Circle 287
Saving Lives 295
Border Patrol Rape Culture 303
Final Thoughts 317

Acknowledgments 327
Author Bio 331

“I swore never to be silent whenever and wherever human beings endure suffering and humiliation. We must always take sides. Neutrality helps the oppressor, never the victim. Silence encourages the tormentor, never the tormented.”

—Elie Wiesel, Nobel Prize acceptance speech, December 10, 1986

FOREWORD

"As a former Senior Patrol agent w/USBP who finally found the right time to stand up & say enough, NOW IS THE TIME TO SAY NO MORE! DHS asylum officers must refuse, resign, strike, whatever. You cannot obey an order that violates non-refoulement and endangers these families again."

I first encountered Jenn Budd on Twitter.

As a journalist who disclosed my undocumented immigrant status publicly in the *New York Times*, my timeline does not lack for people calling out the cruelties of America's immigration system.

But here was a former United States Border Patrol agent doing so—a white, Southern, gay woman, no less—her voice clear and uncompromising.

Define American, the nonprofit organization I founded that uses the power of narrative to humanize conversations about immigrants, reached out to Jenn about possibly working together. We called, and she responded above and beyond, signing on to be an ambassador for us—traveling to El Paso, Texas, to protest inhumane detention centers with our staff and leading a workshop on "criminalization of communities/narratives" for undocumented college students at a Define American event, among other things. Our collaboration led her to publish an op-ed in *USA Today* on anti-immigrant groups feeding Border Patrol agents misleading and false information. She writes: "Mr. President, the hatred of the [2019] El Paso shooting didn't come from our city. The Border Patrol union representatives began appearing at these [anti-immigrant] groups' conventions and meetings after the 9/11 attacks. The groups praised them, asked them to speak and called the agents heroes. Those reps then took the racist talking points and shared them with the entire Border Patrol via their union website. Today, the union has removed the links because they do not want people to know they are associated with these racist organizations."

Voices of American citizen allies—from various racial and ethnic backgrounds, scattered all across the country—are largely missing when we talk about immigration reform, possibly out of fear of eclipsing those directly impacted. But theirs are also necessary voices that politicians need to hear in order to come up with fair, common-sense, and humane solutions to our shared immigration problem. The uncomfortable but necessary truth is, there are no movements without allies.

Being an ally, however, can't just be a symbolic stand in solidarity with immigrants. It's more than just overlaying a rainbow on an avatar or posting a black square on Instagram. Allyship is about taking actions that make the fight for equality a little bit easier. To be a good ally, you have to be active. Allyship is futile if no one knows about it.

It's okay if you don't know much about immigration. (Jenn didn't until working for Border Patrol, and her memoir will help educate you on the issue.) What counts is presence: consistent, forceful, effective presence. Allyship forces you to look outside of yourself, to claim your rightful place with dignity while realizing that you're not the only person in the room. You never are. You never will be. Through her years-long activism—and now, through this daring and soulful book—Jenn models true allyship, inspiring her readers to examine what being an ally means. Nothing about her is performative, and she doesn't sacrifice the truth for an allegiance to any specific agenda, criticizing the Trump administration's horrendous immigration policies, for example, but then also holding the Biden administration accountable for the promises it made. Her firm and fearless voice, informed by her insider expertise and personal LGBTQ+ experience, is invaluable. Her perspective on the U.S. Border Patrol is unprecedented.

In the summer of 2014, when Obama was president, I traveled to McAllen, Texas to participate in a vigil welcoming arriving Central American refugees, most of whom were children fleeing for their lives, not realizing that I would likely be unable to leave the city without "papers." Border Patrol agents handcuffed me at the airport, removed my belt and shoelaces to prevent me from killing myself, and passed me around the McAllen Border Patrol Station like a hot potato. I spent time in a 20' x 30' cell with about 25 inconsolable boys. I spent time in a smaller cell alone, just me and a cold cement floor. Before being released to a throng of reporters, I asked a Border Patrol agent why he became one. "The benefits are solid, man," he replied.

Whereas my experience with Border Patrol was surreal more than anything, Jenn's was downright harrowing. On top of xenophobic indoctrination and human rights abuses, she paints a toxic culture of sexual harassment, misogyny, homophobia, and corruption. What you are about to read is at once deeply personal and profoundly political, allowing us access to Jenn's very raw and vulnerable mea culpa; explaining—though never excusing—her own participation in the brutal inhumanity of America's broken and cruel immigration system; and illustrating an important through-line: Immigration injustice is gender injustice is racial injustice is workplace injustice, and we cannot overcome any of it alone. As Maya Angelou said: "No one of us can be free until everybody's free."

—Jose Antonio Vargas, founder of Define American, and author of *Dear America: Notes of an Undocumented Citizen*

INTRODUCTION

I was once a young Southern girl who believed in God and country. I went to church every Sunday and said the Pledge of Allegiance every school morning with my little hand pressed firmly against my chest. My family and friends called me Jenny. I played softball and basketball rather poorly, read Nancy Drew Mysteries, watched *Looney Tunes* on Saturday mornings and listened to Casey Kasem's Top 40 Countdown on the radio every week. My family had picnics at Monte Sano State Park, went to hockey games, rodeos, and the Ringling Brothers and Barnum and Bailey Circus at the Warner Von Braun Civic Center every time they came to town.

As a teenager, I rode horses and hopped onto the back of motorcycles any chance I got. I drank beer and did a little bit of weed from time to time. I liked studying French, biology, law, and going to concerts and football games. I got my first tattoo of a black panther on my left ribcage from a Vietnam veteran when I was just seventeen. As a senior in high school, you could find me at the large public library in Huntsville, Alabama, curled up in a chair until the librarians finally made me leave late at night.

I often checked out a few library books for the week, stashing them in my car for those nights when my mother was too far gone for me to handle. I locked my doors, rolled my windows up, and read or did my homework just to find peace. I fell asleep listening to punk rock, jazz, or old Ike and Tina Turner cassettes I'd made on my father's stereo. I often woke with the headphones still on my head, the double A batteries of my Walkman long dead. Feeling tired and achy from sleeping in the car was a small price to pay for being safe from my mother's anger.

I was once an Auburn student, an Auburn Tiger, a War Eagle. In college I studied law with an eye towards being a civil rights attorney. Afraid to return home, fearful of admitting who I was, I chose a different path at the last minute upon graduating at the top of my class in the school of law. I felt deeply that I had to serve my country, put on a uniform, and sacrifice some of myself for our democracy, our freedoms, our rights. It was an experience I looked forward to and trusted in because I believed that ours was an exceptional country, and I felt blessed and proud to be an American.

I trusted in that and had faith in it.

I was once a federal agent, a Border Patrol agent. A social security number to my employer. No more, no less. To Campo station, my assigned duty station, I was a star number or a call sign. It changed as I rose in rank. My last one was charlie-one-seven-eight. It is the one that sticks in my mind the most. If you wanted my attention over the radio, you would say my star number and I would repeat it back to you, so you knew that I was listening. If we were in the station, you'd likely call me Budd. First names were reserved for friends, and I had only a handful of them. If I wasn't within earshot, you'd likely call me bitch or cunt. Zena was only popular once they all discovered I was gay, and even then, only with a handful. Bitch or cunt was more likely, and I told myself that it suited me just fine. It was the price women paid to be in law enforcement.

I once wore the Border Patrol green uniform with pride, the sight of which made grown men run from me through the highest of mountains east of San Diego in the middle of the night. I was proud to wear that uniform even though it made migrant women sit still and tremble, made their children cry out in fear and sometimes wet their pants. The one that made the white people in the east county of San Diego profess their undying love and exclaim, "Thank you for your service!" The same uniform that made conservative politicians ask to have their picture taken with me, because a female agent was such a rare sight. The one I thought would provide me with structure, honor, justice, righteousness, and pride. The uniform that I naively thought could protect me and keep me and my country safe.

I once spoke in another language. No, I am not speaking of the Spanglish barking orders they taught us in the academy, but the codes and acronyms used by law enforcement agencies across the country. The ten-fours and ten-nineteens, EWI, LAPR, I-826, 1326, and code fours rolled from my mouth fluently, most comfortably back then. So much so that I sometimes forgot that not everyone understood or used them. Like binary code, it's a language that intentionally strips away any sort of humanity or sympathy.

I was once a master woodworker, a custom furniture and cabinet designer and maker. Folks from all over called on me to design and handmake their kitchens, tables, Murphy beds, libraries, entertainment centers. I hand-selected the raw woods to use: sapele, padauk, elm, walnut, ash…I knew them all by look, by feel, by the smell once the blade cut into them.

I used table and panel saws, line borers, edge banders, drill presses, joiners, biscuit cutters, Kreg machines, sealers, lacquers, and varnishes. It was a finished product in the end, a conclusion I'd never experienced in my other line of work. It gave me a sense of satisfaction and a feeling of worth I so desperately craved. No hurt, no pain of life-long struggles ever entered the transaction like before. No questions of morality or ethics to ponder. It was a simple request, a quote, a job well-done.

And you could have just called me Jenn then, because I preferred to forget all about my other life, the federal one in green that was. I wanted to just walk away from it all, as if it'd never happened. I kept all those memories tucked away behind a wall in my head that I'd been building since I was a small child. My commemorative badge, my original black leather gun belt, a few gun holsters, a pair of handcuffs, an accommodation or two, all my excellent or outstanding evaluations, less than a handful of pictures, my name plate that read "J H BUDD"—it all sat in a plastic box under the house. It was from a person I no longer was, from a life that I was not entirely sure I understood anymore.

No, I preferred to think of myself as someone who worked with her hands for a living, who got them dirty and full of splinters. I was producing a product people needed and wanted. It was honest work, but not easy by any means. There was no security of a government agency, no easily affordable healthcare, no sick leave, no vacation time, no excuses for when things went wrong.

It scared me to give up the security of my Border Patrol career even though I knew that I desperately needed to leave it. I couldn't lie to myself anymore about what the agency was, what we did, what I did. I craved honest work, wanted to see if I could do it, wanted to challenge myself, even if it originally started as a necessity, a minimum wage job after I turned in my badge and gun. Woodworking started as simply somewhere to be, somewhere other than the border. My soul needed a rest, a mending from the Patrol. Truth was, I'd long ago stopped believing in the Border Patrol, even while I still wore green.

I was once lost in my memories. My thoughts had become mostly nightmares and daymares, bits and pieces from the past, sometimes mixed in together in the strangest of ways. Standing at the helm of a ship in my green uniform and my cowboy hat, I hear my mother complaining about my dad, my sister scared and crying in the corner, an agent yelling at me to go after the load vehicle and the ship was now a Border Patrol sedan, faster and faster…everyone just needed to calm down, just calm the fuck down. It would all be okay eventually if we just slowed down, if we just took a step back and figured it out. We didn't have to chase migrants until they crashed or push them out to the desert. There had to be a better way.

I was once a patient in a mental ward. When it was completely dark, and I'd thought I was done, when there was nothing left to grab onto, nothing to excuse my choices and actions, when I had nothing but a hospital gown and two hands that no longer worked, I stared at the ceiling tiles for days…that was not the end but the beginning. It was the start of listening, of hearing, of accepting, of feeling, of loving, of seeing, of being. It was the start of my healing, of tearing down my mental walls that hid the memories I feared.

It was there that I started to see my walls and how they prolonged the hurt, how I'd built and maintained them, how I'd thought they could keep me safe, how I thought they made me strong. The wall I had mentally erected to hold my family back was the first, the strongest. The second wall cornered from the first and helped keep me safe in the Patrol. Only with relentless trauma and drama could I maintain them. It was only when I left the agency that I began to think that all I knew how to do was build walls. To keep them standing, I had to make everything a threat, treat everyone as a danger to my wellbeing and safety. The higher I went, the more wall I constructed, the less safe I felt. Not facing my problems, not experiencing and working on issues, labeling everything as a threat as the agency had drilled into me, all my training in life and the Patrol made it so that I could not recognize the real dangers from the normal non-threatening behavior anymore.

I was so angry. I hated myself most of all.

There was so much on the other side of that wall just waiting to burst forth. The memories and the pain that I tried desperately not to recognize all those years never went away. It waited patiently until everything felt so big, so painful, until the walls began crumbling and I had no choice but to deal with it. I had to go back and experience it, feel it, understand it, admit it.

Accepting responsibility for my actions, for who I had become, the tearing down of those walls and making myself vulnerable, facing my faults and those I have harmed was and still is more difficult than anything I have ever endured. It is also the most meaningful and rewarding work that I have ever done.

Content warning: This book describes in detail many subjects associated with trauma: rape, suicide, child abuse, racism and police brutality. Readers should be aware that racist terms are used to tell this story. To omit them would be dishonest.

Some names have been changed to protect the innocent and the guilty, as this book is not written for personal revenge, but for institutional reform and accountability.

If you or someone you know is suffering from suicidal ideations, please know that it does get better. Please contact the National Suicide Prevention Hotline for help at 1-800-273-8255.

A minimum of ten percent of any profits I receive from this book will be donated to organizations assisting migrants.

PART I

228th Border Patrol Graduation,
GLYNCO FLETC, November 1995

GAME OF SMILES

When I speak today about Border Patrol rape culture, and how endemic it is to the agency, I remember the initiation I experienced as a member of the 288th Session of the U.S. Border Patrol Academy. It was the first week in July of 1995, late in the evening by the time we all gathered in one of the townhomes designated for female trainees. We sat together on the two twin-sized beds. The mattresses were thin and smelly from the hundreds of trainees who'd slept on them before us. Other women from the class sessions ahead of ours sat on the floor.

There was nothing formal about it. It was not a part of the curriculum, not an official act. There was nothing on the syllabus about Raping 101. The woman speaking wasn't even an agent yet herself. She was just a trainee like the rest of us, there to do the same that'd been done for her when she had arrived months earlier. If we made it, and that would be a big if because no more than two women from the same class ever seemed to graduate from a Border Patrol academy, we would be obliged to do the same. She made us swear on it.

In 1995, the Border Patrol Academy was held at a FLETC (pronounced FLET-CEE) training center located on an old military base in Georgia. Being a Federal Law Enforcement Training Center meant that there were other agencies training there as well: US Park Police, Immigration and Naturalization Service, US Customs Service, Bureau of Prisons, and many more including some foreign police agencies. Each had its own classrooms and living quarters. Sometimes we shared. My townhome was for the Immigration Inspectors that worked at the ports of entry. This was pre-9/11, before the Department of Homeland Security was created, and these agencies were under the old Immigration and

Naturalization Service, or INS. Customs and Immigration Inspectors would become CBP (Customs and Border Protection) in 2003 with the Border Patrol remaining separate but falling under CBP. I was the only Border Patrol trainee in that townhome just because that's the way it worked out. They had a room, and my agency needed it.

"Don't ever leave your drink alone," she said.

"There's a bar?" my new classmate Karen said in disbelief.

"Hell yeah," she said. "You ain't going to have a bunch of cops with no beer. They call it the gay bar because it's all guys." Our class had only six women out of sixty-five or so. We got her point. "If someone offers you a drink and you hadn't had your eye on it the whole time, you best not drink that shit. They'll put one of them date rape drugs in it. Next thing y'all know, you wake up in your room wondering what happened."

"Y'all telling us that rape is going on in this campus? That an academy full of law enforcement officials, soon to be law enforcement officials, has a bunch of rapists on it?" Karen said, astonished. I could tell she took no shit from anyone. She was a tall, thin woman who looked like she'd been in a few fights. Her North Carolina accent was still strong even after years of living in San Diego, California. I liked it, liked her tone and thought my being born in the same state lent some cause for us to be tight.

"Yeah, that's what I'm saying."

"Well, go on then," I urged. "We got class first thing."

"If your instructors ask you out, and you don't go, they'll fail your ass. If it's an instructor from another class, same thing. They're always talking and gossiping about us. That's just the way it is here. You gotta get along, 'play ball' they call it, and lots of times that means putting out. And it ain't just the instructors. Don't let the male trainees in your rooms. Don't you go near their places either, less you lookin' to be raped and all." Her classmate nodded in agreement.

"Why don't women report this?" Karen asked the obvious.

"Who do you think's coming on this base? They tell y'all not to call outside law, right?"

She was right—they did say that they preferred to handle issues like disagreements or fights between agents within the agency. It was a federal academy they said; the feds would handle any problems. "That's to keep it all hush-hush. Besides, it's gonna be their word against y'all, and y'all know which side they'll take."

We did. Just as our sisters knew, our mommas and their sisters knew. Hell, all women knew. Like an animal knows things instinctively to survive, we all knew. I reckoned that was what it was, surviving. We were no different than the generations before us. Different individuals, different stories, different cultures…sure, but it was the same story as old as time.

"My biggest warning to y'all is that you especially stay away from the parties on graduation nights. Instructors get together with male trainees in their classes for graduation. They target a woman at the party, drug her, get her back to their place and play the Game of Smiles. They're all sittin' around a table with their pants off and they push the girl under. She's forced to give them blow jobs and the first who smiles, has to drink. If she passes out, they gang-rape her."

"Oh, come on!" I said in disbelief.

"I ain't lying!"

"Why don't she just bite their dick off?" Karen asked, and we laughed.

"This ain't no joke."

Just then, several women from the Immigration Inspectors popped in. "She's not lying to y'all. Our instructors warned us about staying away from the Border Patrol living quarters."

"Then they all take turns raping her. Look y'all, women this happens to don't come forward. They're gone, like the very next day. They're ashamed. They feel like they were stupid for drinking too much. Likely don't know they were drugged. Who are they going to call? They just pack up their shit and leave," she said.

"Y'all know women this happened to?" I asked.

"Yeah, they're gone before we get up the next day. They call it the Game of Smiles. Y'all gotta look out for each other. Don't let each other alone with them. This is a man's agency. They don't want us here. The only thing they'll allow you to do is file EEO."

"What's an EEO?"

"Equal Employment Opportunity complaint. You file that shit and they'll take years to investigate, and your training will stop while they sort the whole thing out. You'll be out of a job, and he'll be a supervisor before they decide on your case."

* * *

In our first week, they separated us. The men and the women, that is. The six of us females were taken to a small room. The men were left in our larger classroom that resembled a small auditorium. A center aisle split the seats into two groups. The instructors said they wanted to discuss hairstyles and makeup with us. This required a female agent, which intrigued me because we'd yet to encounter such a thing. Instructors said the training would be no different for us than it was for the guys, but I was curious to know if a female agent would describe it the same way when none of the male agents were around.

Whatever ease I felt at the sight of her quickly evaporated when she opened her mouth. She coldly read in a monotone voice from an agency memorandum that dictated the policy when it came to our hair and makeup: off the collar, no heavy makeup, no big earrings, no looped earrings, no bracelets, and no necklaces. A small wedding ring would be allowed, as well as a discreet religious necklace. She left as quickly as she'd come in, taking her large looped earrings and bright red lips with her and closed the door behind her. I couldn't help but feel like she hadn't wanted to give the presentation at all. Female agent camaraderie didn't exist, the instructing agents insisted. It seemed that much was true. We were all the same they kept repeating; there were no male or female agents in the Border Patrol, only agents. Though had that been true, I failed to see why we needed to be separated in the first place.

"What the fuck was all that bullshit about?" Karen asked.

We stayed in the little room for another thirty minutes while we waited for the guys to finish whatever it was that they were talking about. Our male classmates refused to tell us what it had been after we returned to our chairs. Things had changed though. It was more than a physical separation. We were divided in a way we'd not been during the first few days, and I could not tell what or why it was, but Karen, and the four others could feel it too. Whatever it was, it was not a good feeling. It was difficult to explain. It didn't necessarily feel dangerous, but we certainly were not as welcomed as we were before.

* * *

"What in God's name was that all about today?" I asked Zarkowski as he plopped down on my bed while I folded my clothes and put them away.

We had spent the time flying from San Diego to the academy getting to know each other. He was half American, half Colombian. His daddy was a preacher and had a church there. He seemed strong in faith and gentle in speech. He was confident of his choice to join the Patrol and stated that what we were about to do was a blessed and honorable thing. Serving our country and protecting its citizens, working in desolate border areas was something akin to his father's work. And though I'd long ago given up on God, I let him pray for me, for us and our class. Mostly because I could tell he was a true believer, partly because I had never been entirely sure about my religious opinions and thought I could use any help offered.

He said our instructors, our all-male instructors, told them women didn't belong in the agency. The Border Patrol was no place for us. It was too rugged, too dangerous. The work was difficult, and the terrain was punishing. We wouldn't be able to keep up physically on the long hikes, and chances were pretty good that we'd get our asses handed to us in fights. He sat on the end of my bed and looked down at the frayed blanket that he twirled in his fingers. It seemed a confession of sorts to me. He was uncomfortable with the words he heard and was now repeating.

"This one guy, you know, the older guy, balding. He's white." I nodded to say I knew of him. "Well, he asked what would happen if a woman was asking for it."

"What'd they say?"

"They laughed it off. I think we were all surprised. But then he asked it again, like all serious and stuff, 'I mean, what if she's wearing a short little skirt, walking down the street just asking for it?'"

I knew men talked like this, that many men and some women still subscribed to this idiocy that the way a woman dressed somehow gave others the right to rape her. It was not foreign to most women I knew or to me. I just didn't realize that men talked like this in a professional setting. Certainly not a law enforcement official, especially not a federal law enforcement official.

"They put him in his place, right?"

"No. They laughed! Then some guys in the class laughed, and the instructors said he ought to be careful because there's no way women could graduate the academy without cheating. They said women can't pass the obstacle course because it's all upper body strength, and that to run the mile and a half in time, you'd have to be crazy physically fit if you're a chick. They said women in the Patrol cheated by filing false sexual assault allegations against the men so that the agency will let them graduate in exchange for not filing charges."

He looked up at me as if I had an idea of what he was talking about. "And what do you think?"

"I don't know. I don't think you'd do something like that."

"I wouldn't," I assured him. "So, all the female agents had to do this to get their jobs? I'm smelling some bullshit. Why did they even bother to hire us in the first place if they didn't think we could hack it?"

I didn't know what the physical requirements were yet. I was overweight by twenty or so pounds but had assumed I'd lose it easily enough with all the physical training we were required to do. Georgia in July would guarantee that without even trying. A minute in that thick humid air and you could see sweat beading up on your forearms and feel it rolling down the small of your back. Gnats and little sweat bees buzzed around, drawn to the salty taste of our skin. Those who locked their knees while standing in military formation would eat dirt before too long as it cut off circulation to their brain and caused them to pass out. Some classmates didn't even make it a month before their lungs swelled up with respiratory infections. They'd come from the dry deserts of California and Arizona and had no experience with the moist heat of the South that I had known my whole life. I figured I could lose a pound just walking from my room to the classroom every day.

From what I had already seen, it appeared that only the physical training instructors valued working out. All instructors were actual agents, temporarily assigned to the academy as law, Spanish, driving, firearms, and other instructors. There were at least six Border Patrol classes at any given time in 1995. One class or session graduated every two weeks. Those who taught law and Spanish walked around in their green uniforms with their drill sergeant campaign hats pulled down low in front. Their giant beer guts hung over their brass belt buckles and I imagined they could no more run a few miles than I could. Having a penis and more athleticism made no difference as far as I could see. Physical fitness was not a necessity in the Patrol. It was just a means to see how badly you wanted the job in the first place, a way to weed out undesirables. Apparently, women were the undesirables, or at least some of us were.

"They said there are four types of women in the Patrol. Those married to other agents. Those are off-limits, of course. Bitches or cunts, meaning those who won't go out with us. Dykes and fuckbags."

"What's a fuckbag?"

"Don't worry about it." He dismissed me with a wave of his hand.

"Oh, hell no. You can't just waltz in here and tell me all this and then stop. What'd they say it was?"

"It's a female agent who the guys pass around. She's, you know, willing to play ball."

"I see. Are you one of these guys?"

"No. I'm a Christian man. I don't treat women like that. I just wanted you to know what's going on."

"Do you think we don't belong here?" I sincerely asked.

"I think if women can pass the exams and physical tests, they ought to be here. Which reminds me, you got a law degree, right?"

"Yeah, a four year though. Not a juris doctor."

"I speak Spanish fluently. How about we become study partners? I'll help you with Spanish and you help me with law."

I agreed.

* * *

I had no intention of becoming a fuckbag or being raped. I planned to stay away from their living quarters and watch my drinking like I always did around men. Part of what the women had warned us about during that late-night talk seemed to ring true now. The part about us not belonging was backed up by what Zarkowski said, and he had no cause to lie to me. But most of their warnings about sexual assault were no different than what we as women already lived with. Being in the Border Patrol seemed to have little to do with it. That Game of Smiles thing seemed ridiculous though.

This was our lot in life as women. It was not right and should not have happened to anyone, but that didn't mean that it didn't happen in everyday life, in every town, in every space. The simple fact was that the Patrol likely had some bad apples, as they say. Every agency did. I was sure they'd do everything in their power to get rid of those guys. Why wouldn't they?

I knew it happened more often than we heard about, more than we women talked about. I knew women kept their secrets close and their distrust even closer. It was something we all went through in some form or another regardless of our status or our race. Maybe it wasn't outright rape, but maybe harassment. And while our mothers and grandmothers suffered, while our daughters and friends cried, men often sat around debating whether this type of rape or that type was more offensive or criminal than the next.

Should they punish the rapist more if he penetrated the woman's ass instead of her vagina? Which woman's orifice are you entitled to do with as you please before the law gets called on you? What if he just used his fingers? That perhaps shouldn't be as traumatizing as if he used his penis. Right? What if they're married? Should a man be charged with rape if his wife just didn't feel like it? How many of us have been in that situation? Couldn't they all identify with a lame fuck?

I didn't want to think about it. That I knew men sat around debating such things in the halls of justice was disgraceful. There's nothing I could do about any of it anyhow. I would just be careful, as careful as women had always had to be since we were born. There'd be no encouragement on my part. No misconstrued signals or late-night heavy petting gone too far. I was there to become a federal agent and not to find a boyfriend. I couldn't wrap my mind around the thought of an agency condoning such things, much less encouraging it. Certainly not a federal law enforcement agency such as the Border Patrol. Our motto was "Honor First." Not many had been selected to even try and become an agent and fewer would make it. That had to mean something.

HONOR FIRST

My knowledge of the United States Border Patrol history came solely from my instructors at the academy. There was no such thing as Google back then. Every day in the academy was an endless infomercial on why we should all want to be a Border Patrol agent, on why we should be grateful for even being asked to attend the academy. I often wondered if they were saying those things over and over to convince themselves.

It was the most honorable, most admired federal agency for its ruggedness, its American-ness, they said. They claimed it was akin to the Marine Corps. Agents who had resigned and joined other law enforcement organizations like the U.S. Marshals, or the Drug Enforcement Administration almost always regretted it. Our instructors claimed most who left came back and begged and pleaded to be let back in the Patrol. Just as our recruiters who were also agents had told us, we would spend our days out in the great American frontier, riding horses, ATVs, four-wheeling, and hiking areas few dared to venture. There were K-9 units, boat patrols, planes and helicopters if you wanted to be a pilot. You could train to be an EMT, a firearms instructor, a physical trainer, an intelligence agent, an instructor at the academy, and there was even a Border Patrol SWAT team called BORTAC.

It wasn't a job, but a life. It was who we were down to our core. We were a rare breed, called to serve. That image of agents riding horses out in the great expanses of the West, hiking in the mountains and deserts, tracking criminals, having shootouts with bandits and smugglers of drugs and people was what I believed the Patrol to be about. That was the legacy I would inherit if I made it through training. That was what I would be expected to pass on to other trainees down the line. That was our motto...Honor First.

Instructors told us that the enemies of the Border Patrol were many: drug smugglers, human smugglers, and some sort of Hispanic rights group they called La Raza who they claimed wanted us dead. My instructors assured us that the group had bounties out for Border Patrol heads and badges. They said La Raza pretended to be a humanitarian organization, but it was just a cover. It was a criminal gang interested in turning the Southwest back into Mexican territory. This La Raza group said agents were racist, but instructors pointed out time and again how that couldn't be true with over half the agency being Latino. I could see this in the staff at the academy and just by looking at my classmates' faces. This made sense to me.

"How do you square being of Mexican heritage and arresting Mexicans who are crossing illegally?" I asked my Spanish instructor, Agent Ortiz.

"My parents actually came here illegally, but I was born here." He smiled wide under his mustache.

"Excuse me?" I asked, confused.

"It was different back then, less criminals, less drugs. Plus, we weren't as populated back then as we are now. I mean, yeah, it was illegal, but I'm not." He laughed uncomfortably. "I was born and grew up in El Paso. Border Patrol was everywhere. They drove me crazy, fucked with me all the time, always asked my citizenship when I was walking to school. But you know what? When I graduated high school, I wanted to join because they were always the guys with the nice cars and the good-looking women. No one fucked with them, and they got to ride horses and carry guns. *La peinche migra*!" he laughed again excitedly. "Better to be feared than fucked with, you know."

No, I didn't know.

"In Texas, we call illegals wetbacks."

"That's racist," I said as my classmates laughed. "What's funny about that?"

"It's not racist. I use it, and I'm a Latino," Ortiz said proudly with his chin held high. "It's because illegals cross the Rio Grande River and then change into dry clothes, putting their wet ones in a bag they carry on their back, making their backs wet, so we can tell who's illegal."

"So, I can say that word as a white person, and it's not racist?"

"You can say it to an illegal or about an illegal. It's racist if you call me a wetback. It's not our fault white people took the word and used it as a racist word." He and others laughed.

"What about in California? We're all going to be stationed in San Diego. There's no Rio Grande there to cross. Are they still wetbacks?"

"No, California agents call them toncs."

"Toncs?"

"Yeah, T-O-N-C or T-O-N-K."

"Why?" I could hear my classmates from the border areas laughing behind me.

"Well, it means Temporarily Out of Native Country or True Origin Not Known. That's what we tell outsiders anyhow. To the press or people outside the Patrol, you say that's what it means so they won't know the truth."

"What does it mean in the Border Patrol?"

"You'll have to wait until you get to your station to get the answer to that. I've already said too much. Only agents get to know what it means."

"How do I recognize a tonc if their backs aren't wet?"

"You'll know," he said with a slight smile.

"What does that mean?"

"You'll just know," he assured me.

"I mean, I'm not trying to be racist but half the people in here look Mexican. How am I supposed to tell?"

"I ain't no fucking tonc!" yelled a classmate from the back.

"I'm not saying you are, but come on, man. I'm a white chick from Alabama. How can I tell if someone is a tonc or not? Do I just go around asking every Brown person where they were born?"

"We're done talking about this. Let's move on," Ortiz said.

RAPED IN

It wasn't like I didn't know it was coming. Not like I didn't stand a fair shot at being forced to join the club. Mom had warned me that it would likely happen to me. One in three, she said, one in three women. The stories didn't just come from her. I remember those times when adults thought we couldn't hear them. When they whispered late into the night as they sipped on decaffeinated coffee or played board games, when they stood in the halls of church and made sure all the women knew what had happened and why. They didn't know we could hear them when they shooed us off to the swing sets to play and our mommas all crowded together.

Had she encouraged it? Jimmy's momma heard she had. She had that reputation, don't you know. Why any woman thought it was safe to go down in there, they never did know. She liked to wear short skirts. Her life is ruined.

If you expected justice, you'd been wrong to ever think such a thing existed. There was none of that unless you were a rich white woman, and your rapist was a Black or a poor white man. Only then would a perverted sort of justice be assured in Alabama, whether they had the right man or not. Either way, you were forced to relive that nightmare over and over in the press, to your family, to the police, to the judge and jury. They said it felt like being raped again each time they had to talk about it.

There was something that changed in women and girls who were sexually assaulted. I was too young to understand, but I knew it was something men did to women. I knew it wasn't good. From all the things I'd seen on television and in movies, from all the talk I heard on both sides and in the news, it seemed that it was something men and women did not agree on. Men seemed to think the woman or girl was always lying or deserved it, that men had something in them that made it so that some of them could not control themselves around attractive women. But if that was true, why did some men do it to children? Why did some do it to other men, or boys? Why did some men rape old women? Whatever it was, as a young girl I had the impression that some women did something to cause it. That some women had been stupid about the clothes they wore and the places they went to. That something about my body could cause a man to attack me, to rape me, and it was my responsibility to not trigger that in him.

Mom had warned me as I got older. She warned me about strangers as all mommas do. Warned me about boys coming around too much, the ones who got too close. When I started dating at sixteen, she told me about the potential dangers of leading the boys on. How they would expect more if I gave them a bit. How they were different than us. How it was a biological drive for them. How I'd best have my ducks in a row—shouldn't show too much skin, shouldn't permit too much touching, shouldn't encourage them.

You could never tell who would go too far, she said. Just look at that poor New York City girl, that Jennifer Levin. Mom had no doubt that preppy boy raped her, but she also was right that the media and the courts would drag her reputation through the mud. Fancy lawyers painted her as slut crazed sex freak, him as the naïve innocent gent. *What had she worn? Who'd she fuck before him? Did she let him do some things and then blue-balled him? Was she a dick tease?* In the end, you'd been forgiven for thinking he was the actual victim, because that was how they showed it in the media. Some like her joined the club posthumously, and I couldn't decide which I preferred if and when it became my turn. This unfairness, the fact that girls were forced to think of such things, felt unjust to me as a young woman. I hated that feeling.

I learned all the tricks that we girls had to learn. I looked around before leaving a building to see if anyone was near my car or lurking about, kept my keys in my hand with the ends sticking out from between my fingers whenever I walked to my car and told myself to aim for his eyes, tried to go with another woman or a trusted boy when out in an unfamiliar place, told people where I was going and who with. I knew that getting drunk could lead to a "he said, she said" argument, and not to get so drunk that I passed out. I thought it was exhausting to be a woman and wondered how freeing it must have been to be a man who did not have to think of such things.

* * *

When I left the academy bar that night, it was already well past dark. I intended to walk the half mile or so back to my room alone as I often did. FLETC felt more and more like a home to me at that point, and I generally walked most places or rode a cheap bike that I'd bought from WalMart.

I felt him come up behind me before he even opened his mouth only because my childhood had prevented me from ever being oblivious to my surroundings. I was aware even when comfortable and thought I had nothing to fear. He asked if he could walk with me, and I smiled, thinking it was quaint.

"I'm fine, thank you," I assured him.

I saw him watching me at the bar earlier, saw him in the mirror behind the bar, that is. Mendoza was my classmate, although we'd never spoken. He was aloof and quiet most of the time. I was there that night to get a burger and a beer, to watch my Auburn Tigers play. I had wanted to get out of my little room for a bit, get out of my head. He said hello when he refilled his pitcher and then returned to his table with his roommates. I'd forgotten all about him until now.

"You never know," he said.

"Never know what?" I walked as he slid up next to me on my right.

"Never know if it's safe for a woman to be alone."

"Well, if I ain't safe on a campus full of soon-to-be federal agents, I reckon I ain't safe anywhere. If it makes you feel better, knock yourself out."

We talked about our instructors and the academy as we walked past our classroom. I looked up at the moon as we made our way to the cafeteria, where the Spanish moss hung low from the trees. It was October and things had cooled enough that I was wearing a leather jacket and jeans. We passed the little convenience store where I bought Gatorade after long runs and headed down the concrete path that led through the dark woods to our townhouses.

I often wonder why he'd just not done it then and there. Why he waited until we got to the other side of the woods. He likely would have been able to finish it off, finish me off as well if he was so inclined. He could've easily wrapped his giant hands around my thin neck, and I'd been gone in a few minutes, left with my blue eyes wide open, staring up into the pine tree canopy. He could've left me in those woods where no one would have found me until I started to stink as the small animals tore at my eyes. Maybe he had considered it best to wait until we reached the back of my place. Maybe he thought I was up for it, wanted it as much as he had. I cannot reason my way through his thoughts, though I would spend years trying. Sometimes, I still do.

He didn't ask, just stopped talking and held me against the wall as he pushed his tongue down my throat. I could feel the red brick scratching into the back of my head, and it tugged at my jacket as he pushed me around, trying to get his zipper undone and my pants down. I had lost thirty pounds from our physical training in only three months, and I was much stronger than I'd ever been. I'd fought him before during physical training. We always trained at 50 percent, but this time I swung at full strength and landed my right fist on the left side of his jaw. He paused and looked into my eyes as I felt pain spread through my hand. A smile stretched across his broad face. My punch barely made him blink.

"C'mon," he said, as if I would change my mind, as if my fist in his face had been some sort of cute foreplay.

I do not know if I said no or not. I cannot recall if I spoke at all, and that disturbs me when I think back on it. As if saying "no" would have stopped him. As if not saying it meant I had somehow forfeited my right to refuse. He lifted me off the ground for what must have been a full foot, held me against the rough brick, level with his dark eyes. I kicked and punched him with all I had in me, but all I had was nothing compared to his strength.

I knew then, in that moment, that I was going to lose. I was about to be raped right there on that cracked concrete pad next to the cheap red barbeque, amongst the pine needles on a federal law enforcement academy property by a soon to be federal law enforcement officer, by my classmate. I knew that all my training, all of those attempts to keep myself safe, my constant preoccupation with seeing the signs and making the right decisions as a woman…it all came down to this moment and time. My internal wall that helped me separate my emotions from myself, the one I had developed as a child and the safety mechanisms I built up could not—they would not keep me safe from this man.

It felt as if I was six years old again. So small, so weak. Unable to stop my mother from stripping my pants down around my legs. Forcing me into positions I did not want to be in so she could beat my backside to ease her pain. Out it came from her heart, from her soul, into my father's leather belt. It seared into my flesh deeper and deeper until it broke my skin. The pain was everything in that moment. It made me forget who I was, the where and the why. It focused my brain into that one moment of physical pain unlike anything I'd ever known.

I was unable to move, and when I did, he just pushed my arm or leg back to a position he chose, he wanted. My mind was unable to fully understand what was going on just like when I was little. I tried to block it, tried to find the safety feature I used to use, but it only resulted in a familiar frantic array of thoughts like I used to fear when she first started beating me, before I learned to tolerate it, before I learned to float above it.

He suddenly stopped and backed away, grasping at his dick. I didn't wait to see why and assumed I had made contact with my foot or knee. I quickly ran inside and up to my room, locked the door behind me. I jumped on my bed and sat with my back against the wall as far from the door as possible, my knees pulled up to my chest. I stared at the door, waiting, expecting him to come through it any second. I stayed like that for hours and tried to understand what had just happened. I tried to figure out what I should do next. My thoughts were coming and going so fast that I couldn't focus on one thing. I needed to let my thoughts have time to slow down, needed to catch my breath. I desperately tried not to puke from the adrenaline rush and the thoughts of what had just happened to me.

It was long before we all carried a computer in our back pockets, before phones were called smart. There was only a bank of pay phones across the street that I used from time to time to call home collect. I remembered my instructors' warnings—no outside law allowed. I looked out my bedroom window at the pay phones but decided I could not risk getting caught by him again.

This was not just a drunken fight over spilled beer. It was a crime. Right? No, no, it wasn't. He just went too far. He didn't finish. He didn't. There likely was no evidence. Right? I fought him off. Besides, his friends saw him follow me into the parking lot. Probably saw us as we walked off together. They'd say I went willingly, and I had. That I'd walked all the way back with him, and I did. Who knows who'd seen us? I did go with him. He didn't force me to walk with him. It was true. I had a beer or two. I wasn't drunk, wasn't wearing revealing clothing.

Why did I go with him? I should have seen the signs. Should have paid more attention. I should have taken his comment as a warning. How could I have been so stupid? I was conceited with my new training, my new strong body. So stupid. So stupid. So. Fucking. Stupid. Maybe he'll be quiet about it. If he didn't say anything to anyone, maybe I could keep quiet too, and we could just move on. Pretend like it never happened. No police. No embarrassment to the agency. If I called the cops, it'd be all over the academy. I'd lose my job for sure, never get hired anywhere, and end up back where I started. Those women were right! Right? They said this would happen. But I watched my drinks. I didn't go into his townhouse. I was not drunk. I was sober! I knew where I was and what I was doing. So, why did this happen? Why did he do this? It wasn't a graduation party. There was no party. I was just eating a burger and had a few beers. We hadn't even talked until I left.

The disgust of knowing he'd been inside of me suddenly overwhelmed me as my mind raced to figure things out. I have always known that I am a lesbian and had chosen not to have sex with a man. Though I'd not considered myself a virgin for many years, I was in a sense when it came to being with a man, in going all the way. It devasted me even more to think about that, and I jumped up and raced to the shower while my house mates slept. I couldn't get the water hot enough and I scrubbed my pussy as hard as possible, using the detachable showerhead to spray hot water inside of me, praying I'd not gotten anything from him, that he'd not left any reminder that I would discover later on and would have to explain to a future lover. For once, I was thankful to be on birth control pills even if it was just to lessen my menstrual flow.

I didn't sleep that night, or for many nights. I sat in my bed, back against the wall just as I had when I was a young girl after one of Mom's tirades. I hated that feeling, the helplessness, the weakness, the wanting to cry. I hated being a victim. I'd spent so much time trying to get away from those memories, to push them away. So much time trying to become something more. I tried so hard not to be broken, used, or tainted. I did not wish to be defined by my abuse, by my past, and most certainly not by my abusers. Yet, here I was again, that little girl just trying to find my way out of my circumstances, the one with the long blond pigtails and freckles, always fearful of what was just beyond that white door. Still listening to every little sound in an attempt to stay safe.

I didn't call the cops that night because they had told us not to ever call outside police to the academy, and I did not want the Border Patrol to take the blame for the actions of this one piece of shit. It wasn't their fault, I told myself. How could the agency have known? I could just go on, just shut my mouth, just put it all behind me as if it never happened. I would ignore him, sit myself down like I did as a child, and just deal with it. It only had to affect me if I let it. I was strong mentally; this much I knew for sure.

I spent the rest of the night patching the mental wall I'd built long ago and trying to throw this new memory over the top.

* * *

When the sun came up the next morning, I got dressed in my green uniform only to realize just how badly I was hurt. My adrenaline had subsided, and my ribs ached to the touch from what I assumed was a punch or two from him. My lip was busted and split, and a bruise under my eye had started to appear. I stared at myself in the mirror and cried. I cried less for having been the victim and more for the thought of what I was about to endure next. The return to normal that was required of living with my abuser was always the hardest part for me. The shame would be all-consuming, and I knew it was soon to follow.

I had no idea what to expect when my instructors saw me. I knew there'd be no hiding any of this, thanks to the parting gifts Mendoza had left on my face. I wondered what they'd think of me. If they'd think I'd "asked" for it or led him on.

This was the club. It was what I'd been warned about all my life. I felt it then and was starting to understand what women meant. It was less about what was done to me in those few minutes and more about what was to come and what others would think of me. I knew there were pieces taken from me that could never be put back into place even though I had yet to identify what they were. Parts of me felt like they had holes in them now. I no longer felt strong, independent, confident, whole. My sense of being, my sense of self seemed distant, and my hands shook as I pinned my name-plate on my shirt. I was forced to see how small I was, how easily I could be taken, how little I meant to this world, and I wondered how I could even be a federal agent.

How could I protect and serve if I couldn't even protect myself?

I'd joined the club, was forced to become a card-carrying member like all the others. It was foolish to think I would ever have any say-so in my designated label. Those things were not our choices as women in this agency or in life. I understood this now. Bitch, cunt, fuckbag—male agents assigned those titles to us. We had no choice. He made that decision for me, and if it hadn't been him, it was likely it would have been some other guy. Some man who just came along and changed my life forever, without any consent from me.

I knew that my physical scars would heal, but the emotional scars hadn't even begun to form yet. I wanted to untie my soul and let it be free, because it hurt too much to feel, to care anymore. Had I had access to my service gun, I might have done just that.

I skipped breakfast because I could not face anyone in the cafeteria. Sitting in my designated front-row seat, they all filed in from the back of the classroom for our immigration law class which mostly consisted of giving us the answers to the next test. Only the two guys who sat on either side of me could see my face. My body tensed up as I heard our law instructor, Agent Little, say good morning to us all. He set his binder down and removed his drill sergeant hat just like he had every other morning. He looked around the room and right at me several times as he spoke in his slow Texas drawl and spit brown dip juice into his Styrofoam coffee cup. Today's lecture had something to do with people born in the Panama Canal area and how to determine citizenship.

I wasn't listening.

We took our standard ten-minute break at the top of the hour. Instead of hanging around the room as usual, my male classmates all stood just outside in the foyer. I sat alone as if I'd become contagious, as if I hosted some pathogen. Not one of my classmates or a single instructor ever asked what had happened. No one took me aside to ask if the other guy looked worse than me, if I'd given him what for—as we said in the South. I was grateful Agent Little had not called on me during class, and angry that he didn't.

I felt that I had done something terribly wrong. I was drowning in shame that didn't belong to me.

After class, I ran over to the gym and changed into the standard FLETC royal blue shorts and light blue t-shirt just like normal. That day we were scheduled for defensive tactics training, meaning we would fight each other. The object was to learn defensive tactics that we might need someday in the field to take down an assailant if our batons were not available. The Border Patrol had yet to issue pepper spray or tasers to its agents. Mostly, this training consisted of punching each other in the body and the face while wearing the protective headgear and gloves people wear when they sparred in boxing rings.

Our all-male instructors only taught us how to fight in terms of how men fought. Kicking was not allowed, something women often did when faced with an attacker because our lower body strength tends to be better than our upper body strength. Kicks and punches to the groin were never allowed. They were considered taboo and not proper fighting. I'd already decided that if I was ever to fight a man in the field, that's the first place I would hit. Instructors once again insisted that we were all agents, not men, not women. The physical differences between us were ignored to seem unbiased, they said. The reality was that it left many, including men but especially women, without proper defensive training. That was how much they hated us.

One of our physical training instructors, Agent Smith, selected who would fight each other that day. A hard-ass, he reminded me of the kind of guy that'd been lucky to have found the Patrol. The type of guy that would have been on the street dealing meth, tatted with swastikas and white power signs, had he not been recruited by the Border Patrol. He cared none too much for my kind as he often called out sexist cadence on our group runs just to prove it. He once kept me in a sit-up position until all the men had collapsed in pain simply because he was trying to get me to give in. He liked to take us on long runs just as the academy was about to declare it a red flag day, meaning that it was too hot and humid to safely run. I was not a fast runner, couldn't do a pull-up to save my life, but I could power out the crunches and was not afraid of his knuckle push-ups on the hot parking lot asphalt that baked in the Georgia sun.

"Budd and Mendoza!" he yelled. I couldn't believe my ears.

We put our mouthpieces in, red boxing gloves and head protection on. I stood in the center of the mat room and waited for him to finish giving high fives to his buddies. He was every bit of six foot three or four, likely had a hundred pounds on me. All of him was pure muscle. We could not choose our attackers in training, and so I said nothing. Agent Smith reminded us to punch at only 50 percent, and I knew I was about to get my ass kicked again regardless of the percentage.

When I heard the whistle, I came out with a right hook as hard as I could muster just like I had the night before. He popped me in my bruised ribs and my eye before picking me off the ground and throwing me into the matted wall. They all laughed. My breath was knocked out of me when I hit the wall, and I flashed back to the red brick and the flurry of hands from the night before. I slid down landing on my butt, and jumped back to my feet as fast as I could. I ran back to Mendoza, back to my rapist, and threw a few body punches before he wrapped his arm around my neck, pulled me in close with my back to him, and choked me.

"You're going to learn not to say no to me," he whispered and began punching me in the back of my head.

"Let her go," Smith yelled.

Catching my breath, I went for his groin when Agent Smith yelled at me that I was breaking the rules. Again, I was picked up and thrown across the room into the wall, and again, I heard them all laugh. Tears streamed down my face, and I swore at myself because I couldn't stop. I got back up and charged him again. Agent Smith blew the whistle and called the fight over as I slid down the wall for the third time. Out of breath, my ribs screamed with pain. I ripped my helmet and gloves off and threw them to the ground. My instructors and some of my classmates still smirked at my beating. The only other female left in my group by this time stared at the ground, avoiding eye contact with me. My rapist received high fives from our male classmates as I left the room.

* * *

"You've got to go to your instructors and tell them what happened," Karen said. I hadn't seen her all day as our class was split into two sections and we were not in the same section. She heard the rumors and guessed the truth easily enough.

"What makes you think they don't know? They did that on purpose, Karen!"

"Budd, a guy is at the door for you," someone said.

"Look, I just want you to know that Mendoza's in the guy's locker room throwing his hands in the air and yelling that he taught you a lesson. That you learned to never say no to him again." My classmate, Roberts, was the only guy to come to me. "I'm sorry that happened to you. You don't deserve this." He slinked away before any of the guys saw him.

He wasn't even trying to hide it. There was no "he said, she said." It was just "he said," and that was fine by most of them, apparently. My horrible faux pas wasn't that I had accused Mendoza falsely, it wasn't that we disagreed on the events. It was that I had not allowed him to do as he wished to me. I had refused to be a fuckbag.

"If you don't say something, I will," Karen threatened as I returned to my locker.

Still in my sweat-soaked gym clothes, I knocked on the instructors' door and requested to speak with Agent Smith.

"I need a witness with me, so you don't try and accuse me of something," he said.

"Accuse you of something, sir?"

He came back with my other physical training instructor, Agent Thomas. They sat down at the conference table I was at with a chair in between us.

"Yeah, well I don't want you to say I raped you like you did with Mendoza," he said.

"That's interesting," I said, "because I've not said that to anybody, sir."

"You've filed EEO, right?"

"No, sir. I haven't talked with a single instructor, but it seems that you all have done a shitload of talking, which means you knew about this assault before you assigned me to fight him."

"What do you want, Budd?"

"I am not asking to have a say in who I fight. I'm asking that I not fight Mendoza ever again. He fucking sexually assaulted me."

"First of all, don't take that tone with me. Secondly, you can't prove that." Smith always did all the talking. "You need to file an EEO report."

"This is how you handle sexual assault? Is this how y'all bury these things? Is this why there are so few women in the Patrol? File an Equal Employment Opportunity complaint? With all due respect, sir, he's not my superior, and it's a crime. This should be a criminal investigation, not an EEO complaint." I winced from the pain as I leaned forward to rest my arms on the table.

"Did he rape ya, Budd? Why you calling it a sexual assault?"

I didn't want to say that I was raped.

I saw rape as something an unknown assailant did in a dark alley to a woman who'd made a bad decision. Even though I knew that was a stereotype, even though I knew about date rape and spousal rape, the word rape had a specific meaning to me back then. I didn't like it, didn't want to say it out loud. The word rape gave people a definitive picture of what was done, and it somehow felt like being raped again to call it by its name. Sexual assault felt a little more distant to me, safer, a term that could encompass a range of actions. Like it would still somehow give me back a bit of control about the whole thing. It was something that I could admit to without feeling like a complete victim. Not using that word was an attempt to wrestle back a small bit of power over the situation, to not feel so helpless, to have a say in the narrative.

"I will fight anyone, any size; just not him, sir."

"File EEO. You can't call the police on a federal academy. We can handle it by filing EEO."

The only thing I knew about filing EEO came from just a few years before as I watched Anita Hill testify about the sexual harassment she had endured from Clarence Thomas when he was the head of EEO. I learned from that hearing what happened if we women come forward. I watched how she was treated, how they forced her to relive her trauma over and over for each senator, and it felt like I was watching her be sexually harassed by each and every one of those men.

Again and again for the whole world to see, Hill was belittled and not believed. The senators made fun of her as they rallied behind Thomas. I witnessed how the system wasn't only designed and built by these men, but how it protected them, how it prevented others from coming forward, and how it punished those brave enough to ask for justice. The lesson I learned from Hill's treatment was clear—assailants would never be held accountable. They could even become a Supreme Court Justice. Filing an EEO complaint meant that victims would be violated again and have their reputations dragged through the mud for all to see. Anita Hill was way smarter and far more educated than me. There was no way I'd ever file EEO.

"I know that if I file, you all will stop my training to investigate. I cannot do that, sir. I have to graduate. I need this job."

"No, you will file EEO. That's how we handle these things. We prefer to handle them internally. It's just your word against his. No witnesses. If you don't file, then we all know you're lying."

"You all will think I'm lying even if I do! I am not filing EEO. I am not stopping my training. If you force me to fight him again or put me in a position where he can harm me, I will fucking sue all of you!"

I would not be their fuckbag or marry another agent. If they thought I was a bitch or cunt because I refused to sleep with them, then a bitch or a cunt was what they would get. What did I have to lose?

Reports were written about it, I assumed. Memorandums were likely filed by my instructors on how I'd threatened them and how I refused to file a grievance. I never saw any of the reports, but I thought they existed. I did not know either way. I was not asked to document anything as they did not care what my side of the story was anyhow. No one came to take my statement, to photograph my injuries. No one asked if I needed counseling or wanted a rape kit. No one interviewed Roberts about what was said in the locker room. I wondered if Mendoza was interviewed at all. Maybe they never documented a thing.

I don't know.

The following morning, our class supervisor stomped up the aisle and addressed us all. I could tell he was pissed because he failed to remove his drill sergeant hat as was custom when indoors. "Anyone of you women have a complaint against anybody, you will file an EEO complaint! That is an order!"

He avoided eye contact with me, but we all knew exactly why we were being dressed down. I felt all eyes on the back of my head. I'd have crawled under the table if I thought it would help. "I'm sick and tired of women coming to my academy and whining and crying. If you don't like it, if you can't hack it, you can get the fuck out!"

GETTING BY

When Karen asked me to go out for dinner, I wanted to say no. I'd spent many of my nights trying to forget my circumstances by getting drunk and visiting a woman training to be a Park Police officer. Ann's classroom was across from ours, but her living quarters were on the other side of campus. It was as far as I could run from my troubles and my classmates.

When I was with her, I was in a different world. I could, for a little while, forget all that waited on the other side of the door. With her, I was valued because I was a woman and not punished for it. She saw and understood that there was strength in me. That my usefulness and purpose weren't measured in units of spit and testosterone or "playing ball." I wasn't undeserving because I was a woman. For at least a handful of hours a week, I felt accepted, encouraged, and at the very least, loved physically.

I told Karen what I was, that I preferred women. It was no surprise to her at all. She could see that I didn't flirt with the guys. She noticed how I was uncomfortable with their lewd comments about how we looked in our uniforms and gun belts, and how they talked about what they wanted to do to us if given the chance. She also knew about Ann and why I sometimes did not sleep in my own room.

"I just need you to go with me. I'll explain on the way," she said.

She had rented a red Chrysler convertible during those four months we trained at the academy. It gave us more freedom to go into town and out farther to the beaches on St. Simons Island for long runs in the rainstorms that so often seemed to spring up out of nowhere. Some weekends we spent in Savannah, down by the river, drinking and eating raw oysters that came in giant buckets with Corona beer. Savannah was where she took me to my first gay bar. It was three stories tall: one floor for men to dance, one for women that was always empty, and one for drag shows. We partied into the night and sobered up at the all-night Denny's with greasy eggs and hash browns. That ugly car helped us feel less trapped on that campus.

Karen was nervous that night, which wasn't like her at all. She was the most brazen and straightforward person I'd ever known, and I wondered what happened to her to make her that way. She would never say. Her secrets were always held so close that I imagined her mental walls were made of steel and not red brick, like mine. We had each other's backs as much as possible, and I thought of this as one of those times, one of those things I should do for her simply because she asked me.

"They're really nice guys, and I just want a girlfriend there, you know, in case."

Yeah, I knew.

It was one of those chain restaurants like so many others found in or near shopping malls. The kind with crappy watered-down drinks, fried potatoes, burgers, and cheap beer. The kind of place high school boyfriends used to take me to on the weekends. The kind that had the same exact menu and service all across the country as if that was somehow a good thing.

I saw them as soon as we walked in. Sitting in one of those semi-circle booths were Agents Little and Ortiz, my law and Spanish instructors. I knew they were from the same station in Texas and best friends in that odd couple sort of way. Little was tall, lean and quiet. Ortiz was short, chubby and always laughing. "*Cerca pero no puro*," he always told me when I made a mistake. *Close but no cigar.*

"Hey Karen, my instructors are here," I said discreetly to her.

"Yeah, they're who we're having dinner with."

"What the fuck, Karen!" I grabbed her arm and pulled her back outside. "Karen! Jesus fucking Christ! I don't want to get involved with my fucking instructors."

"And I do?"

"I guess, yeah. You're the one that dragged me here. I don't want to be known as the woman who got her badge because she slept with her law instructor."

"No. He's mine. Ortiz is yours, but don't worry. He knows you're not interested. Just here for a backup."

"They already think I accused Mendoza of sexual assault to get my badge!"

"Yeah, so what does it matter? They're going to think whatever they want about us. They talk like a bunch of women sittin' around a kitchen table," she said, trying to get me back inside.

"It matters to me," I pleaded, standing my ground.

"You think I want to do this?" She turned and faced me. "Because I don't, but I got a shit Marine husband back home who beats the fuck out of me every week. I got three boys who I can't raise on my own without this job, Jenn! I'm fucking thirty-four years old, for Christ's sake. What the fuck am I going to do? Not everyone has a fucking college degree like you. You got options. I don't. I need this job, just the same as you, only more so."

I'd been wrong; I had judged her and the other women who I knew were dating instructors as if I was somehow better than them. I thought I was different because at least I had not gone off willingly to sleep with instructors to assure my position. I assumed that for them, for women like Karen, that it was a choice, but it was no more a choice than it had been for me. Karen was doing what she knew she had to do to pass her tests, to become safe, to provide for her babies, to not be raped. She "played ball," as they said, but only because she had to, because she was forced. I had no doubt she would have passed her exams on her own. Hell, they gave us the answers to most of it. I also had no doubt they would have failed her if she didn't do this. The women who filed EEO were often fired for bullshit reasons. I knew it. She knew it. We all knew it. His actions were a declaration. In this version of "playing ball," he possessed her, planted his flag on her body for his own to say to the others, *she is mine. You may not touch her.* She felt this was her only way of staying safe after she saw what had happened to me.

And that was perhaps the most frustrating part of it all; that for us to wear the badge, we had to be their property. For us to be safe on a campus full of federal law enforcement officers, we were forced to give ourselves over to them. It was another layer, another challenge or test that many female trainees had to complete to graduate. Run the obstacle course in under two minutes, pass your firearms qualifications, your law and Spanish classes and oh yeah, fuck one or more of the guys. Our only choice was how we wanted to complete the exam, politely or violently.

Did we want to give it willingly or have it taken from us?

We were all in the same boat, us women, that is, and it felt like there was but one oar. That even if we had two oars, we didn't know which way to go or how to get there without throwing each other overboard to save ourselves. We had no one to guide us through those treacherous waters, no map, no light. Most didn't make it, and the few that did felt that they owed the others nothing for their sacrifice. In whatever way it happened to us, we kept it to ourselves and a few close friends. Our only choice was to keep our mouths shut or file EEO, be retaliated against, and possibly lose our jobs.

The men had each other. They looked after one another, lied for each other, and kept one another's secrets. They had the mostly male instructing staff to guide them, to tell them how to get through, how to deal with us. The talks about how we didn't belong, that we couldn't hack it, those weren't just about boys being boys. They were about men protecting men. They were about men teaching other men how to get away with sexually assaulting and raping fellow classmates. These were the agents who told female trainees that if they wanted to be part of the gang, to be accepted, they had to "play ball" or go under that table. Our assaulters, our rapists, were free to brag and engage in their locker room talk without any fear of being held accountable.

I guess I couldn't really blame her for fucking my law instructor.

* * *

Agent Ortiz took me back to the academy that night after dinner. He was kind enough to turn his headlights out and parked away from my townhouse, knowing that if anyone saw us, there'd be rumors that I was sleeping with him.

"I know what happened to you, Ms. Budd." I stared at the floor, not sure where he was going, what his intentions were, and I wondered if I was going to have to fight him too. "I know. I've seen this a lot in the Patrol. It's an ugly secret, but I want you to know that I believe you. I don't know how you see him every day and continue, but you do. That takes strength. It takes a big heart. Courage."

I did not expect this to come from him and had no idea how to respond. I did not want to be in that place, the part of myself behind my mental wall where the memory of that night lived. I certainly did not want to tell him that I already knew how to survive living with an abuser. I spent every waking moment trying to move on. It was a broken record that I never wanted to hear again, but again, that was not my choice to make.

Every place I went, he was there. Every class I took, he was present. I looked past Mendoza whenever possible, never acknowledging him, never making eye contact. I ignored his taunts and his stares. I pretended I couldn't see the looks from my classmates as I walked past their tables in the dining hall. Monday through Friday, from morning until evening, I saw my attacker every day, every class, on the shooting range, in the gym, in the pool, on the driving track, in the cafeteria.

And when I went to sleep, he invaded my dreams.

"I think you're a good person," Ortiz said. "I want you to know your supervisor told me to fail you on your Spanish exam so they could terminate your employment, but I said no. That means they will try and fail you on your physical training. Be sure you pass them with time to spare. Hang in there; we're not all bad."

Maybe joining the Patrol had not been a good decision, but like so many others, I had nowhere else to go. It had taken me over a year to get hired. The thought of quitting, going back home and starting over with another agency, or going to law school was not an option for me. I knew what waited for me back there, and I was more afraid of my family than I was of what may come my way in the Patrol. The unknown of what was ahead had to be better. I had to make it work.

After all, it wasn't like every male agent was a rapist. Agent Ortiz was an example of this. A small few were faithful to their wives and girlfriends back home, though not most. *What happens in the academy, stays in the academy,* they often said. Infidelity did not necessarily mean sexual predator, but then again, none of them bothered to stand up for the women that they knew were being assaulted or forced into such situations even if they had not agreed with it. Yes, Ortiz refused to fail me, but he never came forward and said he thought what they were doing was wrong either. He never called for an investigation or said a word to my rapist.

I could not let myself think too far ahead. I had no idea what it would be like out at my station in southern California but simply hoped that there were more agents like Ortiz there. I had to take each day as it came, survive the best I could and do it all over again the next day, just as I had when I was young.

I patched my mental wall like I always did and tried to move on.

* * *

I got to know Armando as we sat in the non-descript office building in Spring Valley, California, that the Border Patrol had rented for new recruits of the 288th Session. He was a San Diego native, Mexican American, fluent in Spanish, and had worked at the city zoo prior to joining.

As I patiently waited for everyone to fill out each portion of our paperwork, the agent in charge of our class walked around checking and rechecking to make sure we'd done everything correctly. It reminded me of being in middle school and those classmates who were unable to follow the simplest of instructions. In the agent's defense, there was always one who could not. Stopping in front of me, he pointed to my form and told me to correct it, thinking I'd entered the wrong date.

"But today is my birthday," I said as I felt Armando kick the back of my chair. I tried not to laugh.

We walked across the street for lunch, and he ordered for me in Spanish, paying in honor of my twenty-fourth birthday. He'd said something about the place having the best tacos ever, real Mexican food, and he laughed when I confessed that I'd only ever eaten Taco Bell or homemade ground beef tacos and when I admitted I thought guacamole was avocados mixed with sour cream. He spoke mostly in English with a few exclamations and curses in Spanish, which made me laugh. "*Aye guuueeeey*!" was something he said a lot when he talked with his best friend, Juan. He rolled his R's and his eyes at the same time.

I guessed that Armando was at least six foot five, nearly a full foot taller than me. His face was wide and that made his grin seem huge. His hands were at least twice the size of mine, and he laughed all the time. I'd never met someone so funny and lighthearted, always joking and cracking up so intensely that he would bend in half and twist sideways in pain as tears rolled down his face. I thought he'd choke to death from laughing so hard after he told me what *tacos de cabeza* meant. It was pretty good if I didn't think about what it was.

Armando was one of a handful of exceptions in the 288th, in the academy as a whole. I never heard him say a bad thing about anyone or gossip about who fucked which female trainees or who he thought was fuckable or who was a bitch or a dyke. After hours at the academy, I often practiced on the obstacle course that gave me and many others a challenge. It was Armando who pointed out to me that it was based all on upper body strength, and that was what gave most women a difficult time.

There were tricks, ways to beat the obstacles. It was Armando who taught me not to waste my upper body strength on trying to pull myself up over the eight-foot wall like the men did, and instead to use my feet to climb up it as I held onto the top with my left hand. He showed me not to cross the monkey bars in the traditional style of swinging forward and back as we did when we were kids, but to swing left and right as doing so propelled my body forward faster by gripping the outside of the bars instead of the center. As tall as he was, he didn't even have to leave the ground to touch the monkey bars, but our instructors still demanded he lift his feet.

Most men could easily pass the physical tests even if they were only 70 percent fit, according to the government's statistics. A woman my age had to be over 100 percent physically fit to pass the Patrol's tests in the times that I did on the final. Many of the guys' bellies still hung over their belts even after four months of training, but it was different for Armando. It was difficult to get that giant body over the course or even run a mile and a half.

Armando knew about the night Mendoza walked me home, and he knew why my face had been busted up. He knew why the guys laughed and snickered behind my back. I imagine that he'd heard Mendoza brag about what he had done to me in physical training that day because of the talk in the locker room afterward. He knew they lied when they said I filed a complaint against him. He knew that I did the same hard work they did to pass the exams and that I never filed EEO for fear of losing my job. He knew that I got through the academy even after I was raped, something none of them could attest to. That I did it while I stood next to my assaulter day after day, always fearful it would happen again, always on the verge of a panic attack that I just had to fucking swallow every single day. And though he never said anything to me about it, he always had a kind word, a smile, a nod, a joke or two.

He had my back at times when the others went too far. Like the time when we had drills to clear a stairway of an active shooter, and I was the lead. My job as primary was to look directly in front of me, around the nooks and corners of the stairway. My three partners were supposed to look up and around me. They were supposed to keep me safe, to warn me. Only they'd already made a plan amongst each other to leave me on the stairs when we encountered the shooter. Without warning, I heard their footsteps clamor down the stairs and their boyish giggles echoed in the stairwell behind me as I heard the gun go off just before the rubber bullet hit my spine. It laid me flat on my stomach, and I hoped I'd not been seriously injured as I rubbed my back.

"They just left her in there and never warned her," he said to the head firearms instructor afterward. "They abandoned an agent and she got shot!" The look of disgust on his face was real. It was just another way they told me that I didn't belong and that I could expect as much in the field. Still rubbing my spine where the rubber bullet hit me, I tried to tune them out, tried to just get through another day.

"We don't leave anyone behind!" yelled our lead firearms instructor as he leveled his gun at them. Two took a rubber bullet to the thigh and one to the stomach. "Anyone else think it's funny to leave a fellow agent behind?"

I couldn't blame Armando when he became a bit distant at the academy. If they were willing to let me get shot in practice, one had to wonder what else they would be willing to do in the field. He probably had to wonder if they'd come after him. Plus, I assumed he wanted to fit in like I wanted, like we all wanted. I was labeled toxic, a complainer, and he needed the job as badly as I did. So, I took the little bits and pieces of his kindness when they came and held on tight.

I was happy to know we were both assigned to Campo, California, with eight other classmates. I hoped I might be more accepted with him there. At least I didn't have to work with Mendoza, who was sent to Imperial Beach with Karen and most of our other classmates.

* * *

When the time came to take our final physical tests, I had planned to pace my run so that I did not spend too much energy on the mile and a half. I knew I would need to have energy for the obstacle course and final sprint. In addition to our physical training classes, I'd spent hours on my own time running and lifting weights to get in shape. At least three days a week, I did four hours of physical training in addition to my eight hours of other training each day. Come finals, I kept pace with a guy that had always made it in the past, but I decided to back off on the last lap as it felt like it was too fast. We had thirteen minutes, and I felt that I was good for the mile and a half at about twelve or twelve-thirty. As I crossed the finish line with several people behind me, I stopped dead and turned to Agent Smith. He paused for a few seconds and looked at his watch.

"Well?"

He chuckled. "Fuck, Budd, you just missed it by one second. You're done," he said with a big shit-eating grin.

"Wait! What?"

"You fucking failed. Hit the showers, loser!"

I turned to look at Agent Ortiz, who came out that morning to watch our class. He shook his head in disbelief. Later he said all the other instructors agreed that I made the time, but none of it mattered. I failed, according to Smith, and he was the one with the stopwatch in his hand. Ortiz had been right; they were trying to get rid of me. I had one more chance. Along with those who came in behind me, we were all offered a retake per policy in case a trainee had a bad day.

A few weeks later, I made sure I smoked the run. I felt strong in the mile and a half and especially in the obstacle course as I climbed the ladder to the top and rang the bell, clocking the fastest time I had ever done. Even faster than many of the guys. At the sprint, Avila and I were the only two left and we lined up, side by side, at the starting line. We were neck and neck until the halfway mark when he pulled ahead, but I still came in way under the time.

Our entire class waited for us at the end of the sprint. They cheered and surrounded Avila and patted him on the back like he'd scored the winning touchdown. I tried to catch my breath as I stood there next to Karen and watched them cheer. My classmates all walked past me to shake Avila's hand. They had no intention of shaking my hand or patting me on the back.

"Shake her hand!" Ortiz yelled.

I didn't wait around to see if they followed his order and ran to the showers. There was nothing I could do to become one of them. I was branded, and that was the end of it. I may have passed the tests, done better than some, like when I won the shooting obstacle challenge against the entire class, but I was not part of their family and knew then that I never would be. It was a familiar feeling, like the one I'd grown up with. I suppose I should have been thankful for that. I knew what it was. I had felt alone most of my life and had become accustomed to it.

Still, it hurt.

The day before graduation, I phoned my mom to see what time they'd be in for the ceremony. "We're not coming. We've got to move in a month and don't have the time."

I slammed the phone down on the receiver, picked it up, and beat the phone box with it. They didn't know all that I had endured in the academy. How hard it was to keep going, after I was raped and then see my attacker every day and work right beside him. I never said anything to them because I knew my mother was not capable of mothering, and my father was too busy having another affair. I knew the outcome whenever I shared my pain and triumphs with them, and I told myself that it was better that they would not be there. Having pride in myself was enough; should have been enough. I did not need their approval or praise and did not require their witness or applause when my badge was pinned on me. That's what I told myself.

I made sure to take a graduation picture with Agent Ortiz in our official dress uniforms before I left to drive across the country with Karen. It is the one picture I always make sure to hang on the wall in all the places I have called home. A few years later, Karen told me he was murdered. She said he was found in his basement in Texas, tied to a chair with his head blown off by a shotgun.

STARTING ANEW

We had a few weeks before we were to report to our duty stations. Karen and I decided to rent a Ford Taurus to drive across the U.S. She kissed Agent Little goodbye as I waited in the car. "Thank God that's over," she said. Neither of us ever talked about it again.

We stopped overnight at my parents' place in Gulf Breeze, Florida, to pick up my clothes, a VCR, and a small television I had in college. My father was off working or screwing that gift shop manager again. I noticed that there were no moving boxes or any packing going on. My mother and sister sat watching CNN and simply wished me good luck as I headed out the door to my new life in San Diego.

"They ain't big on goodbyes, huh?" Karen noted.

We stopped in Baton Rouge for what I was sure would be my last decent etouffee and sweet tea. Driving about twelve or thirteen hours a day, we stopped and stayed in the cheapest hotels we could find. I was jolted awake in New Mexico one night by a trooper's siren pulling us over for speeding. Our .357s were under our front seats within reach, fully loaded with Border Patrol-issued hollow-point bullets meant to cause the most damage as they flattened or mushroomed out upon hitting a target.

"Should we tell him?" I asked.

"I dunno. No one talked with us about this," she said quietly.

"Just keep your hands on the wheel."

"License and registration," he said and immediately returned to his car.

"We should tell him. I don't want to get shot. I would want someone I stopped to say something," I said.

He reappeared at her window within ten minutes with a ticket and simply told us to slow down and have a good night.

"Well, I guess that's a good lesson. You think he just assumed we were not armed because we're women?"

"I guess," she replied.

* * *

As we drove, I thought about all I was leaving behind. It was all I'd ever known, the good and the bad. I was born in North Carolina but never called it home, as we left when I was just a few months old. Huntsville, Alabama, was my hometown. It was somewhere between a small town and a large one like Birmingham. Its claim to fame was that Nazi scientists from the war were brought there to work on the Saturn rockets and other things that I never much understood. The civic center is still named after one of the Nazis, Wernher von Braun. People from all over the world came there to study engineering and to work for Boeing like my mother's parents. Dad's father was stationed at missile command on Redstone Arsenal. That's how my family came to be there, how my parents met.

I never did have that thick Alabama marble-mouthed accent that many who come from there do, though I wanted it badly. A few smaller marbles are in there, I've been told. My only southern relative was Grandma Budd, and she was raised on a farm outside of Nashville, Tennessee. Chimneys were "chimleys," and the governor was pronounced "guv-a-na." If I came home from her house or from school mumbling, turning my o's into a's, or excessively using the word "done," Mom made sure to slap it out of my mouth. No, I could not call Grandma "mee-maw" as she wished. If I have a bit too much to drink or get around folks with such accents today, I can slip back into it as if I'd never left. There is something about it that makes me happy, makes me smile, and I feel most expressive and real when I let it roll off my tongue. It warms my soul and is what my inner voice, my thoughts sound like to me when I think back on my childhood.

I was not raised in the country, mountains, or hollers, but in the city. I do not have tales of cotton fields or Klan meetings as I've found many think I should. Never been on a hayride or a plantation. I did not grow up running barefoot through cow pastures or playing in the streams in raggedy overalls, never used an outhouse nor shot my own dinner. Not that I would have minded any of that; it just wasn't my life. I was raised in an average house on an average street. First on the poor side of town, then on the other side in my teen years. Which is to say, the Black side and then the white side. That much was true and is still true today.

My earliest memories are of baking chocolate chip pecan cookies with my mother. We'd put them on cheap paper plates, wrap them in holiday-colored cellophane and tie them up with red and green ribbons, then load them all into my mom's avocado green Maverick. We headed out to the wealthier parts of town where our fellow parishioners lived. I can easily remember running up to their front porches, placing the plates down before my brother rang their doorbells, and running as fast as our legs would take us back to the car, stealing away into the night, laughing and giggling. To give and not expect anything in return was the lesson my parents wanted us to learn, and it made me feel better than anything else.

Our congregation was not large by any means. To be a Mormon in north Alabama in the early seventies was rare. Most of my friends at Lakewood Elementary were Baptists. I wasn't born into our religion like so many in our church. Neither set of grandparents practiced any sort of religion, but all their kids did. My mother's sister joined the Jehovah's Witnesses, and my dad's sister became an evangelical who spoke in tongues. So, my mother upped the ante and chose to become a Mormon, which naturally meant we would too.

I always felt safe in church. Always felt comforted by knowing what was expected of me, how to behave. There were rules, commandments, and if I followed them, they said I could be part of the Mormon family forever. I tried as best as I could to be a good Mormon. I prayed every day, never even let a curse word enter my thoughts, was careful not to watch the *Planet of the Apes* or drink Dr. Pepper, and always helped when we gathered the corn and sweet potatoes from the fields out in the country to donate to those poorer than us. My parents didn't curse back then and never said that they hated anybody because hate was an unforgiving word. They wore the onesie underwear that the church said would keep them on a righteous path. We were thankful for our food, our home, our family, and our God. We were a forgiving, loving people who did unto others as we would have them do unto us.

Our little three-bedroom, red brick house on Sullivan Road was where Mom taught me to read when I was only three or four. I can still remember how she pulled me up onto her big bed with her, wrapped her arm around me, and held me close. Her long, blond hair curled around my little shoulders as her finger touched every word. I sounded them out with her help, her sweet voice and mine, and we turned the pages together. Again and again until we fell asleep, always waking in time to pick up my brother from school.

That house was where I learned to ride a bike, sled in the snow, catch lightning bugs and caterpillars, and shoot a basketball. She used to take me out to her garden and show me how to make a small hole with my index finger in the dark, newly tilled dirt, then place a seed and cover it up softly as if putting it to bed. She showed me how to tell when the tomatoes, cucumbers, zucchinis, and squash were ripe enough to eat and how to get them off the vine without destroying the whole plant, how to pull the stem from honeysuckle, bite the end, and suck the sweet nectar out. She showed me how to crack a pecan from our neighbor's tree by stepping on it and separating the buttery nut from its shell, how to knead bread, batter and fry chicken, and make homemade ice cream and biscuits.

Some weekends I got to spend at Grandma Budd's house down the street from our church on the other side of town. It was a split-level house, much bigger than ours, with four bedrooms and two full baths. Great -Grandpa Budd lived with them. He was a grumpy eighty-something-year- old man who took evil delight in teaching me how to whistle so we could both drive Grandma crazy. I'd been his favorite, the only one allowed to sit on his lap while he napped, and I can remember him taking out out his teeth after eating to rinse them in the kitchen sink.

He liked to make clocks—grandfather clocks, ship's wheel clocks, any kind of clocks. They hung throughout the house and would strike every hour a few seconds apart, filling the entire house. I can remember him coming home, asking Grandma to drive him to the hospital because he'd accidentally cut off another finger or two using a table saw at the neighbors'. He'd just put it in his pocket and walked back home. Both hands were missing some fingers, but it didn't bother me none. I was used to it.

Weekends at Grandma and Pop Budd's house meant biscuits and sausage gravy in the morning with fresh-squeezed orange juice for my brother and me. Both pantries were always stacked high just in case another depression ever came along. A can of bacon grease sat permanently on the white stove in a big old coffee can. We never went without in that house. Grandma was the best damn cook and made most things from scratch just like she'd been taught to by her momma. She never wasted a bite, always ate the fat I left from my meat, sucked the eggs out of the fresh fish Pop had just caught at the lake, and gnawed on frog leg bones until every bit was gone.

My brother and I spent our days swimming and nights watching *Hee-Haw* while covering our sunburns in Noxzema, laughing at Buck and Roy because that's what Grandma liked to watch. Summertime meant getting up early to go fishing for bass in Guntersville Lake, learning to shoot Pop's .22 rifle, and picking raspberries, blackberries, and strawberries out of Grandma's garden in the backyard. What didn't end up in my mouth was used for making jams.

What we didn't grow we bought at the farmers market, over yonder, as she liked to say. It was just a roof and supports, open for all to see and smell. There were piles of peaches, apples, plums, and every fruit or vegetable you could want. She'd drive us all the way out to the country in her red Cadillac just for a few dozen brown chicken eggs because she said they were the best, and then over to the commissary on base for meat. Everything took time; everything was slow and done with love.

Winter weekends at Grandma's were spent watching college and pro football, playing pool downstairs in the den as the smell of cedar wood burned in the large fireplace and filled the house. There were plenty of books lying around. I liked the big collections and special-edition picture books on Native Americans and cowboys that they bought from *Time* and *Life* magazines. The kind with the faux leather binding. Every edition of *National Geographic* sat on the bookshelf in the order that they were printed.

It was hard to be bored there. Pop spent the mornings in the garden or worked on his model trains that ended up being featured at the Huntsville Railroad Museum with their own room: "The Colonel Gene Budd Room." The house was filled with souvenirs from their travels, from when they'd been stationed around the world. Camel saddles from the Middle East sat at the end of their bed, Arabian swords were displayed on shelves, ceramic green elephant statues were used as end tables, and giant Turkish rugs covered the solid oak floors in every room. The army had taken them around the world, and they brought it back home with them, to us.

In the afternoons, Pop drank cheap beer from a can and worked on his stamp collection or hovered over a jigsaw puzzle that he picked up from the flea market. Grandma could make a home-cooked meal no matter how many showed up at her door, and no one ever left hungry or dissatisfied. I can still see her standing in front of her stove, sipping on Fresca and gin served in tumblers with pictures of space rockets that she picked up from the Huntsville Space and Rocket Center where they volunteered every week. My mind can picture them in their bright red jackets, Grandma ringing up souvenirs at the gift shop, Pop assisting people with directions on where to find the space monkeys or the Apollo capsules displayed over yonder.

Sometimes when Pop took my brother fishing, Grandma and I went to lunch at the Piccadilly in Parkway Plaza mall. It was a cafeteria style restaurant where you grabbed your tray and asked the ladies in white uniforms, aprons and hair nets for some of this and a bit of that. Then she'd take me to the movie theater to see the latest Disney film.

I thought they were the best grandparents, that my family was the best in all the world. Not just because of the things we did or the fun we had, but because they'd always taught us to consider others and to be compassionate to those in need. There was no yelling then, no fighting, no hitting, save that one time when Grandma slapped me for calling Dad the N-word. I'd heard it at school and heard Pop say it a few times until she yelled at him to stop. I can't say as I blamed her after she told me what it meant.

Those were the stories I preferred to think about. The only ones I was willing to share with Karen as we drove across the country.

JOURNEYMEN

Campo, California is a high desert, meaning it gets just enough rain to maintain the thick mountainous brush, sage, and some oak trees, but not wet enough for much else. It is the last bit of greenery before you drop off into the sandy, flat desert of Calexico, where only the most adaptable creatures dare to live. Behind the original Campo Border Patrol station that I was assigned to is the Pacific Crest Trail that Lewis and Clarke explored. The same trail I'd learned about in all those books I used to read as a child at Grandma's house. The ones that said the explorers and settlers were brave because they risked their lives and the lives of their children by migrating across the dangerous Southwest in search of a better life.

I knew some of the history about America's genocide against Natives even though it was never talked about at school, simply because my third great-grandparents on my mother's side were pure Cherokee and forced to walk the Trail of Tears. My maternal grandmother and her siblings visited the Cherokee reservations from time to time and always came back with stories that I could not identify with. Native reservations still dot the landscape of the Campo area, down this dirt road and that one over there. Tribal lands are common along the border.

We were given a basic introduction to our individual field training agents known as journeymen. The midnight supervisor gave us a synopsis of Campo station's area of patrol before heading out. It was roughly thirty miles of border from the steep mountains of Tecate that were thick with brush, boulders the size of cars and beautiful manzanita trees, to the flat valleys and sandy arroyos of Boulevard, California. We could drive and hike north all the way past Interstate 8 into Julian, where it snowed every winter, and where we'd be sure to find the tracks of deer in and around Corte Madera Ranch and the Laguna Mountains. In the summer, rattlesnakes were everywhere on the open roads or curled up waiting to strike on the rocks or hiding under the brush that most hikers routinely passed by without ever noticing. Occasionally, we could expect to see a rosy boa, a California king, or a gopher snake that, although not poisonous, liked to chase people. He warned us about the bobcats, mountain lions, coyotes, scorpions, tarantulas, and other predators. We would rarely see them but would know they were around because of the tracks they left behind.

If you were lucky enough not to meet your fate with any of the predators, the heat of the long summers could easily kill you. Campo generally hovered above 100° and below 110°, with several days a year of record temps. As long as you were still sweating, you were fine. It was when you stopped sweating and got chills that you needed to worry. By the time most realized they were in trouble, it was too late. A simple momentary pause to catch one's breath and cool down while sitting on a rock could develop within seconds to flushed skin, headaches and nausea, or diarrhea. Trying to stand and walk it off, victims often discovered their vision blurred, and their leg and stomach muscles cramped in excruciating pain. Even if we found them before they died, even if we gave them water and life-flighted them to the hospital, it was likely that they would not survive as their organs would already have begun to fail. Heatstroke and dehydration are horrible ways to die.

We should expect to find bodies, our journeymen warned. Only the ignorant or truly desperate would cross our area, and there seemed to be a lot of them. Sometimes the bodies of migrants were found shortly after passing, but mostly the bodies were days or weeks old. Members of their group often posed them lying on their backs, arms crossed on their chests, with a cross necklace or rosary in their hands. Before too long, the digestive gasses built up and exploded their stomachs, attracting critters and bugs from miles around. Larger animals and birds often carried away parts of the bodies before devouring what was left. Cell phones did not work in those desolate mountains and the Patrol did not have any emergency water stations at the time. Migrants either made it or they didn't. It was our job to collect as much of their remains as possible and wait for a county medical official to fly overhead and declare the person deceased.

In the winters, the farther north the migrants climbed, the more their chances of freezing to death increased. The sweat on their clothes from the beginning of the hike quickly turned into ice. Agents often found them naked as they suddenly believed they were burning up. Their minds had become frozen with confusion, with a sort of dementia that occurs just before passing away from hypothermia. It made it impossible for them to seek help even if they wanted. When you found a jacket, then a sweater a few yards away, then shoes, and pants—you knew they were just around the corner, frozen, fallen face first in the snow after taking their last breath.

When I arrived in November of 1995, Campo station consisted of only one double-wide trailer that housed management, one cinder block office for the administrative assistants and an old cinder block garage with asbestos coated ceilings for the migrants in processing. We had five supervisors and one boss at the station who was called a patrol agent in charge or PAIC in Border Patrol speak. Everything had a thick coat of light brown dirt on it brought in from the dust that clung to our uniforms and boots. Tables were littered with Styrofoam cups of dip spit and nude pictures of women torn from *Playboy* and *Hustler* were stapled to the walls. A frozen bobcat in the freezer of a small refrigerator in the kitchen was posed to stare right at the person opening it. An old coffee tin sat next to the pot to collect money for the maker that was constantly brewing.

There were only about fifty or so agents assigned to Campo when I first arrived. With many on temporary training details, others on sick or vacation leave, we were lucky to have more than five or six agents per shift. Once we passed our six months of post-academy training, we were expected to drive alone, hike alone, apprehend groups of five to a hundred or more alone. We would each be assigned a training officer for two weeks, evaluated, and then passed on to a different agent. Once a week, we met with our post-academy instructor for Spanish and law classes meant to prepare us for our six-month and ten-month exams. If we failed either, we were fired instantly.

* * *

It felt cold enough to snow my first night on patrol, and when I looked north, I could see under the bright moonlight how the snow dusted the peaks of the Laguna Mountains. The noise and light pollution of San Diego could not reach that far east. The only sounds were the hum of the giant San Diego Gas and Electric towers, howls of coyotes, and screeching owls.

I listened for the occasional movement of the group that we had been tracking all night from the border. I could hear them as their clothes scraped against the brush. Occasionally, I heard whispers in Spanish to be quiet. Their footfalls that landed on leaves or sticks stood out the most. It looked to be about six or seven, women and men, maybe a few children, judging by the size of their footprints. My journeyman and I followed them quietly for miles. Occasionally, he stopped to teach me about the sign they had left. I was in the best shape of my life from the academy, and still my thighs burned from the steep climb.

"See the color difference in this footprint versus that one? It's because the one with color is fresher, has lifted the moisture from below, and that moisture has not yet dried. This one is soft, all muted colors. It's dried out, which means it's older and not the group we want," he whispered and then spat his chew in the print. He let me lead for a while after he showed me how to hold my flashlight low to better see the footprints. This was the art they called sign cutting, and he taught me all the tricks that he knew on how to hunt humans.

I stopped at the beginning of a large piece of rock they crossed. "How do I track across rock like this?" We turned off our flashlights and waited for our eyes to adjust to the darkness.

He pointed ahead. "Look at what they are looking at in the dark. Where would you go?" The path was clear under the moonlight. We crossed to the other side, and I picked the sign back up once the trail went back to dirt. "Do that for leaves as well," he said. Six hours later, he stopped again and pointed to the ground. "See how deep the toe is now? How the dirt is kicked back? They are running. They hear us." And we started running too, stopping here and there to see if we lost them. We circled until we found their tracks again and continued until suddenly all went quiet.

"They laid up," he said. "Laid up" was Border Patrol slang for a group hiding in the brush, hoping agents had lost them. "Busted them" meant the group scattered everywhere. We followed the sign until we heard a baby cry. At the end of my light, I saw a woman's face. She was maybe in her late twenties. Her long brown hair was filled with broken brush, and her face was covered in the same dirt that covered my own. She held her baby close to keep him warm. I had my hand on my .357 revolver, and my heart raced as they all dropped to their knees and raised their hands in the air.

"It's a family, Budd. It's all good," he told me. I took my hand off my pistol. Agent Thompson never yelled at them, never cursed them.

Mom, dad, two kids, a baby, and grandma and pop. A family? A family. I was confused. "I thought we were chasing drug smugglers or single criminal males crossing illegally," I said in my ignorance.

"We chase everybody. Don't know who they are until we catch 'em. But most are single males looking to work the fields and to send money home. Sometimes, it's families. Search 'em."

I did as he ordered, as I had been trained to do in the academy. There were no drugs, no weapons. Only a change of clothes, water, and some tortillas in plastic grocery sacks. They avoided eye contact, always looking down in what I assumed was their shame for breaking my country's laws, never saying a word as I patted their bodies. I recognized their fear and could feel it.

"Why are they so afraid?"

"Because we're La Migra. We have a reputation for not taking shit," my journeyman said. I put them in our transport van, and we returned to the station where I took down their names, birthdates, birthplaces. "Let's get back in the field and catch some more," he excitedly said. In the morning, when the small Tecate Port of Entry opened, we returned the family to Mexico after buying baby formula and diapers for them using our own money.

Sitting in a hot bath the next morning after working for thirteen hours, I thought about how good it made me feel to find that family. I thought about how they might have frozen to death that far north or how they could have fallen and gotten hurt. I felt good when I took the young mom in to pick out things for her baby. I was glad that my journeyman wasn't a dick to them like I knew others were.

I called Mom a bit later, and she asked me how I liked my new job. I liked the hiking, the four-wheeling, and tracking, and added, "But I feel like a fucking Nazi hunting people down like that. Families. Babies. But I'm sure I'll get some real criminals soon."

"Well, my parents said the Border Patrol is the butthole of the federal service, that they're racists," she said.

I bit my bottom lip trying to choose my words carefully. "I don't know, Mom. I just started. I don't know about that. Besides, over half the agents are Hispanic."

"They said you need to join the FBI or something else."

"Well, that's not what I did, Mom. Can y'all just be proud of me for doing this? Can you just give me that?"

It was eleven in the morning, which was nearing bedtime for me. I turned on my old television set, microwaved a frozen chicken pot pie, and sat on the floor of my new one-bedroom apartment that I had rented in town. Furniture, a couch and a bed, would have to wait until I earned more money. I laid awake most of the day, thinking about her comments and wondering if I'd made a mistake.

The good feeling that I had for finding the family didn't last. I couldn't help but wonder why they had decided to take such a dangerous journey. They certainly did not seem happy that I had found them.

* * *

On the days I did not have a journeyman to ride with, I was assigned to the I-8 checkpoint located several miles north of our station. Campo did not have enough agents at the time to fully staff the new checkpoint and was forced to detail agents from Texas to man it. I found the old faded green Crown Vic parked in the back of our station parking lot. It was the only service ride left, and I understood why no one took it as I drove up Buckman Springs Road toward the interstate. The brakes were so soft that the pedal nearly went to the floor, and the steering wheel bounced left and right, even though I was driving in a straight line.

At the checkpoint, there was one port-a-potty, a couple of gas-powered lights, an old white school bus that had once been used by the Immigration and Naturalization Service to deport migrants, and an old oak podium with the U.S. Border Patrol seal mounted to the front. All the Texas agents wore cowboy hats and the brown leather jackets that we as trainees were not allowed to buy until we passed our post-academy training. Like most things in the Patrol, this was not a written policy but a part of the culture.

"You just stand here behind the podium. Ask them what their citizenship is first, cause that's the law. We might be able to arrest people for drugs and other crimes, but we have to be doing our immigration inspections first before we can get into any of that," Agent Olson said. "We ain't got no dogs here. So, you can't rely on a dog hit to search for drugs. If it ain't obvious, don't worry about it."

"Do I stop everyone?"

"You can, but don't let traffic build up too much. If it starts getting heavy, wave most through. You'll know when you see a wetback," he said.

It was one in the morning and traffic was light. I stood behind the podium, wondering to myself if it made me more of a target for oncoming cars when another agent pulled it aside and confirmed my thoughts. As cars pulled up, they lowered their driver's side window and I asked them to state their citizenship. Most were locals, citizens heading into San Diego. They were used to us and simply waved and said, "U.S. citizen." I could always tell those from the local Native reservations as they often refused to roll down their windows and just stared at us. I was warned to stay clear of them, as it wasn't a fight worth having.

When the old Cadillac pulled up, the first thing I noticed was that all four males in the car appeared Latino. I asked in English if they were U.S. citizens, and they replied with a blank stare. I asked the same question in Spanish, to which they replied, "U.S. citizen." Before I could ask anything more, the Texas agents surrounded the car and began pulling them out.

"You are so new you can't tell a wet when you see one," Agent Jenkins laughed.

While they searched and interrogated their subjects, I had a young man who'd been sitting in the back up against the car, facing away from me. I told him to place his hands on his head and then placed my left hand on top of his hands while I reached down to pat down his pants. Suddenly, he removed his right hand from my grasp, and I quickly grabbed it and forced it back on his head.

"Don't do that!"

"My wallet is in my back pocket, ma'am," he said in Spanish.

"I don't care," I replied in Spanish, and I realized the Texas agents were watching to see how I would handle this guy.

"Don't move. Do you understand?"

"Yes."

I started my search again and he removed his right hand again, nearly getting it down to his side, which was also the side my gun was on. I grasped his left hand still atop his head with mine and pulled his arm down behind his head, causing him pain, and slammed my body into the back of his as I again grabbed his right hand in mine. With all my weight and strength, I pushed him over until his face slammed onto the trunk of the car. He cried out in pain and started saying something about his nose as I quickly cuffed him and then patted him for weapons. I then turned him around to look at him. His face was splattered in blood.

"I told you not to fucking move!" I yelled in English. He nodded and said he was just trying to give me his wallet.

"Do you have a green card?"

"No," he cried.

"Then I don't care about your wallet! You're reaching right where my gun is! You gave me no choice!"

He simply nodded, and I went through his wallet and his other belongings, established he was in the country illegally before uncuffing him and giving him a paper towel to wipe his face. He sat in the front of the bus while I filled out their paperwork, trying to calm down. The adrenaline rush was like that of being in a car wreck.

"Should I take him into the hospital? Report that I injured him?" I asked Jenkins.

"Being a Border Patrol agent means never saying you're sorry to a wetback. Never. You did what was right. If he accuses you of anything, you just follow our motto: deny, deny, deny, counter allegate, deny." This would be repeated far more often than "Honor First" ever was. He leaned into the bus and asked in Spanish if the young man wanted to file a complaint and tell everyone that a *guerita* beat him up. The bus erupted in laughter. "Looks like he wants to go back to Mexico. You, little lady, can kick some ass!"

It felt weird to receive praise for busting someone's nose.

* * *

The point of post-academy training was to get a well-rounded education into the different ways of patrolling the border. My new journeyman liked to hike, but he didn't seem to like me none too much. Rarely did he say anything to me. We rode around in silence for hours on the dirt roads with our heads hanging out, looking for signs of crossings. Every road north had hundreds of footprints in the dirt. There were so many crossings that most didn't even bother to hide. The smarter smugglers put sponges or rags on the migrants' shoes or came back with a piece of brush to wipe the footprints away. So, we dragged large tractor tires attached to towing chains behind us to smooth out the dirt so we could see the faint impressions of the brush-outs. It was better to get the freshest prints of the shift or the most recent crossers instead of wasting time chasing a group that had already loaded into a car.

The midnight supervisor called over the radio for all trainees to return to the station, and we immediately stopped our hunt. We got back to the station at around 2:00 a.m., and I took a seat at the end of the long, dark wood laminated government table. The building was deep enough to pull a truck in and long enough to hold three of them. The garage doors had been replaced with the white concrete cinder blocks that comprised the rest of the old building. In the corner were two small alcoves. Each one had a filthy toilet and a small bench that could seat about three people. The alcoves were surrounded by chain-link fencing from the floor to the ceiling. The chain-link door was locked with a standard Master Lock and was the only way in or out. Every agent had a key to it. It smelled like the bathrooms at a zoo or county fair—heavily used and hardly cleaned. It reminded me more of a dog or animal kennel than a human detention cell.

Older agents had tracked down a group of thirty Mexican migrants crossing the border illegally that night, and we as trainees were brought in to learn how to process them or clean them, as some said, as if they were trout. Name, date of birth, place of birth, where they crossed and when were all handwritten on their I-213 officially called the Record of Deportable/Inadmissible Alien. My classmates who spoke Spanish fluently were done within minutes while I struggled to simply understand the names that came to my ear like a machine gun. "*Otra vez, mas despacio, por favor*," would become my most repeated phrase in Spanish.

All migrants have rights. They all have a right to have a hearing before an immigration judge if they believe they should be allowed to stay in the U.S. If they want to claim asylum, they can request it. Border Patrol agents are not asylum officers or immigration judges, which requires more education and training. We just did the paperwork concerning their crossing and their biographical information before sending them down to town for the asylum officers. Illegally crossing the border was a crime under 8 USC 1325, but it was an administrative immigration violation and not charged criminally back then. It was sort of like being arrested for jaywalking. Yes, we documented it, but we did nothing about it other than to return them to Mexico.

If the migrant was not a Mexican national, we referred to them as "OTMs" or Other Than Mexican. OTMs required an immigration hearing because Mexico would not take a non-Mexican back then. It wasn't a big deal to do asylum paperwork, but it was more than a simple voluntary return to Mexico. Most agents and many of my journeymen did not like doing paperwork and often never bothered to learn how to complete a simple asylum claim. Most of my journeymen returned OTMs as voluntary returns, falsely stating on their paperwork that they were Mexican. Even though this was against the law, even though we officially lied on government forms, even though we were violating U.S. and international laws, my journeymen did this every morning once the port opened by hiding them within a crowd of Mexican migrants and then shoving them through the small Tecate Port of Entry so that Mexican authorities had less of a chance to realize they were not Mexicans.

This denied the OTMs of their hearings and rights, but my journeymen knew no one cared and no one was watching. I did this too. I violated OTM's rights under the orders of my journeymen. This was illegal. I knew it; they knew it. Once I passed my trainee status and became a full agent, I never did it again. Not because I did not want to violate their rights, but because I knew it was illegal and feared someone would turn me in for doing it, even though I had been trained to do it. Those agents who went after me for reporting my sexual assault could have turned me in for this, and I would have been fired.

Most people who crossed illegally in the mid-nineties were Mexican migrants looking for work. They were not claiming asylum. They did not bring their families and intended to return to their homes in Mexico after the harvest season. Their only choice, once apprehended by us, was to claim asylum or waive this right and take a voluntarily return back to Mexico, known as a "VR" in Border Patrol lingo. This right was written in Spanish on their I-826 forms they were required to sign if they did not want a hearing and preferred to return to Mexico voluntarily. Most chose a VR because they could turn right around and try again. I was told that it usually took three tries before they succeeded in getting through.

But not everyone could read, and not everyone spoke Spanish. Many migrants from Mexico spoke only their indigenous languages, for which we had no translators. So, we pointed to the signature line and handed them a pen telling them to put an "X."

"Read this form and sign it if you agree," I fumbled in Spanish.

"What the fuck, Budd?" Agent Diaz, my post-academy instructor, yelled. "Don't fucking tell her that. She'll ask for a damn hearing, and then they'll all ask for hearings. Do you know how much paperwork that is?"

"No. I don't. Isn't it their right to ask for a hearing?"

"Yeah, but we don't tell them that. They'll fucking fill up the detention space if we tell them that!"

"I cannot read," she quietly said as she handed the I-826 back to me. I looked up at her curiously, and slowly it dawned on me that this was a kind of poor I'd never seen before in my life.

"*Usted tiene derecho a comunicarse con un abagado o otro representante…*," I began reading out loud.

"Goddammit, Budd! What did I just fucking say?"

"You said not to tell her about asking for a hearing."

"Then why are you reading her those rights?"

"Because those are her rights, and she cannot read. You know, read 'em their rights. Like in the movies. Like all cops do."

"She's a fucking tonc!" he yelled. "Do you know what a fucking tonc is, Budd? That is a fucking tonc!" He pointed at her, making her jump back because she knew he was talking about her. "Say it! Fucking say it!"

"She's a tonc."

"That's right. That means she's got no fucking rights. Have her sign the damn form and move on."

I wasn't shaken for being yelled at. I was used to my instructors yelling as if they were military drill sergeants. I was more concerned that we were not reading people their rights and about his insistence that they had no rights. These rights were not the same as the Miranda rights we'd all grown up hearing on television cop shows. These were immigration rights that the academy had taught us were under a different but equitable system of justice. That, I supposed, was a matter of opinion. The academy taught us that migrants who crossed illegally were not afforded the right to an attorney if they could not afford one for immigration violations because immigration violations were charged as administrative immigration violations and not criminal. Even so, I couldn't understand his point. Why bother having rights if we didn't tell them what they were? Why were we asking them to sign something that many could not even read?

My classmates who spoke fluent Spanish had already left by the time I finished my last person. Diaz closed the gate and locked the men and women in separate cages, crammed like sardines.

"How long do they stay there?"

"Until morning when Tecate opens, then we'll VR them. The inside supervisor will look after them from time to time."

"So, what does tonc stand for? They just said it meant an illegal in the academy."

"It's the sound our flashlights make when we hit them in the head," he said without hesitation.

"What?"

"You fucking heard me. You don't tell anyone that. It's for Patrol agents' ears only. You tell outsiders it means Temporarily Out of Native Country or True Origin Not Known."

"Why the secrecy?"

"Because they'll say we're racist or some bullshit like that. Look, Budd, if you want to be an agent, you have to say tonc. If you can't say that, if you're some kind of fucking liberal crybaby, then get the fuck out. We're family here and we have to protect one another. We bleed green."

Agents claimed that anyone who crossed the border illegally were "toncs," but there was no denying that the word was used exclusively for those coming from Mexico and Central and South America. I have never heard an agent call a Canadian a tonc. Not someone from China, Haiti, Israel, Russia, Australia, Germany, and yeah, we had those too. Just not as much as the Mexicans. The word "tonc" was used for Latino crossers; the term "illegal" was for all the others.

I had no problem using the word tonc.

* * *

The checkpoint had been closed for a few days, waiting on the latest snow to melt enough that it was safe to reopen. Bad weather or less than four agents was enough to temporarily shut it down, which was often. After throwing the heavy orange traffic cones out of the bed of a truck for the Texas agents to set up, I stood at the podium, waving cars through without checking, just as they had ordered me to do until everyone was back with me at the primary position. It made me nervous standing there as my bulletproof vest had still not arrived. All my classmates had theirs. It would have been easy for someone to drive up, shoot me, and just drive away. From all the academy stories about how violent migrants were, I thought that this was a real possibility.

"Alright, Budd, whenever you're ready," Jenkins said as he started up the outdoor heater that kept only our legs from freezing. There wasn't much traffic since it was just after midnight. I saw two cars approaching in the single lane that we had made for them with the traffic cones, and I raised my left hand to signal that I'd intended to stop them. Agent Jenkins stood on the passenger side as my backup and would search any vehicles that I ordered to pull over into the secondary inspection area.

As the driver rolled down his window, I could tell he looked confused when he saw me. I had already learned that this was not uncommon for people who'd never traveled this close to the southern border and was mentally preparing my speech when he leaned across the passenger seat, and began telling Agent Jenkins that he was a U.S. citizen. Jenkins did not even look at him because he was watching the next car coming and said, "Tell her that, not me."

"I ain't talking to no split tail," he said. "She should be in the office. Why they let you put on a uniform and come out here and play with the big boys, honey?"

"Please state your citizenship, sir," I ordered.

"I told him already." He started to put his car in gear when I grabbed a stop stick that had thick, needle-like spikes all around it and was covered with a black, hard plastic case that would break away once a tire ran over it and threw it out in front of his car.

"If you go forward and not over there to the right into secondary inspection, you will be running a federal immigration checkpoint, which is a felony. You will be placed under arrest, and I will be sure to show up for your court date," I assured him.

"Well, ain't she a bitch," he said to Jenkins.

As he pulled into secondary, Jenkins yelled to Olson to take secondary. "Watch this old Ford truck, Budd. Something's off. See how he's sitting back. I think he's giving himself enough room to gun it and run the point. Look for a place to run if you need."

I glanced around to my right, looking for a place to run as I heard him hit the accelerator. I ran backwards onto the side of the road and watched as the truck's driver blew the stop sign at the primary position and just missed the stop stick that I had thrown out before. I saw people lying face down throughout the bed of the truck as it passed me.

"Bodies in the bed!" I yelled at Jenkins as we both ran for a sedan.

"Go! Go! Go!" Jenkins yelled as I threw the running Crown Vic in drive and floored it, hitting my lights and sirens.

The old truck was already at the top of the hill west of us and going down the other side toward San Diego. It took me a couple of miles before I even started to catch him.

"Wooooooo! I love this shit!" Jenkins screamed, and I could feel the adrenaline flowing in me.

The pursuit policy of the Border Patrol at that time was that if the driver of the vehicle drove dangerously or entered a densely populated area, we had to terminate the pursuit. Years before I joined the agency, agents in San Diego had chased a car into the city and innocent pedestrians and others were killed. Public outrage caused the agency to change the pursuit policy, making it stricter about when and where we could engage in a pursuit. I agreed with what agents nicknamed the "No Pursuit Policy" simply for the fact that I did not believe that stopping a vehicle was worth risking anyone's life. Especially considering that we stopped vehicles simply for immigration violations. This was an opinion that I kept to myself because I knew most of my colleauges did not agree.

By the time I looked down at the speedometer, we were already up to 110. "We need to terminate," I said.

"Fuck that! Keep going!" he ordered.

In the few seconds that it took me to realize he was ordering me as a trainee to violate policy, the truck's engine caught fire and began veering to the left of the four-lane interstate towards the median. He was headed straight for the Pine Valley Creek bridge, which spanned a four-hundred-and-fifty-foot drop to the bottom. It was not survivable.

"He's going to drive off the fuckin' bridge!" I yelled.

"No, he ain't!"

"Fuck!" I yelled as I saw the truck's hood fly open and block the driver's view. He stood on the brakes, but the truck skidded as he was on the dirt and gravel median between the east and westbound lanes. There was no guardrail in front of him. I stood on the brakes and stopped within inches of the truck's bumper, which created a large cloud of dirt that Jenkins disappeared into. Everyone in the bed of the truck jumped out and started running in all different directions.

"We need backup at the Pine Valley Creek bridge!" I yelled over the radio.

An old Campo agent and two California Highway Patrol officers showed up immediately as they'd been following along on the radio and had already started heading our way. We began rounding everyone up and sitting them near my car when Jenkins ordered me to stay with them while they looked for others. The Highway Patrol officers used their fire extinguishers and quickly put the fire out.

I looked at the people sitting before me, and all I could think about was what could have happened. They could have wrecked, going that fast in the old truck. Some of them could have fallen out because they were in the open bed. They could have gone over the side of the bridge, and then they'd all be dead. Some could have run over the side because they couldn't see from the smoke and the dirt cloud or because they were terrified of *La Migra*. My mouth filled with saltwater and the glands in my cheeks began tingling. It took everything I had not to puke.

"We got 'em all, I think," Jenkins said breathing hard.

"You think?" I asked.

"We got 'em all, Budd," said the old agent who I did not know. "Next time this happens, next time a load crashes on you, you need to say over the radio that you've terminated the pursuit so that it is on record. You say, 'I'm terminating the pursuit because the driver is driving erratically or dangerously. I'm stopping on the side of the road and have turned my sirens and lights off.'"

"Yeah, I didn't do it soon enough. I should have done it once I realized we were speeding," I said, not understanding his meaning.

"Fuck that, Budd!" he said. "You chase 'em until they crash. If you say that you've terminated the pursuit over the radio, and it's out here where no witnesses are, then no one knows that they've already crashed. Hell, get up beside them and make them crash. Intimidate the fuck out of them. When you say that over the radio, sector dispatch has a recording of it. As long as it's like this—late at night in the middle of nowhere, you can still pursue them. Wait a few minutes after you say you're ending the pursuit, and then get back on the radio and say that you were looking to make sure the car did not crash when you suddenly came upon them crashed. That way you're not responsible for the crash, the injuries, or any deaths, and neither is the agency."

"But the people in the load vehicle know, right?"

"Yeah, but no one listens to wets," Jenkins agreed.

"So, if I'm in pursuit and the car crashes, I just turn off my siren and say to sector dispatch I've terminated the pursuit?" I asked.

"Right. Then wait a few minutes, come back on the radio, and say you are going to drive around to make sure no one got injured. Then you suddenly stumble upon them," Jenkins said.

"But what if someone is seriously hurt or dead?"

"Who the fuck cares? They're just toncs!"

On the drive home that night, I thought about how thankful I was that nobody was hurt in that chase. I didn't agree with my journeymen that night. I didn't believe people should die for crossing a border legally or illegally.

* * *

Two weeks later, I followed my third journeyman into the thick brush just as he ordered me to do. I had no idea where we were or where we were going. There were no streetlights to guide our way, no signs or landmarks that I recognized. It was just somewhere in Campo, on the side of a mountain along a dirt road. He ordered me to jump out halfway up the steep incline and turn the hub locks on the front tires to place the truck in four-wheel drive. We jumped out once parked at the top.

"The sign's here," he whispered back at me.

I followed him for a bit, crawled on all fours under the bushes filled with thorns that sliced at my face and hands. I stood up when I came through to the other side and brushed myself off, only to no longer see my journeyman. There were no answers to my whispers. No noise I could perceive. Just a wall of thick brush and darkness. I pushed on, never hearing or seeing a thing.

"Charlie one eleven," I radioed to him.

For them, the male agents, leaving me in the middle of nowhere was a bonding experience. I'd not yet learned how to tell my position from the stars or from the terrain, nor did I have a compass on me. GPS locators were not given to agents back then, and in the dark with no wall designating the border yet, it was all the same. I climbed to the top of the next hill, hoping to see something, anything at all, but there was no car in the distance, no electrical tower, just brush and more mountains.

I heard them laugh on the radio, laughing at me. So, I turned it off. I didn't want to key my mic and ask for help. It was my first time alone out there with the mountain lions and the drug smugglers that they said were everywhere. And though I'd seen no evidence of rampant criminality in my short time there, I still believed all my training and that the migrants who crossed the border were dangerous criminals waiting to steal my badge or take my head to La Raza.

I knew they wanted me to quit because I couldn't be trusted to keep my mouth shut. That's why they left me out there alone. That's why I had been assigned to that station in the first place. It was one of the last "Old Patrol" stations as they called it, where agents tracked groups on foot for hours, entire shifts, and sometimes even days, passing the baton to the next shift. Campo agents, they said, were the toughest and best-known trackers in all the Patrol. Instructors at the academy were jealous I'd been assigned there. They told me how lucky I was, that I should have been grateful for such a station in one breath and that I'd likely die out there in the next.

I zipped up my jacket, pulled my collar over my chin and mouth for warmth, guessed which way was north and headed out. I had about an hour to find my way out before the sun rose and the day shift started. I found a trail and stuck to it. Many people who got lost and confused out there had done so because they second-guessed their decisions so much that they ended up going in circles. I thought about them while I hiked. I thought about the stories I heard of people dying within hundreds of yards from where they started. Most often they died of falls, dehydration, or freezing to death. These were all likely outcomes for me as I had no water or food and just a pack of smokes, a flashlight, a gun with six bullets, and a baton. Against all urges to turn this way or that, I stuck to the well-worn trail as I figured the migrants had been doing it for many years and knew best.

Jesus, I hope I'm going north, I thought every time I crossed a barbed-wire fence. It could have been the border marker for all I knew. Up and down I went, across giant slabs of rock and around boulders, through the brush, past some cows that seemed none too concerned by my presence, through the thick grass, and skidded down the packed dirt to the edge of a cliff where I stopped just in the nick of time before going over the side. I kept going for four hours, never sure if I was heading in the right direction until I saw the lights of a few cars on what I recognized as Highway 94, the first east-west paved road north of the border. The sun started to come up as I hit pavement, and I began the walk west back to the trailer park on Forrest Gate Road that was my station.

Agents flew past me in their Ford Broncos as I walked on the side of the old highway. A couple of guys pulled over and waited, but I just walked past them. I thought if I made it that far, I'd make it the rest of the way. *Fuck them!* Day shift had already started. As I entered the fenced compound, I could see my journeyman who'd left me out there and some of my classmates sitting in the back of the station parking lot, drinking beer after shift and laughing it up when I walked in. My legs ached and my whole body shook from the cold. I poured a cup of coffee.

"Go sit in my office," Supervisor Donner ordered.

Gladly, I thought.

"Her facial expressions give me the impression she does not like me," he read aloud. This was what my journeyman, the one who'd just abandoned me, had written on my evaluation. I didn't deny it. I did not like him, but then again, I was not aware that liking him was part of the job requirements.

"He says we should fire you on your verbal Spanish boards," Supervisor Donner warned me.

"What do you want me to do about it, sir?"

"What happened last night?"

"It doesn't matter."

I'd been at Campo for only a month. My first post-academy law and Spanish exams were not far off. If I didn't get good reviews, what they termed "recommended for retention," they would fire me on my verbal Spanish boards, whether I passed or not. That was the only point in having the Spanish boards, to get rid of people they didn't like. Management claimed it was a fair and neutral process because they brought in assistant chiefs from other sectors to administer the test. They claimed that these chiefs didn't know anything about us, that they couldn't be biased in any way.

What they didn't tell us was that our post-academy training instructor had gone in before us and told them if we should pass or fail. I'd soon be sitting in a small room with two of them as they asked me to repeat thirteen memorized sentences in Spanish and answer a few questions. It had nothing to do with being able to speak or understand the language and everything to do with getting rid of what they deemed to be troublemakers or trainees that did not fit in. I'd seen fluent speakers fail and guys from the bayous of Louisiana who couldn't speak a lick of Spanish pass. I just hoped they wouldn't hold my having been sexually assaulted against me and fire me.

As I sat across from Donner, I could feel my blood start to warm from the anger brewing inside of me. I stared at the cheap government linoleum floor, so I didn't have to see his nuts being squeezed against the seam in his pants. Everything on him was tight, and I guessed he was easily over three hundred pounds. He was a Vietnam vet, about my father's age, with a large combover, a poorly trimmed mustache, and dandruff that covered his shoulders. He probably thought I didn't notice him looking me up and down through his thick bifocals my first day, but I had. I felt it. I sensed it every time I saw him. A little smile here, a brush against my shoulder there.

I was the only female working at Campo back then. Although there were two other women assigned to the station, they were always gone on special details to the academy or at the San Diego sector headquarters. Both were married to Campo agents. The bullying started the first day. Every time I showed up for work, the only women's toilet was full of shit. So full that I didn't dare flush it or use it. My station mail drawer was often stuffed with used condoms and magazine pictures of women fully spread. When assigned to our processing station in Tecate, I often walked in to find lingerie hanging from every camera stand used to take mug shots. I could hear them giggling like little boys in the offices as I threw the panties away. The sticky smell of sweat and cum was sprayed around in the trucks we shared, and I was forced to wipe my truck down before I even started my shift with cleaner that I carried in my duty bag.

"I know things have been hard for you. I know about the academy. About what happened." Donner explained that he was the one who picked up the phone at the station back when one of my instructors called from the academy to warn them. "The academy said you accused a classmate of sexual assault because you were afraid you might fail the physical training. They said you filed a false allegation, and we should fire you on your Spanish boards."

"That's not true. I didn't file an EEO complaint."

It had followed me to my duty station and was affecting my post-academy training. It was something that I had no control over, something that was not even my fault. And thanks to Karen, I knew that no one was giving Mendoza any shit over at their station in Imperial Beach.

Donner didn't care what had happened at the academy. He was making a point, seeing an opportunity. "I'm trying to help you. Do you want my help or not?"

He saw me hesitate. *Help, as in an honest-to-God, legit, fair shot of passing my post-academy training, or a this-for-that type of trade?* I wondered. "I'm not going to have sex with you if that is what you are going for," I said quietly, not believing I was in this situation.

"I'm not asking you to do that. Your classmate...the Black kid..."

"Johnson."

"Yeah. Well, he's having trouble too. Seems some of the agents don't want to work with a Black guy. Most don't want to work with a chick who's not their cheerleader either."

"I'm not here to be their fucking cheerleader!" I said angrily.

"Well, maybe you have to be," he seriously said. "I'm going to assign both of you to midnights on a drug lay-in with Simpson and Anderson. You all do what they say, and they'll give you both a fair chance."

Simpson and Anderson were what we called "crusty," meaning they were older agents.

"I don't have a bulletproof vest yet. All my classmates got theirs the first day."

"Do you want to pass or not?"

I assured him that I did. "Why are you doing this for me? Hardly anyone has been fair to me at this station."

"You don't think I know that? You think I can't see that? You don't think I have a hard time here because I'm fat? You think I can't hear all the jokes and comments?" He paused. "They don't want to give you your vest because they want you to resign. I'll look into it."

"Has a woman ever filed an EEO complaint and still kept her job after failing the physical training exams?" I asked.

"Not that I'm aware of."

"Then why do y'all accuse us of that every time we say we've been assaulted or harassed?"

He didn't have an answer for me.

* * *

Johnson and I laid in the snow on this trail and that one, night after night, for the remaining months of our trainee status. It was a "fair chance" that felt more like punishment as it meant we had to lay in the snow for ten to thirteen hours, waiting on drug runners to come up a trail.

"They're trying to kill us," Johnson said one night.

"Oh c'mon!" I whispered.

"You're the only chick. I'm the only Black guy. Think about it."

"They haven't called you the n-word, have they?" I asked.

"Yeah, I heard my journeyman call me that when he thought I wasn't around."

"You should file a complaint! They can't do that! That's racist," I whisper-shouted at him.

"There's a lot of other ways people can be racist, you know. How'd that go for you when you filed?"

"I never filed. Didn't want to be booted out for it."

"Well, there's your answer," he rightly pointed out. We sometimes spent the night spooning each other, trying to stay warm.

"At least you have a vest. I just have this stupid jacket," I reminded him. As trainees, we had a limited budget for uniforms every year, and I didn't have enough money for any more than the one jacket. After a couple of nights of freezing, I went to K-Mart and bought thermal underwear and big, thick tube socks that I wore two at a time.

There was no need to compare insults, to have a discrimination battle of who was treated worse. They hated him for his dark skin. They hated me because I had the nerve to report my rape. Everyone had their own hurdles to get over, I guessed. Looking back over the past graduating classes, we noticed there were never any more than two women and two Black trainees who made it. It may not have been written policy, but it was policy, nonetheless.

Night after night, we did as we were told. We hiked into the densest brush and waited. The hour-long drive back to my bare apartment in Rancho San Diego was excruciating. I turned the heat on high in my used '93 Camaro I'd bought with my savings from the academy, but I still couldn't stop shaking. Every morning when I got home, I ran a bath as hot as I could stand before dropping my heavy belt with my gun still holstered in it onto the floor and stripping down. Brush fell out of my uniform and covered the linoleum. Occasionally, I noticed a scorpion crawl out from the pile of clothes and tossed a heavy boot on them before they got too far. I had to soak in the hot bath for thirty minutes, sometimes more, before the pain went away. I contemplated why I was doing any of this while listening to Janis, Billie, and Dolly.

This was what it took for the only Black guy and the only female at the station to graduate. It was unfair, unjust, and outright discriminatory. While our other classmates rotated through different journeymen and learned different areas and trails, how to conduct safe vehicle stops, how to track groups through the mountains, practicing their Spanish, Johnson and

I stayed in place and listened to every single piece of brush breaking, every little whisper. Not once did we apprehend a drug smuggler, but we passed.

I wonder if he, too, thought he was paving the way for others.

HONOR FIRST IS A LIE

I spent our post-academy graduation evening working the night vision scope truck, setting up the heavy camera on its tripod stand wherever agents requested. Animals and humans glowed green on the small screen inside the truck as I radioed to agents on foot, telling them where the groups were and where they should go to apprehend them. I didn't mind running the scope after several nights of constant hiking. I was still running five to six miles a day after working, and my legs needed a rest.

None of my classmates were working that night. I imagined they'd planned a party and as usual, I was not invited. The next evening, when Zarkowski returned to work, he informed me that I was right in my assumptions. He stopped hanging around me at the academy after Mendoza assaulted me, stating that he couldn't be sure I wouldn't accuse him of sexual assault as well. He had changed his mind after we arrived in Campo and was willing from time to time to hitch a ride to work with me since we lived in the same apartment complex, and it saved him money on gas.

As I drove us to work the next day, he told me all about what they did on graduation night, about how the supervisors of the station took up a collection to throw them a party in Tijuana.

"Why Tijuana?"

"Uh, well, cause that's where the whores are," he said like I was stupid.

"Whores? What are you talking about?"

"All the stations do it. We saw the others from our class; you know, the guys from Imperial Beach were there too. Same thing. Their management took a collection and treated the graduating class to a night of drinking and pussy." He said this like it was common sense, like it was common knowledge.

"Alcohol and prostitutes?"

"Yup."

"You did this?"

"Jenn, everyone does this. Well, most of the guys do. A few don't. Some even do drugs. It's like everything and anything goes down there. You know, it's like the academy; what happens in Mexico stays in Mexico. It was awesome. We got so wasted!"

"What about your faith?" I asked.

"Faith?"

"Yeah, how are you doing this when it violates your faith? Also, how are y'all doing this when it's against Border Patrol policy? What if someone at San Diego Sector Headquarters finds out?"

"First off, those guys at sector were once trainees too. From trainees to chiefs, they all do it. It's tradition. Graduate, go to Tijuana, get drunk, watch a girl suck off a donkey, and get laid. If we're all doing it, then no one can rat anyone else out for it. Secondly, you have no right to question my faith. My faith is none of your business."

"So, you're not concerned that management knows you're doing this? That those whorehouses are probably owned by the cartel, and they know who y'all are now?"

"Ummm…no. If the bosses do it, we do it. That's how this family works; it's the green line. We look out for each other, and those that don't go down there keep our stories to themselves," he stated.

"What did you say about donkeys?" I yelled as he got out of my car and ran into the station.

Bachelor parties, graduation parties, birthdays—any excuse to party and visit the brothels of Tijuana soon became the norm with many of my male classmates and every class before and after them. Zarkowski had been telling the truth. Agents openly bragged about their trips and compared stories, often visiting the same women when they found a particularly good one. Ten, twenty, thirty guys fucking the same prostitute so they could add her name to their list. It was a competition among some.

All the agents, male and female, knew this. For the white guys who did not feel comfortable going to Tijuana because they could not speak or understand Spanish, they simply learned which massage parlors in San Diego were covers for prostitution. They often ran into local police officers in the strip clubs. Badge to badge, they saw themselves as brothers in blue and would exchange information. Border Patrol agents told the local cops where to go to find action in Mexico, places where they would be safe, and in exchange, they gave our agents info on the safe massage-prostitute parlors in the county, the ones they didn't intend to raid any time soon.

It wasn't too long before I learned that many agents set up dates with the women they arrested. Zarkowski was one of these guys too. After apprehending a group, he often selected the females he wanted to fuck by setting up a place and a time to meet them after work in Tecate or Tijuana. He promised the women that he would consider making them his girlfriend if they went out with him. Desperate to get into the states, many migrant women fell for these schemes. Male agents had a never-ending supply of desperate women.

Agents did this so often that they openly discussed it with no fear of being caught even though it was against policy and the law. Countless stories were told while standing at the checkpoint, after work, in the processing centers, on the firing line. Management always looked the other way and encouraged this behavior because the majority of those in management had done it too. Some still did and saw it as a "boys will be boys" kind of thing. Chiefs often claimed that the men needed to blow off steam, that it was how they bonded. To openly criticize them invited ridicule. Bragging about how they used their positions as law enforcement agents to get sex was viewed as one of the perks of the job.

One night as Zarkowski and I walked a group of women down the railroad tracks back to our trucks on Highway 94, he quietly asked me if I thought he should ask one of them out. He wanted to meet one in Tecate later that night for some drinks and a blow job.

"I think you could get with any one of these ladies," I responded.

"Yeah?"

"Oh, yeah. You'd probably have a chance with all of them. Maybe at the same time." He looked at me curiously, almost hopefully as I suggested he turn his light on and look more closely at them.

"They're all men dressed as women, you moron!"

"Oh, come on, Papi!" they cooed at him, blowing him kisses and making smooching sounds. He quickly ran off, leaving me alone.

"Sorry ladies, you're stuck with me."

"Take us to the station to meet more agents, girlfriend."

"No, that would not be good for y'all."

I did not want to think of what my male colleagues would do to them if I took them to the station for processing. Instead, I headed over to Tecate and quickly voluntarily returned them to Mexico. It was my only option to keep them safe from my co-workers who despised the gay and transgender migrants above all others.

* * *

I eagerly transferred to the day shift after graduation, as it was easier to learn our patrol area. Supervisor Donner started by assigning me to inside agent, where I issued the trucks, shotguns, M-16s, spike strips for deflating tires to agents going out to the field, and then answered phones and ran errands. I helped in processing whenever agents brought in groups by taking their pictures, scanning their index fingers, and sending them back to Mexico. I weighed and recorded the occasional narcotics seizures and then secured the bundles until the Drug Enforcement Administration guys came to pick them up.

I learned immigration casework inside and out and quickly became the go-to agent for processing criminal migrants, human smuggling, and dope cases for the courts. Casework was something I liked, and I found it strange that most of my coworkers did not care about putting smugglers in jail. There were agents with over twenty years in the Patrol who barely knew how to turn on a computer, and others who never bothered to learn how to write up a case. If they ever encountered a dope load or a migrant load, they mixed the smuggler in with the group so they did not have to write up a case for court. They lied and routinely wrote "driver absconded" on the paperwork.

It wasn't long before I complained to Donner. I told him I was not hired on as an administrative assistant, that I was not there to be his personal secretary either, and pointed out that I had graduated the same academy as the men. I wanted to be in the field more, as I had trails to learn, mountains to climb, tracking skills to work on just as my classmates did. Reluctantly, he gave in and allowed me to take a truck into the field after I finished assigning everyone else their gear, but it was never long before he called me back in for one reason or another.

He used any excuse he could come up with. There was a woman who needed to be searched, a child who needed comforting, a problem with the computer, no one to answer the phone. Could I help with a case? Would I take a vehicle up to the checkpoint? Did I remember how to speak French? He told me he was writing a book and had decided to use me as the inspiration for the main character. I passed on his offer to let me read the raw manuscript.

He liked me because I was blond, young and thin, intelligent, and had an education. He recognized my writing skills and legal training, adored my freckles and the way my .357 hung low on my hip, and how my right hand always pushed against the grip when standing at the checkpoint. He commented on how my hair always fell out of its tie, giving him the excuse to touch it and then remind me to pull it up.

But most of all, I think he liked that I was his subordinate and that I could not defy his orders, that he had me trapped and there was nothing I could do about it. I'd already seen what happened when they thought I filed a grievance about being assaulted. I did not want anything worse to happen. As it was, I still had to clean out my trucks and mail drawer of the crap the men left behind for me. Aside from me getting used to their behavior and being a full agent, not much had changed since post-academy graduation.

My male colleagues spent a great deal of time spreading rumors about Supervisor Donner and me. Were we dating? Fucking? He was probably the only reason why I wasn't fired on the finals, they surmised. Before muster, after shift, at weekend parties, in training—all they did was gossip and tell stories. Especially if they thought it involved sex and a female agent, which their stories almost always did. I tried my best to simply ignore it.

When I wasn't assigned to Donner's regular shift, he often pulled me back into his orbit by requesting the PAIC assign me to work on a detail or temporary assignment with him. During my first year, he made me enter the station's time cards for payroll even though the station had two administrative assistants. Every two weeks, I came in on a Sunday dressed in normal street clothes and spent the day sitting at a computer. It was an excuse for him to try and buy me lunch, ask about my life, tell me about his. I knew he was married, had become traumatized by his service in Vietnam when his foxhole buddy was shot in the head right before his eyes. He didn't care for drugs or alcohol but ate his emotions. For that, I felt sorry for him. I could not hate him even though he drove me crazy.

He ordered me to work inside on this special project or that one. Some assignments helped me become a better agent, to understand the system better, to see the bigger picture. Others were simply busywork. I had little choice either way. This was a man responsible for my evaluations, a supervisor who could eventually affect my promotions. The guy who finally got me my bulletproof vest. It was more than the heavy pets of boys at the end of a date in high school or the constant calls from guys in college. It was harassment, and I started to understand it.

I realized the systemic nature of Border Patrol misogyny once more females were assigned to our station. It wasn't just being done to me. Female agents constantly had to navigate the advances of male agents who didn't necessarily believe that no meant yes but hoped that it meant maybe. Most of the guys didn't see anything wrong with any of it simply because they were not normally the victims of it and because they saw their superiors engaging in the same behaviors. When women complained, they were told to file EEO. The men went along with their work, were promoted and moved to other stations or sectors. After five, six years of waiting for EEO to conclude the investigation, they simply gave the female agents a right-to-sue letter. Most women agreed to a settlement, just wanting to be done with it. They would never know what happened to their abusers. Like pedophilic priests, predatory agents were simply moved around the country.

Some victims believed that it was part of their hazing as agents, but it was more than that. The men in the agency had figured out how to use the EEO system to hide their sexual assaults against female agents and the smaller male agents, the guys suspected of being gay. And though complaints were supposed to be confidential and private, the agents who were union stewards would quickly tell everyone. As a victim, you either had to hire your own attorney or use one retained by the union just like your accuser. Both sides were represented by attorneys paid by the union, making it impossible for confidentiality. This is still the system today.

Donner's actions signaled to the other agents to leave me be. I was his even if we weren't having sex. He'd marked his territory. Again, I had no say. It was the same as Agent Little had done to Karen, and I understood then personally how it had not been a choice for her. I resented the attention not because I was not interested in Donner as a lover, but because I needed him in the beginning just to get a fair shot at keeping my job. Without Donner, I would not have been given that chance to pass my post-academy training. Without him, I would have been fired. I was turning into a Border Patrol agent on the outside, but inside I was desperately afraid that some other agent may do what Mendoza had done.

Donner's mark on me, to some extent, saved me. I knew it as well as everyone else. No, I had not slept with him or any other agent, for that matter. I never asked for his help, but I took it when he offered it because I had to. There'd been no choice.

I started to believe that "Honor First" was just a lie.

* * *

I was only a few minutes away from the arroyo just east of the Tecate Port of Entry when dispatch called the sensor out. I raced along the dirt border road and skidded to a stop that kicked up a large cloud of dust. Without thinking twice, I jumped from my lifted Bronco and ran up the wash just north of the cemetery until I came to the general area where I knew the sensor was located.

"What you got, Budd?" came across the radio.

"One set of fresh sign. Looks like a dog with him."

I hated it when they used my name over the radio. It was bad enough that I was one of less than three women working at the station. Saying my actual name for anyone to hear, for smugglers to hear was irresponsible if not dangerous.

"Well, I'm north and I don't see any sign, or dog tracks. Check and see if they went west into the field," Beltran said just as I was climbing out of the arroyo and heading west, following the sign.

"I can hear someone yelling something southwest of me," I replied as I neared the top and leveled out. As I walked south toward the voice, I could see only the top of a man's head about fifty yards away. A few more steps up the embankment, and I could see his right arm was extended towards me. He was aiming a .44 magnum revolver, the kind Clint Eastwood carried in those old westerns, straight at me. Having nowhere to go in the open field now, nowhere to find cover, I dropped to one knee as I pulled my .357.

"U.S. Border Patrol! Drop your weapon!" I yelled as I'd been trained. As quickly as my gun came up from my side, he had dropped his into his left hand. He held it backward with the barrel pointed behind him as he grasped it by the cylinder. "Drop your weapon!" My .357 had a long trigger pull, and I relaxed my trigger finger, realizing that I had instinctively already pulled it about halfway.

"Where are you, Budd?" I heard Beltran ask.

"In the field south of you. He has a gun. I drew but he's holding it backward, not aimed at me." The radio suddenly became flooded with a handful of agents all asking my "10-20" or location. Beltran answered for me as I continued to follow the man as he walked away from me with his German Shepard trailing behind.

"You ain't got no right to threaten me! I'm a fucking U.S. citizen! Fucking bitch!"

"Drop your weapon, sir!"

We continued walking west towards some trailers as he yelled obscenities at me, and I kept him in my gun's sights. Beltran came roaring up behind me in his truck once we reached a dirt road, and I holstered my gun and quickly jumped in the passenger side. "Dude, what the fuck is that guy's problem?"

"I don't know. I think he's crazy. He says he's a citizen, but he had the drop on me when I came out of the wash," I replied. Other agents circled around him but kept their distance. I heard Donner over the radio say the San Diego Sheriffs had been notified, and within minutes we were all at his trailer.

"He pulled a gun on me! Don't let him get in his house!" I yelled at agents and deputies.

"Well, ma'am, he's a white guy. He's an American. He can own a gun, and he can walk around out here," was the response from one of the deputies.

"He set off one of our sensors and then pointed his gun at me as I came out of the wash!"

Eventually, the deputies talked him into letting them come into the trailer. The walls inside were wallpapered with pornographic magazine pictures. As they handcuffed him, he asked if they thought I would mind posing for him so he could take pictures of me.

Back at the station, one of my former journeymen ordered me to write up the arrest. I insisted that I could not write up the case because I was the victim but was told to shut my mouth and do as ordered. The other agents who had come to back me up all sat in the same room as me, rehashing the events as they typed up their witness statements. I knew this was wrong. I knew from my education and internship as a Mobile County District Attorney's Office investigator that witnesses were not supposed to talk with each other about the incident. As other agents from the next shift came on, many of them my classmates, the talk turned to how they believed I should have killed the man. They spoke as if I was not even in the room.

"Yeah, she should have shot and killed him," Beltran said.

"I drew my weapon to shoot, and he lowered his…"

"So, she should have still shot him. The shooting would have been justified. He had a gun," said a classmate.

"You weren't even there!" I replied. "And if all y'all think I should have shot, why didn't any of y'all get out of your fucking trucks and shoot him?"

"You would have gotten away with it. That's the problem with letting chicks in the Patrol; y'all are too afraid to shoot."

I did not want to shoot anyone. If I could end the confrontation without taking a life, that was what I would do. That is how I was raised. That is what I believed in. To my colleagues present that day, it was more about getting away with shooting someone or justifying the killing instead of doing the right thing.

I did not have my bulletproof vest on. I had grown accustomed to patrolling without it.

PROVING MYSELF

Agent Martinez was like most male agents I knew in that he never believed that I or any woman should have been an agent. It was nothing against us personally, he insisted. He just didn't think women had what it took to be agents, much less a Campo agent. When a male agent lost a fight in training, he shook their hand and said, "Good fight." When a woman lost, he said it proved we shouldn't be allowed in the service, that we couldn't hack it.

One morning, he started after a group just north of Lake Morena that had gone into the high mountains in the summer heat. My ears perked up when he said he was giving up over the radio. He decided it was too dangerous, too hot at over 112° and he descended back down the rocks to the lake and then drove back to the border. Always looking to prove myself, I snuck in where he started and went after them alone.

If you measured straight from where I started to where I ended up, it was probably only a few miles, but when hiked, those mountains had a funny way of multiplying the distance traveled. I don't know how long it was, step by step that is, but it was one of the harder hikes I did, steep up and steep down. The group curled around the mountains, switched back and forth as they tried to reduce the incline that I knew had burned their thighs because it burned mine too. I saw their empty water bottles and guessed they were laid up ahead of me somewhere, trying to get through the heat of the day, waiting for the cool of the night. Anyone who ever followed a group of migrants through that terrain, in that heat, would have to respect what they were willing to go through to find a job, a better life. If they didn't, then they lacked a soul.

When my radio went off, it was Martinez looking for me. He wondered where I was hiding down on the border.

I ran up to the highest point I could find to get out on the radio towers. "I'm chasing a group."

"What group?"

"Your group. The one you quit on." I could hear the other guys clicking their mics in laughter as I jumped back on the sign. It'd been two hours and my legs were on fire; my Camelback water bladder I'd brought was strapped to my back and was already half empty.

"I'm calling the copter. You're going to die out there," he insisted in his thick Puerto Rican accent.

"I know what I'm doing. I'll be fine."

I heard him ignore me and call the bird in anyhow. Then he called the station and told Donner that I was lost, maybe injured, which caused me to have to veer off the trail again and scurry up a hill to set him straight. I ignored all his other calls as I decided that I didn't have the time, or patience to deal with him anymore, and instead concentrated on getting to the group. I was worried that they may have had dehydrated members. I made sure to scan around under the brush and trees for bodies as I continued but thankfully found none.

After about four hours, I found them asleep under a big oak tree. I sat on a stump and smoked a cigarette to rest and waited for them to wake. My pale skin burned from the sun because I was too stupid and stubborn to carry sunscreen. At least my new cowboy hat had helped keep it off my neck. I counted fifteen men, likely all Mexican, sleeping like babies. Their eyes lit up when they realized they'd been caught by a woman, and they told me how tough I was to have followed them through the mountains like that. It made me smile, and I wondered why most of my coworkers couldn't see this in me. They said no one was left behind, which eased my worries a bit about dead bodies. I shared my water like always, and when I heard the bird, I waved for the men to get up and follow me. I only had one pair of cuffs and did not even bother with those.

"Are they giving her a fight? Is she okay?" Martinez came over the radio acting as though I needed to be saved.

The pilot laughed. "Naw, dude, she's good. Relax. Just follow that trail you're on ma'am. Your boys are up ahead."

I stuck my hand in the air and waved, too tired to get on the radio, thankful I had not died myself. Armando's face was the first I saw off in the distance. I could never miss that wide grin. "I got her over here," he said over the radio. He had just started the next shift when he heard me on the radio south of our checkpoint and came to help.

Before I could get to him, Martinez barreled down the road and cut me off with his truck. He jumped out and started screaming that I'd put myself in danger, that I shouldn't go after groups alone in those mountains in that heat.

"What do you think I should do? Sit in the office? Be your damn secretary? I'm a fucking agent, just like you. I trained just like you! I passed just like you! Hell, I'm senior to you!" I yelled at him, pushing him backward with my voice.

"They could have hurt you! Raped or killed you!"

"We'd never hurt a woman. Certainly not one that can hike like her and catch us. Much respect," one of the members of the group said as he patted me on the shoulder.

Armando held Martinez back with his big hand and told him to calm down. "You're just pissed because she showed you up, son."

"She doesn't belong out here," he seethed.

"Hey, Martinez. I ain't got time to go around and around about how I just kicked your ass. Maybe you don't belong out here! I gotta get back to the station and change my tampon," I joked.

"See! That right there! That having to go in and change your tampon is another reason they shouldn't let *putas* out here!"

"It was a fucking joke, asshole! I change my tampon on the trail just like every other agent!"

Everyone laughed.

* * *

When I came through the back door of the supervisors' trailer, I was pissed. Supervisor Donner had called me in out of the field once again. I was the only woman on day shift, and it often required me to do all the female searches and interactions. It did not matter that policy stated that men could pat down women for weapons if they used the back of their hands or that they could deal with kids as well. Male agents made excuses not to do their jobs and always claimed that female migrants would make allegations against them if they searched them.

So, when Donner radioed for me to return to the station that day, I figured it was for something one of the men refused to do again.

"There's a ten-year-old child that needs your attention," Donner said.

I was no longer afraid to get into it with him. "You know I have no children. There's no reason why I should—"

"Just fucking do as I ordered you to do. Will ya just do that? We're waiting on the Mexican Consulate. She's been wandering the mountains for three days. Agents caught her group, and her mother was apprehended, but she was not. Have some sympathy, for Christ's sake."

"Oh my God," I replied, ashamed.

She was in processing with the others, sitting in a cell alone. I knew that Acosta was assigned to processing that morning. That meant he was in charge of entering every apprehension through IDENT, our new computer database. Names, birthdates, places of birth, index fingerprints, and photos were all captured by this new program, and we could finally see how many times migrants had been apprehended and where. He usually volunteered for this position because he did not like hiking or making arrests. He was a station rat, a slug.

To avoid time-consuming paperwork, he often entered their thumb or pinky prints instead of their index fingers so that it would not identify the print of a migrant with a criminal record, forcing him to do more paperwork. The guys thought it was funny as many of them were guilty of the same malfeasance. I thought it was a dereliction of duty, if not outright criminal, and wondered how many rapists and pedophiles were simply returned to Mexico because the agents were too lazy to do the paperwork.

Acosta was a perve. He had a large porn collection of videos and magazines that he rented out to other agents. They could find him before shift and get a different magazine every time they worked. His claim to fame was that all the cum sprayed on the large yellow scraper tractor down by the border, above Highway 94 and the RV park, was because of him. He spent most of his time in processing, accessing porn websites on the government computers, jerking off and ogling the female migrants.

If I had been assigned processing that morning, I would have had her sit out with me at the desk, let her play games on the computer or draw. A filthy, stinky Border Patrol cell was no place for a child. Certainly not for a child who was alone. As it was, I reckoned she was safer in a cell alone than sitting next to Acosta.

"I'm taking her to get clean clothes on the inside Supe's orders. Call me in the front office or on the radio when the Consulate is ready."

"Whatever," he said without looking up. It occurred to me then how easy it would have been for any agent to just take her. There was no documentation required, no record that I picked her up.

Our processing center was new and much bigger and located in its own trailer now. Still, the smell always hit me like a ton of bricks. Our cleaning service only came once a day and the migrants were always sweaty and dirty from hiking for days, sometimes weeks. It took many miles of hiking in Mexico just to reach our area, then many more once they jumped the invisible border line and made their way north. I would stink too if I had made that journey. We did not have showers or clean clothes for them. They were in our custody for only an hour, maybe four at most, before transport officers picked them up and took them back to Mexico. We rarely returned them to Mexico ourselves anymore. Juice and crackers were all they got from us. Sometimes we gave them a blanket to keep warm if they needed. That was if the processing agent wasn't a dick.

I knelt in front of her and untied my blond hair to soften my hardened sunburnt face to her. Her dark hair had broken brush bits stuck in it and it was tangled every which way. The little jacket and jeans she wore were torn and her knees were scuffed from when she fell on the same rocks I often fell on. She was coated in dirt, and when she looked at me and smiled, I could see it stuck in her teeth.

"*Guera*," she said, and we laughed together.

She told me her name was Claudia, that when the agents came upon her group, they yelled at them, and her mom told her to hide. She waited there under the brush until it was quiet, until she heard the trucks drive away. Hours later, when she stood in the darkness, she realized no one else was left. She called softly at first for her mama, then screamed. Yes, she said she was scared when she heard the coyotes cry in the distance. Sometimes, she could not see anything but the brush directly in front of her. She stayed there that night and hoped her mama would return.

Migrant parents do not often abandon their children. More likely, the agents involved in the arrest were not fluent Spanish speakers and could not understand the mother's pleas. Agents routinely criticized and blamed the parents, as if they somehow loved their children less than Americans did, never willing to consider that their circumstances were different from ours.

By morning, Claudia figured the agents had taken her mom. So, she decided to walk in the direction they'd been going. She stayed on that trail, followed it up and down, slept under bushes when she was tired, drank from bottles and milk jugs of water that she found along the way, and ate from plastic grocery bags she found with old tortillas in them that had been left by the migrants before her. On the third day, she said she heard some cars on a road and went toward the sound. She popped out on Interstate 8 and was picked up by a passing agent.

I knew from making that same journey myself many times that this little girl was a strong soul, a brave soul. I asked Donner to order her a big breakfast and milk from a local diner, and we walked across from the station to a little hole-in-the-wall Catholic Charities thrift store.

"Anything you want. You pick," I told her.

"I have no money," she said as she held my hand and stood on the toes of my boots looking up at me.

"I do."

"But you're *La Migra*," her eyes widened, and she laughed.

"That's true, but it's okay."

Back at the station, I gave her shampoo, soap, and a towel in the new women's locker room and pointed to the shower. I did not know the word for shower or bath in Spanish. I turned on the water for her, tested the temp, and made like I was taking off my clothes, then pointed to her.

"I wait over here. No one will come in," I promised in my broken Spanish. I put my gun belt in my locker, holstered my gun in my off-duty holster now on my pants' belt and waited by the sinks on the other side. I heard her cry after a while; softly at first, then more desperately, she sobbed. I asked if she cried because she missed her mama, and she said that she did. I told her it was okay to cry, that it was good for her to cry. It was something I wished I'd been told when I was her age.

I thought I understood her, because I'd known the feeling of being alone at that age. That is to say that I knew the loneliness of not having a mother when you most needed one. Not that I had ever known the feeling of being a child in a foreign country, of being tended to by a person in a uniform that I'd been taught to distrust, of being so desperate to flee my home country and venture into the unknown. I realized then that I could not identify with her in that respect. I'd been born over here, and I was not her color.

"We will find your mama," I assured her. She dried herself off and got dressed in her new clothes, a pink and white dress, and cute shoes. I bought her a pair of jeans, shirt, extra undies, and tennis shoes as well and had them in a plastic grocery bag. I combed her hair with my brush and added that to her bag as well. I made her stop to look in the mirror before we left.

"How pretty," she said quietly and smiled.

We ate breakfast together in the station's old break room, and I gave her coloring books and crayons. Eventually, she fell asleep sitting in my lap.

"That is why I called you," Donner whispered to me peaking in from his office.

I was a Border Patrol agent, a *pinche Migra*. I was trained to stab water jugs, to tear up and stomp on the food they left behind on the trails for other migrants. I believed that these things only furthered their illegal entry into my country, that migrants could give up if they needed help.

After Claudia, I never again stabbed another water jug or destroyed another bag of food I found left behind on a trail.

* * *

I could tell by the way Zarkowski slammed the hatch of my car that he was pissed. He looked like he'd not slept in days and asked me to stop at the 7-Eleven on the corner near our apartment complex before we made the long drive to the station.

"Can you fucking believe that guy?" he yelled as he sat back down in the passenger's seat with his coffee. "Don't ever go to that store again. They hate Border Patrol!"

"What the fuck are you talking about?"

"That guy in there wouldn't give me free coffee!"

"And?"

"And he should always give us free coffee when we're in uniform," he insisted.

"Are you serious? Why should he do that?"

"Because we protect him. That's how it works. We look after their stores, and they give us free coffee. Don't you take free lunches and shit?"

"Ummm, let me think," I said sarcastically. "No, I don't take free stuff. No one's even offered me free stuff, but even if they did, we don't work in this area. We're not deputies or police. We're Border Patrol. *La Migra*. The immigration cops."

"We protect this country from drug smugglers and all sorts of criminals."

"You mean migrants?"

"Yep. Any one of them could be rapists."

"Any one of us could be too," I reminded him of our classmate.

"I'm not hearing that. Besides, you know what I mean," he insisted. "I have to tell you something, but I don't want you to tell anyone else. Okay?"

"Sure."

"I'm serious. Swear."

"I swear! It's not like I'm one of you guys constantly blabbing everyone's business!"

"I took an AIDS test, and it came back positive," he blurted out.

This did not get much of a response from me as I knew he was still visiting the brothels in Mexico on weekends in between fucking his apprehensions. He had a habit of insisting that the women he had just paid for sex kneel and pray afterward for forgiveness because he honestly believed it saved their souls. Not his soul, mind you, their souls. According to him, it was expected for men to have sex outside of marriage, but never for a woman.

Zarkowski dated American women from time to time to find a wife, but only those he met at his church. He required a potential spouse to be a staunch conservative, vote Republican, and a strict Christian. She must see him as the head of the household, and she must also be a virgin. The virgin part was the hardest because he was in his mid-thirties. I assumed he intended to marry young as I'd never known a woman to keep her virginity that long.

"Do you think you got it in one of those whore houses?"

"Where else would I get it?"

rotection?"

es that mean?"
n. Look, I prayed with my dad, and I just hope it
ething. Can you pray for me?" he seriously asked.
he was crazy and quickly looked back at the road.
thoughts, but no, I won't pray for you. It would be disingenuous."

"What does that mean?"

"It means I'd catch fire. I'm not a Christian. You are the one that took the risks. You are the one that chose to do this without protection with God knows how many women."

"I put my faith in God," he exclaimed. "Plus, men don't normally get it from women. It's more common for men to give it to a woman."

"Wait, are you saying that you knowingly had unprotected sex because you thought men could give it to women but not the other way around?"

As it turned out, Zarkowski's test was a false positive. He spent some time trying to sue the maker of the test and the Red Cross, who had discovered it when he donated blood. He claimed that they had caused him emotional damage. I told him that he was the sole cause of his emotional damage.

For this, he never spoke to me again. He is now an investigator in the Office of Inspector General in the Department of Homeland Security, tasked with investigating crimes committed by Border Patrol agents.

* * *

In my second year as a Border Patrol agent, my parents came to visit me after I begged them. As in college, I almost never heard from my father, and only heard from Mom whenever I made the call. I once tried to see how long it would take for them to notice that they had not heard from me, how long it would take for her to pick up the phone and call me. I made it two months before finally giving in and calling them. They were my parents after all, and I missed them.

I took Dad on a ride-along one day so he could see what I did as an agent. I wanted him to be proud of his little girl, riding in those big trucks, running through the mountains alone, chasing down large groups of men who entered our country illegally. While hiking a trail, we stopped for a break and some water under the hot sun. Though he was skinny, my father was never an athletic man. Even though it was a relatively easy walk, I still worried about him.

As we sat on a boulder to catch our breath, he said, "I think you would do well to forgive your mom and me."

The shock of his words bounced around in my brain. W really talked about my childhood. I knew that he must have known Mom did to me all those years ago. The physical and emotional abuse cou not have escaped him even if he was away most of the time. I cannot recall her ever whipping me in front of him. Maybe he didn't know the severity of it, maybe he did.

"And what exactly is it that you think I should forgive you for?"

I wanted him to say it out loud.

"You know."

"No, please enlighten me, Dad. What is it that I should forgive you and Mom for? Just say it."

"I read this book that said forgiving is what sets you free. That it helps you to move on and gives you power. I just think it would help you," he said.

"Yeah, but forgive what? How am I supposed to forgive you if you won't even acknowledge it? Or is it that you would rather I forgive you so that you can just move on and not feel guilty about it?"

We walked a bit more down the path until I stopped and clicked my mic attached to my shoulder, "10-15 with thirteen."

"What?"

"You just caught your first group, Dad."

He looked into the brush, around back where we came from through a small valley. "I don't see anyone."

"*Levantense!*" I ordered. My fathered jumped back as the group of men and women stood up from under the brush. I told them he was my father and to not cause any trouble. Some smiled and waved at him as a transport van that had been circling us appeared.

"Wow, Jenn. Are you always alone when you find this many people?" he asked.

"Yes, but usually it's at night and usually way more people."

The transport agent and I patted each person down, checked their bags quickly for drugs or weapons, and loaded them into his van. My father never said if it bothered him that I hunted people for a living. I expect it didn't. We continued working the rest of the day, made the hour-long drive back to my apartment, and ate my mother's lasagna she made for us without ever bringing the conversation back up.

* * *

I was ten years old when she started drinking in the open. She kept the bottles of amber liquor on the open kitchen shelves. She later told me she'd been drinking for many years, drinking alone in her bedroom whenever she locked us out of the house. One day it was hidden, and the next, it was displayed proudly. It had a black label with country-style writing on it. Number seven, it said. She trained my three-year-old sister how to make a whiskey and Diet Coke and had me help her with the heavy bottles as she stood on a kitchen chair. Mom always commented on how cute my sister was when she brought the glass out to the den, slowly so as not to spill a precious drop.

I watched as she sipped down one after the other, holding it more tenderly than she'd ever held my siblings or me. It smelled awful, and I couldn't understand how she drank so many of them or why anyone would. Sometimes it made her laugh at every little thing. Other times she spent the night crying and talking about all the babies she'd lost. These were the moments when I had to be careful what came out of my mouth. One misconstrued word or sentence could land me in an hour-long battle of her going around and around about all the horrible things I'd done to her, how I did not love her enough or show her the respect she deserved. Arguments only ended when I stopped fighting and admitted how terrible I really was. I was six years old.

By the time I'd turned ten years old, we no longer went to church, which was fine by me since we weren't following the Mormon rules anymore. Losing my religion had the added bonus that I could now drink Dr. Pepper. Besides, I did not care for listening to her lie to other church members about how great our family life was, how happy we were. Her secrets were not just hers, but all of ours. Alcoholism, after all, is a family sport. We all had to play the game, put on a performance as it were. We did not talk about her drinking, not even her smoking. We never mentioned the beatings and the fights, or the yelling that the neighbors could easily hear, or the times when I could not wake her to tend to my younger sister.

She could not control her emotions any longer and had become just as dangerous when she was happy as when she was angry. Like when she kneeled over me and pinned me under her and tickled my sides until I laughed, then tickled harder until I cried. Her fingernails dug into my skin until I could not breathe and tears ran down my face. I was a bitch she said, just trying to make her look bad, pretending she was hurting me. Something that had once been a fun thing became what felt like torture, and I tried to keep her from doing it, which made her angrier.

Every morning, I listened for the slamming of cabinet doors or dishes being thrown in the sink, for clues on what to do, where to go. If it was Saturday, I knew to get up and start cleaning the bathroom. If it was during the week, I knew to get dressed and walk to school right away. I spent the whole day hoping she'd slept her anger off by the time I returned.

I learned to translate her sighs, to tell if she was just tired or mad, and watched for when she grabbed something to throw—a glass, an ashtray, the telephone, the dog. But I could not anticipate everything her mind came up with, like the time I came home and found out she'd given all my stuffed animals and toys to the neighbor's kid. My life was about surviving the day without a beating, without being told how horrible I was, how I had ruined her life simply by being born.

I was excited when Mom told me he was coming home that night. Dad had been gone for many weeks in Tennessee, training for some new job managing another chain of restaurants. I was old enough by that time then to understand that he used work to get away from Mom by constantly taking the jobs that required him to travel, to stay overnight. My memories of him are few and far between because of this. Their phone calls to each other only ended when she started screaming at him for leaving her alone with us for so long. The neighbor kids who heard her screaming often teased me about her hollering. So, I told them that she was a schizophrenic and could not help it. It was the only psychological term I knew at that age, because she had forced me to watch a documentary on it and then told me I would likely get it in my twenties. That and cancer, diabetes, and anything else she heard about.

Dad being at home was such a rare occurrence that his returns often became a celebration. Mom made her lasagna instead of the Hamburger Helper or the macaroni and cheese that she fed us night after night when he was gone. She liked to cook for him, but only him.

I met him at the door with a big hug that nearly knocked him over. His moustache and beard were fuller and hid his pock-marked skin and lack of a chin. He looked handsome with a beard. I smelled the flowers he had behind his back for her and giggled at his gesture. They sat in the living room on the white, faux leather couch that her mother had given her many years ago, while I sat on the floor and listened to his adventures. It felt as if I hadn't seen him in months. I missed him whenever he was gone.

He made me laugh because we had the same sarcastic sense of humor. We talked about music and cars whenever I helped him wash his old rust-colored Chevy Nova. I listened to all his stories about when he used to play guitar or trumpet for bands touring around Alabama, and all the muscle cars Pop had bought him as a teenager. From time to time, I rode with him over to Florence and to Muscle Shoals. I can remember listening to Lynyrd Skynyrd's "Sweet Home Alabama" and Smoky Robinson sing "Cruisin' Together" on the Nova's radio with the windows down, staring at myself in the side mirror as my blond hair blew in the wind.

He would always point out the little places he used to play at, and the famous recording studio that all the stars like the Rolling Stones, Etta James, and Aretha Franklin had once come to cut albums at. Something about those places brought out the soul in people, he said. Maybe because they were surrounded by history that had been so violent and intolerant, the sundown towns and the Klan rallies, towns where people kept their mouths shut lest they swing from a tree. It was a form of protest to let their voices be heard, I imagined, to say they would not be quiet any longer. He told me about all of it.

There was an unspoken connection between us. We could sit for hours waiting in the lines to buy gas during the shortages, listening to the radio, feeling the groove, tapping our hands to the same beat. He always quizzed me on which artist sang this or that song. It was because of him that I fell in love with jazz, rock, country, blues, and classical, because of him that I found Big Momma Thorton and Janis Joplin late in those warm southern nights.

I thought I could feel Janis through those big headphones as I lay on the floor of our den with my eyes closed. I thought I'd felt her pain, whatever it had been. It seemed familiar, and I felt bad for her when I heard her scream. What a wonderful release it must have been to be able to put it into her voice, to throw it out there into the world, letting bits and pieces of it go each time. And I knew that when he heard her and closed his eyes, when he leaned his head back to take it all in, that he recognized it too, though he never talked about it with me. Whatever it was, it always made him run from us into the arms of others. He'd always come back and try again, only to get right back in that car and drive away.

"Go get your dad some of that candy on the shelf in the kitchen," she said to me.

I had to stand on the kitchen chair to reach it and when I pulled the glass candy bowl off, the other side of the shelf tilted because the weight was not evenly distributed. Everything came crashing down. Every single bottle broke into hundreds of pieces, and the floor was soaked in alcohol. I froze with the candy dish still in my hand for what seemed like an eternity and felt my throat would close off with fear when I saw my mother standing before me, yelling. Her mouth moved and her arms flailed about, but I cannot recall what she said. I jumped down, walked on the shards of glass with my bare feet, trying to scoop up some liquor in my hands to save it for her, when I suddenly felt my father's strong hands lift me through the air.

"What the fuck is wrong with you?" he yelled at my mother. "She could get hurt!"

"Good! She deserves to get hurt. Look at my whiskey! Little fucking bitch! Do you know how much money that is?"

I ran to my room and pulled my pillow over my ears, only to hear the front door slam and my father's car drive away.

"Jennifer, come here," she called. "I want to talk to you."

I did as I was told because I knew it would be worse not to do so. I sat on her lap just as she asked me to, even though I felt too old for such things, even though I was terrified of her. She ran her hand down my long hair and twisted the ends in her fingers. I waited for her to rip it out.

She told me that they would likely get a divorce. Her voice was soft and sort of singsong. I had caused it. They were fighting over me. She knew I didn't mean to do it, but that my accident had made her yell at me, which made my father hate her and, in turn, hate us. For the rest of my life, I would look back on this moment as the day that I caused my father to leave us. My brother and sister, all of us, would likely never see him again. She said that we may not ever see Grandma and Pop again. She said it all tenderly, as if she'd been sorry for me, as if she felt for me. She said she wanted me to remember that moment for the rest of my life.

I sobbed in her lap with my whole body. She was right. I was a bad child. I was stupid. I'd done this not only to myself but to her and my siblings as well. I had put my mother in a difficult situation; she could not ignore my actions any more than she could not breathe. I knew this. It was my responsibility not to make such mistakes, not to make her lose her temper. My life was over as near as I could tell. Those I loved the most were going to leave me. I cried because I thought I'd never see him again, because he was the one good thing besides my dog in that house on Sullivan Road, because I loved him so much and he left me there, again.

Mom rocked me back and forth in her chair. She didn't know how we'd make it without him. She'd have to find a job, wouldn't be home when I came in from school. We may have to move out to the country or into an apartment. I wished then she would be quiet and whip me. So much so that when she got up, I felt hopeful that she was going to get the belt. I wanted to see her walk in with it, motion for me to strip down and take my licks, split my skin, beat me so hard that I would go far away in my mind and not be there in that place, feeling that emotional pain. I needed to feel the physical pain, the pain that took my mind away, to float away on that familiar cloud of nothingness.

When she came back, she had Dad's gun in her hand. A small black pistol with a wooden handle. "Maybe this will make you feel better," she said quietly.

I watched it all—her movements, the tears streaming down her face, the barrel going into her mouth, her finger on the trigger, her blue eyes that looked just like mine watching me. When her finger twitched, I fell to my knees and screamed for her to stop. Covering my face with my hands, I begged her to stop. Told her not to kill herself. That I loved her and would do anything to make this stop. I felt so weak and done at that moment.

"You do love me."

I WAS RUNNING AWAY

By the time I heard the group breaking brush ahead of me, I'd already climbed a few mountains and slid down the back side of them before I climbed back out of the ravine to the pavement that is Highway 94. I ran past the emu farm and chicken coops that nearly made me vomit at the smell of them, walked down around where the cows stood in silence. I turned off my flashlight and stood still to listen. Something tugged at the giant heel of my Red Wing fire boots, and I heard what sounded like a soda can being opened after shaking. I looked down to see a baby rattler spewing venom all over my boot. "Go on," I whispered, knocking it loose with my light.

The sound of breaking brush had stopped. I knew if they made it past here, it would be a world of hurt. It was a vertical drop hundreds of feet down to the bottom and a thigh-busting climb through thick brush on the other side before they would pop out at the Lake Morena Reservoir. If they tried to run, some would no doubt fall and get hurt, if not die. *Please stop,* I thought to myself as if I could mentally will it to be so.

In front of me was the last little twenty feet of boulders. They had to be on the top. I scrambled upward without my light as there were no footprints to follow, and I needed both of my hands to climb. When I reached the top, they stood across from me, peering over the other side.

"Please don't go. Very dangerous," I said in Spanish. The group of women and men all turned and looked at me, then back at the drop-off. "Everyone okay? Come on, sit," I pleaded. I'd learned not to yell at them like most of the male agents did, like they taught me to do. Yelling only scared them and made them run in different directions, increasing the chances that they would injure themselves. I found that if I asked if everyone was okay or if they needed water in a calm voice, they mostly stayed and gave me little trouble.

"We're lost," he said in perfect English.

"Supposed to get a ride on the highway back there?"

"Yes, ma'am."

"Please, do not go over the side. It is very dangerous. Someone will get hurt or die. You all can try again tomorrow," I said, lighting a cigarette.

"The fucking *Migra* telling us we can try again tomorrow?"

"Well, you shouldn't, but we all know you will. Your life is not worth this."

He translated the situation for the others as I patted each down quickly. They all sat down together while I radioed for a transport van. Every shift now had one or two transport vans because we had so many new agents at the station. It was a busy night. Everyone worked their own groups, and I was on a waiting list. It would be an hour or two wait.

"Sit, eat, drink. It will be a while." I poured my camelback water into their empty bottles and watched as they snacked on tuna from cans and tortillas that I politely declined. His name was Pedro. He was better dressed and had softer, cleaner hands than most of the migrants I'd encountered. He said he had a four-year degree in law, the same as me, which was odd.

"Why the hell are you crossing the border illegally then?" I asked as I lit his cigarette.

"Have you been to Mexico, *guerita*?"

"Nope."

"Ahh, well, you should go. Then you would understand that there are no jobs there. Even for someone like me, you have to know someone to get a job. You would see that we need to feed our families, our children. How else can you understand why the people you arrest every day come here? How else can you sympathize with them?"

"I don't believe I need to go there to sympathize with them. Plus, the law is the law..."

"Well, maybe it's an unjust law," he said, interrupting me. "You know, like the laws your government used to have about slaves."

"It's not the same," I replied quickly, feeling offended.

"No, not the same, but similar. Tell me, do you treat the people up north the same? Do *Migra* run around the woods chasing families and people who are only looking for work like they do down here? Do you track them and hunt them like animals? The Canadians?"

I looked down at my boots and kicked some loose rocks around, thinking on it, wondering who this tonc thought he was, questioning me like this. I was uncomfortable with how it made me feel. I knew that many Canadians worked illegally in the states and that no one was that concerned about it. "There are agents on the northern border, yes."

"Yes, but do they hunt Canadians like you do to us? Do Canadians have a hard time getting work permits to come over? Are they forced to hike the mountains and deserts?"

"No," I said. I was getting more and more irritated with what he was getting at. I was uneasy with his questions and assumptions that I was somehow a racist just because I was white and enforcing my government's laws. I had grown accustomed to stupid questions from Californians whenever they learned I was from Alabama, but Pedro had no idea where I was from. My thoughts turned toward thinking that he should not ask me such questions because I had authority over him.

"Why not?"

I knew why. I had been in the Patrol long enough to understand the inequities of how immigration laws were enforced. I knew that no one hunted down Canadians or Germans or Australians who overstayed their visas, that most of those who were undocumented had come here legally on a plane and did not in fact cross our southern border illegally, that politicians on both sides used pictures and videos of poor Brown migrants like these sitting before me to scare white Americans into voting for them, that the Border Patrol said that migrants were dangerous, even when the vast majority were not. More and more, I had the feeling that my job was nothing more than a show, a game of pretend law enforcement, a game of cat and mouse. I knew that Canadians were not vilified like the Mexicans, the El Salvadorians, the Guatemalans, and others. More than any of that, I knew exactly why we treated them differently but did not want to admit it.

Out there in the dark on top of that rock in front of them, I said the quiet part out loud for the first time, "I reckon it's because they are mostly white, and you are Brown."

I saw the van's headlights down below us as it pulled up and felt relieved that I would not have to listen to his questions any longer. I radioed for the agent to climb up and help me get the group down safely. I turned and asked Pedro to tell everyone that I would not use the plastic flexicuffs to tie them all together because I did not want them to fall and get hurt.

"What if we run?" he asked me with a smile.

"Then you run. I'm not going to allow anyone in my custody to get hurt. You are my responsibility now."

The group stood and followed the transport agent's light as he often stopped to turn around and light their way, making sure no one fell. I gave Pedro my light and placed him in the middle of the group as I brought up the rear. We all made it down safely. Everyone was searched again and placed in the van when Pedro suddenly jumped back out, something that normally would earn him a baton or punch from most agents. I held up my hand to tell the young transport agent it was okay.

He shook my hand and thanked me. "You need to think about what you're doing. You are better than this. You are a good person."

"Good luck," I told them all in Spanish.

"What was that all about?" the transport agent asked.

"Nothing. Just another fucking tonc who doesn't know what the fuck he's talking about," I said, half embarrassed that he had seen and heard our conversation.

He laughed.

I was angry. Pedro didn't know the first thing about me or why I did this job. He saw my white face and just assumed he knew me and my life, but he didn't. No one did because I never talked about it.

When I got back to my truck, I pulled up to the San Diego Gas and Electric tower we called the Nine Tower. It overlooked the Tecate beer factory, and I waited for Jacob to meet me. We parked our trucks door to door, and he watched while I closed my eyes for twenty to thirty minutes. I needed to take a break, let my legs rest. If he needed the same, I would do it for him once he woke me up. My mind would not turn off, though, and my anger at Pedro caused me to reach over my mental wall and grab at anything I could find to justify my choices in life.

* * *

I graduated at the top of my class from Auburn University with a bachelor of science in criminal law with an emphasis on policing and law enforcement, with the intent of going to law school to become a civil rights attorney. I believed that being the first in my family to earn a college degree meant something. My parents had always said it would, after all, and I believed them. School had been my sanctuary as a child. I felt relatively safe there, and it was the one area of my life where I excelled and made my mother proud of me. She often commented to my brother and sister that they should study more like me, and then they too could get better grades and earn her approval—which was difficult to come by.

More than anything, I saw that education was a means of getting the hell out of there, out of my home, out of Alabama. I believed I could find myself, learn who I was, if I could just get away from her. Maybe then I would be able to spend some time discovering who I was and what I wanted my life to be.

Auburn had become my home. I felt safe there and had unknowingly grown protective of it, of all it had given me, of the way I felt walking the streets and the campus, of the laughs I had watching the free movies for students, cheering at the football games, covering Toomer's Corner with hundreds of rolls of toilet paper whenever we won, of the way I could walk down any street and instantly be invited to join a party. Of all the campuses I had visited before enrolling, Auburn was the one college where I felt I would belong.

It was a pathway to a better life for me. At that age, I knew that I wanted a career, to provide for myself, be free and independent of my family. I had watched my father move from job to job and concluded that I did not want to follow him into the restaurant management business. I assumed the financial instability we so often lived with was caused by the type of work he did versus his own doing. All I knew back then was that my mother's tantrums became worse whenever he was unemployed, whenever we needed something from the doctor and had no health insurance, whenever she didn't have enough money to pay the bills. I needed the stability that I had enjoyed at my grandparents' house. The stability that I knew my mother was jealous of and that had come from Pop's lifelong career in the army.

I chose college.

My first two years were spent at the University of Alabama in Huntsville. Tuition was free because Dad had lost another job. His misfortune was my luck in that it allowed me to apply for Pell Grants, which were more than enough to pay for the tuition back then but not enough to go to my first choice. By my junior year, he'd finally gotten a new job, and I was no longer eligible for that free money. So, I went to my local bank and was relieved that they allowed me to take out student loans with my father as a co-signer. Those loans allowed me enough money to transfer to Auburn and pay for tuition and books. I went to school full-time while working two, sometimes three, part-time jobs.

Auburn was hours away from my family, and for the first time in my life, I lived alone. I found an old, run-down apartment complex near campus that had previously been a cheap hotel. The walls were cinder blocks painted white, and my bed was a mattress on the floor. The refrigerator and stove were that avocado green from the 1970s. All I cared about was that they worked. The couple that lived next to me complained any time I turned my country or blues music on. The young women who lived on the other side played hip hop as loud as they could all Saturday night and Black gospel Sunday mornings. I didn't have a car and walked or rode a bike to my classes. Sometimes I tagged along with my friends when they went to the grocery store to stock up on toilet paper and other essentials. During the week, I could snag a free lunch on campus when friends were working at the burger joint in the basement of Haley Center, where most of my classes were held. On Saturdays, during football season, I could hear the stadium from my apartment. There was something wonderful about waking up on a football day in the South. The smell of the air, the coming of fall, the tailgating and great food, the excitement and tradition of it all made me happy.

My senior year, I moved farther off campus into an even older trailer with faux wood paneling that smelled of cigarettes and beer. My father bought me an old Toyota pickup with a camper shell so he wouldn't have to spend hours driving me back and forth during the holidays. Even so, I rarely went back home and chose instead to take classes every quarter.

Auburn was my home, and I loved it. I could stay out as late as I wanted and go back to my apartment when I chose. When I came home and opened my front door, I didn't have to worry anymore about the fury and fists that used to await me. I didn't have to move around my home as if walking on eggshells, afraid of hearing doors slam or seeing my dog thrown into a wall. I no longer had to make excuses to be away from my home or spend the night sleeping in my car as I had in high school. I didn't have to listen to her drunk diatribes about how horrible my father was. The only time I heard her voice was when I called her. I considered that to be a blessing, though not once hearing from my father during those years left me deeply hurt. I'd been mistaken in thinking we were close.

On graduation day, I was sincerely happy to have my parents and my little sister there with me. We stood outside Stamford Hall, one of the last old red-brick buildings from the original school that was built in 1888. In front of the building, there is a large stone monument with "Auburn University" written on it where graduates usually got their pictures taken with their parents. It was cold and windy that day as we stood waiting in line with the other families underneath the infamous large oak trees that had already lost most of their red and yellow leaves to the change of season.

The line moved slowly, but I imagine it was truly no more than ten minutes or so when I noticed her shifting her weight from side to side, putting her hand on her hip like she always did. I could feel the heat crawl up the back of my neck as saltwater rushed into my mouth. The glands in my cheeks gave that sharp tingling feeling like biting into something extremely sour, and I suddenly realized that I had not had that feeling ever while at Auburn. I'd had a little over two years of respite and had chosen not to remember her ways by pushing them over the first wall I had built inside my head after the beatings began. At Auburn, there'd been no need to be keenly aware of her body language, on alert for all her signals that I'd learned to decipher in my younger years.

She sighed loudly and ran her tongue across her teeth as she looked back at me. I knew then that it was close. There'd be no escaping it. *No, no, no,* I thought. I didn't want her anger, violence and nastiness at my graduation. I'd forgotten how living with her required my full attention. It gobbled up any mental energy I had and there was never anything left for me. Hopes and dreams did not exist. I could not be. It was no wonder that I spent so much time sleeping whenever I visited my parents. I could not cope as I had before, and I realized now why it was that I tended to just close my eyes and bury myself in books as I had as a child.

I touched her elbow, and she turned to look at me as I twisted my head to the side. It was my nonverbal way of saying, "Come on now, please don't be that way."

"What the fuck is taking so long," she said loudly, smiling back at me, knowing full well I would be mortified. This game she played was what bothered me more than anything else. She'd become manipulative, enjoyed the cruelty she could dish out and the lies she told. It gave her power to know that I knew she was lying, right in front of me while I stayed silent in my shame. My only choice was to tolerate her making a scene or leave.

I turned and walked back to our old brown Lincoln station wagon that barely ran. I didn't say a word, and we never took that stupid picture. I could not handle her that day, would not play her games at that moment, my moment. The embarrassment that she could make me feel with just one look, the shame, that sense of helplessness I used to know as a child, all came flooding back into my body and filled every tissue of my being, making me want to scream it out.

Once everyone was back in the car, she turned from the front passenger's seat to the back, slapped me across my face hard, looked at me for a brief second, and then slapped me again. "What? Do you think this day is all about you?" she screamed.

I was dressed in my black cap and gown and stared back at her in disbelief. My years away had changed me some, made me more independent, stronger, and I realized that I was not nearly as afraid of her as I had been before.

"Yeah, actually, I do think it's about me. All about me. It's my fucking name on that degree. My fucking name on those loans. So, yeah, I fucking think this entire day is about me!"

I'd never spoken to my mother this way, never used so many f-bombs. She reared back with a fist and started coming over the seat when my father grabbed her and pushed her back.

"Both of you, stop this. Jenn, you stop antagonizing your mother!"

"What the fuck?" I exclaimed.

"All of you, shut up!" he said. "We're going to see Jenn graduate and then go home."

But home for them was no longer home to me. They had moved to the other side of Alabama, all the way to Mobile while I was away. It was a city I had never known until my internship during my final quarter of college as an investigator with the Mobile County District Attorney's Office. I'd already moved all my stuff to their new place, and there was nothing left to do, no other place I could go. It would be a long four-hour drive back to Mobile.

She'd always done this to me, always made everything to be about her, and when it wasn't, she ruined it for me. There was never a graduation or award ceremony where she didn't make a scene. It was as irresistible to her as that bottle was, and deep down, I knew it was only a matter of time before it showed itself again. I should have known better than to put myself in that position. I should have never invited them, and had my diploma mailed to my new address.

I sat in the large auditorium with the other six hundred graduates as they went through the various speakers, the graduate programs, and then each college. Everyone was smiling and laughing; parents stood proudly next to their graduates and asked others to take their pictures as they all posed and said, "Cheese." Soon-to-be graduates were making final plans to party one last time as I sat, staring straight ahead, too afraid to look up at her.

I could feel her eyes on me when they announced how long it would take; thought I'd heard her sigh from the balcony floor above me. When I finally got the courage to look up and to my right, to see what I already knew to be the case, I saw my father as he held her back and forced her to stay. She shook her head and had her thin lips pursed as if murmuring threats under her breath, as if I'd planned this just to upset her. She pointed her index finger at me like she would get me for it, like she was calling me outside for a throwdown. It was as if she thought I'd somehow gotten all these people to graduate the same quarter I did just so she would have to sit through a long ceremony, away from her best friend, chardonnay.

I vaguely remember a friend sitting next to me, chatting about how she was going to Washington, D.C. to work at a senator's office the following month. I cannot remember who spoke that day, what words were said. I do not recall any graduates and their funny antics pulled on stage one last time before heading off to the cheers of their friends and families, to adulthood. When I topped the last step, I did not hear my name but knew that they had called it because whoever shook our hands and handed out diplomas reached out for me. I remember crossing that stage, shaking his hand, and grasping the degree with the other and turning to my parents so they could get a picture.

I don't know how long I stood with that man or what he was wearing or what he looked like, but I recall feeling his hand on my shoulder, urging me to cross to the other side and go back to my seat. I was floating, like I was watching from the outside, like I used to do when I was small, and she whipped my naked body. When I looked for her, I saw the back of my mother in her black dress and high heels as she disappeared into the halls. No one had taken my picture. She had not even watched me graduate, had not cheered for me, did not clap when my name was called. She walked out on me; the moment was forever lost in time.

I thought that it had been the cruelest thing she'd ever done to me. I hated her then because I knew this would forever be my memory of my college graduation. Honors degree, cum laude, dean's list—none of it mattered. I hated her meanness, her pettiness. How could anyone be so harsh, so brutal, and nasty to their child? I thought I understood her pain, her insecurities, but I never could comprehend her anger. The meanness, the manipulation and intentional pain she caused me was beyond my grasp as a human being.

* * *

It'd be wrong of me if I only gave the impression that my mother never did right by me. She sometimes did. She didn't start changing until I was six, and my memories before then were the only ones I allowed myself to think much about, the ones I clung to. Those were the good memories, the better times. I never knew when or why she would be nice to me, but truth be told, she was sometimes, and I think that's what made life with her so difficult. I couldn't just be angry with her for the horrible things she'd done. I'd known and loved her better side, even if it was few and far between.

It was because of her that I had a passion for social justice, history, education, art. She introduced me to things I never learned much of in my Alabama public schools: the women's movement, the Equal Rights Amendment, the Holocaust, and the great Dr. Martin Luther King Jr. She taught me the truth about the place we called home: the cotton fields, old plantations, double water fountains still visible at the Birmingham Zoo, George Wallace and the four Black girls killed at that church. My folks had always voted Democrat and made sure we knew about the awfulness of the South as well as the good.

I heard it all, even if I still did not fully understand it. This part of me, the social justice part, came from her. Justice was something I was obsessed with, for myself and for others. I thought it was the best part of my character that I'd gotten from my mother. It was the one part about myself that I did not loathe.

She softened to me a bit after I graduated college, even though I was back living with her and Dad again. It was almost like she felt sorry for me because I had worked so hard in school and not been able to find a job for over a year after receiving my diploma. My parents and grandparents expected me to go to law school, and I thought about it often as I still wanted to be a civil rights attorney. I took the law entrance exam a few times but didn't have the drive to follow through with the applications. I knew that southern lawyers were lucky if they made enough to pay their law school loans. Looking around at my parents' new place in Mobile, a city and a house that felt foreign to me, I couldn't imagine putting myself through another two years of school, being further in debt, and the possibility of having to go back to living with her.

My older brother was already long gone. He left immediately after barely graduating high school and joined the Army. He wanted to be like our Pop and make a career out of the military. After Sylvester Stallone played a Vietnam veteran in *Rambo*, he started to talk and walk like the character and began collecting large hunting knives. He was like Mom in so many ways, always seemed to be searching for a personality, a character he could emulate, so he didn't have to be himself. Just like me, he was horribly abused. I assume he had a difficult time knowing who he was too.

Prone to arguing and violent outbursts like she was, he ended up doing time in Texas somewhere for stealing weapons from the Army's armory. If I remember correctly, a grenade and some other weapons were found in his apartment closet in Waco. He had lived near the Branch Davidian, during the siege, and the feds thought he might have been involved, though he wasn't. He was just stupid.

"Does she whip you?" I asked my fourteen-year-old sister, who was in middle school at the time. We sat across from each other at the Waffle House near their new neighborhood in Mobile. Mom had been screaming and throwing things at Dad again, and I felt I had to get her out of there if just for a few hours after I saw her crying and holding her hands over her ears.

"No. She just drinks, yells, and passes out. Dad's never home. Always off fucking his gift shop manager."

"Don't say that!"

"Why not? It's true. You know it. I know it. Everybody knows it," she said, pouring more syrup on her pancakes.

She was right, and I could tell she was growing up faster than she should have, just like I had. It didn't matter that she wasn't physically beaten as I had been. She had my brother and me to thank for that when we confronted Mom one day about hitting her. She wasn't allowed to do that unless she wanted to face the cops. Our mother had many weapons in her arsenal. The pain that could come out of her mouth could cut as deep as any leather belt. This, we all knew.

"You just up and left me there. You abandoned me," she said.

"When?"

"When you went to Auburn," she said.

"You're not my child. I didn't give birth to you," regretting every word as it fell from my mouth.

"You know you were more like my momma than her. You took me trick-or-treating every year. You set up the Christmas tree every year. You came to my plays at school and picked me up in the afternoons when she was drunk. You took me to dance class."

"I know, but you've got to understand that I had to take that opportunity and get out of there," I explained, feeling guilty, selfish.

"What are you going to do?"

"Get a job."

"So, you're just going fucking leave again?"

"Yes. I am, and you should too when you're old enough."

* * *

As an intern investigator at the Mobile County District Attorney's Investigative Unit, I was mentored by an old investigator by the name of Bob Eddy—a tall, lean man, who was as southern as they come, judging by his thick accent and his red neck. He talked of times past, when he'd been the sheriff of Madison County where I'd grown up and then in Birmingham on special investigations that he did not want to talk much about.

Mr. Eddy taught me everything I knew about conducting investigations: to take the time to listen, not to form an opinion and avoid trying to make the evidence prove me right, value everyone's testimony, and follow the law and policies. A badge wasn't an excuse to do whatever you wanted, he said. It was something that required you to hold yourself to a higher standard, to treat everyone equally under the law. We were the investigators, not the judge or jury.

I continued working for him privately at a law firm after graduation for about a year, driving all over southern Alabama, digging up old property records and such. I was forced to quit when Dad moved us again down the road to an island called Gulf Breeze in the panhandle of Florida. The twenty dollars an hour Mr. Eddy paid me was a lot back then, but it was sporadic, and I knew I would not be able to pay rent and stay there in Mobile. One afternoon I saw him on Oprah Winfrey's show, talking about how he'd been the one to discover which Klansmen had done the Birmingham bombing in 1963 that killed the four little Black girls. I realized then how fortunate I'd been to have him as a mentor. He said I was a natural investigator.

I applied to every police department I could find that was hiring and many who were not. I sold my truck to pay for a flight and a two-day stay in Austin, Texas, to try out for their department. The recruiters told me that they had to hire more Blacks or else they'd get fined by the feds. When I pointed out that they seemed to have no problem hiring lots of white ex-military guys, they let me know it was better for them to hire a Black female and "kill two birds with one stone." It seemed to me that they were only willing to hire just the number of women and minorities they needed and no more. It didn't matter to them what our education or experiences were. They simply did not hire any more women or people of color than required. Whether true or not, all it meant to me was that I didn't get a job. Some small-town departments called me from time to time, saying they needed a female to meet their quota so they could get more federal funding but could only pay less than fifteen thousand dollars a year. This was far less than what I needed to live on and pay my school loans, even in the Deep South in 1994.

So, when Mom mentioned that she'd heard the U.S. Border Patrol was hiring, I was interested, although I had no idea what the hell the Border Patrol was. I'd never heard of it. Most federal law enforcement agencies required more experience than an internship and a degree. Those lucky enough to enter the FBI or CIA right out of college had studied the more difficult languages like Arabic, Russian, or Chinese instead of the French I'd studied for years. The agencies would also hire recent graduates with accounting degrees because they tracked many criminal organizations through their financial transactions. There was little call for those of us who had a four-year degree in law. The Border Patrol, however, would take anyone, it seemed; they were on a hiring spree.

I borrowed Dad's red Mazda truck and drove the five and a half hours to Jacksonville, Florida, for an interview and entrance exams that consisted of a basic civil service test and a faux language test. The faux language was a made-up language, and we had to apply the grammatical rules they'd given in the directions. Those who passed were then given a lecture on what the agency was all about.

It was the days before Google and government websites, and I had not had any time to research the agency at our local library. The recruiters were agents themselves and sharply dressed in their official green dress uniforms, the ones with the blue stripe down the pant legs and a cheap clip-on blue tie. They told our small group of prospective agents what would be expected of us if we made it through the tests, physical exams, and background checks. I thought it was odd that they did not have a psychological test like every other state and local agency I had applied to.

The recruiters told us there were lots of ways to apply and enter the country legally, that those who crossed illegally simply did not respect our laws and were looking for jobs where they would be paid in cash and subvert the tax system that we all had to pay into. This took jobs from hard-working Americans and forced them to get on welfare, they said. The government did not know who or how many migrants entered the country illegally. They had not submitted themselves for inspection. For all they knew, many of these migrants could have been murders, rapists, and drug dealers in their communities before coming to our country.

President Clinton started Operation Gatekeeper in October 1994 in a bid to appeal to Republicans by being tough on immigration. They had already started building his version of a wall where the Pacific met the sand in Imperial Beach, California. Now they were hiring the agents with which to saturate the area north of that steel-paneled wall. At the time, the Border Patrol was within the Immigration and Naturalization Services department led by Commissioner Doris Meissner. She stated the sole purpose of Operation Gatekeeper was to "deter" migrant men who did not obtain work permits from crossing illegally and push them out to the more desolate and dangerous terrain like the high desert east of San Diego and even farther east in the actual sandy deserts. Operationally, they said it would cause most migrants to give up and to not even try to cross illegally. Those who risked it gave the Border Patrol more time to track them down and apprehend the groups before they could get into the cities.

I could see myself in that uniform with a cowboy hat and a gun on my side, riding a horse in the vast expanses of nothingness. I rode horses as a teenager, drove trucks, and even wore cowboy hats when I went two-stepping with my college boyfriend. The Border Patrol seemed like a natural fit for me.

Every morning, I gathered my fishing poles, stopped at the bait shop for some live shrimp, and sat out on the old bridge that spanned between Pensacola and the island of Gulf Breeze. It was not an entirely horrible place to be unemployed. Between catching stingrays and pompano, I spent hours inside my head preoccupied with what I should do next. I felt helpless and stuck waiting on some agency, any agency to give me a shot. I'd done all that'd been asked of me. Kept my grades up, got that degree, and now...what?

I often thought about how when I was young and I'd wanted to be like my mom, to be there for my kids as she'd been for us every day when we got home from school, but I believed that was not possible for me as a gay woman. There was never going to be a courtship, an engagement party, a bridal shower, a wedding in my future. Marriage was illegal for us. My future, whatever that was, would require me to take care of myself. My sexuality was something I'd been aware of since second grade, though I dated boys and men throughout high school and college. My parents never came out and said that being gay was a sin or wrong. They didn't have to. I learned it from television and the ways kids hurled terms like "faggot" and "dyke" at each other. I did not want to be gay, but the older I got, the less it felt like a choice to me.

I worried more than anything that the feds who dug into my background would find out I was gay and not hire me. It was legal to discriminate against gays and lesbians in federal employment at the time, and even though I was not officially out, even though I could pass for straight back then, even though I'd listed my ex-boyfriend on my application, it was all I could think about. That someone in my past would talk about that brief fling I had with a friend back in college. That we'd not been as discrete as we'd thought we were. That my mother would tell the background investigators about it to sabotage my hopes and dreams of getting out of there. About how she'd been so ashamed and demanded I go back in the closet because she could not bear the thought of what people would say if they knew her daughter was a lesbian.

Depending on how you looked at it, fortunately or unfortunately, no one mentioned it.

WHO DO YOU LOVE?

I was back at the checkpoint working the swing shift when my supervisor came out of the new double-wide trailer that was now our office. The old white bus was gone, and the checkpoint had become a small station with computers, a separate processing building, and temporary detention space. We even had men's and women's bathrooms and soda machines. When agents finished their hour on primary and then secondary, they could rest inside and play games on the computers if nothing was going on. Most of the guys spent the time watching either porn or videos of people getting hit by trains and cars or blowing their own heads off. I had learned by then to tune it out.

"Budd! Come in here!"

We had just finished a Greyhound bus check and pulled several people off who did not have documents. Another agent took my spot at secondary as I ran up the steps to the office.

"Yes, sir."

"I want you to deal with that guy over there," Supervisor Watkins ordered.

"Sure. What's the deal?"

"He's a homo and no one wants to get near him."

"Huh?"

"He's a faggot, Budd. Guys don't like to be around them. We know how guys are. He might hit on us or something, and then there'd be some punches thrown. I don't need that shit. I want you to process him," he said seriously.

Only a handful of agents that I considered to be friends knew that I was gay, and none of them were working with me this night. Because I was the only woman at the checkpoint, it meant I had to deal with it. I rarely got angry about it anymore because nothing ever changed.

"I'm trying to get to San Diego to see my partner," he said to me in perfect English. He was handsome to the point of being pretty, and his voice had that higher, softer pitch that is often associated with gay men.

"Put your index finger on the scanner," I said. "Now the other one."

"I was living with him for six years when the Chula Vista Border Patrol caught me at the trolley. Girlllll, I thought I was safe because I wasn't close to the border but in the city."

"We're everywhere, man. Look into the camera, please."

"Yeah, well, I got returned to Mexico, and now I'm trying to get back to my man. Do you know how unfair the immigration laws are? How they discriminate against us?"

"Why didn't you just get a worker's permit or a fiancé visa? What are those called? I can't remember."

"K-1 visa," he replied.

"Hey, that's right. K-1 visa. Why not just get one of those?"

"They do not recognize gay couples. Even if they did, I don't have the money for it." He frowned.

I stopped typing and looked up at him. "Yeah, I guess they don't. I've never really thought about that."

"I'd pay you if you could help us, you know."

I stared blankly at him, thinking about what he said. "You're not offering me a bribe, are you? You know that's a serious felony to bribe a federal agent."

"No, no. Of course not," he quickly said.

I shut down the computer as his prints did not come back with any warrants or a criminal record.

"What are you going to do?" I asked.

"What should I do?"

"I can't give you advice like that. I mean, obviously I would suggest you not cross again because it's illegal. I suggest he visits you in Tijuana on the weekends."

"Would you be happy having to live most of your time away from your partner?"

"No, no, I wouldn't," I said as I closed him in the cell. He clung to the wire fencing as I walked to the exit door. "I also wouldn't date someone who was illegal, though."

"We can't help who we fall in love with, right?"

I turned back to him and nodded in agreement. "They say the third time crossing is the charm. You know what I mean?"

He winked at me as I shut the door.

"He's all done, sir," I told Watkins as I entered his office. I leaned against his desk with my arms folded as he watched the inspection area outside.

"Thanks. It's a guy thing, Budd."

"I just want you to know that this idea that gay men are going to see y'all and suddenly try and have sex with you is ridiculous."

"Really? You know how we men can be with sex," he insisted.

"Yeah, I do, but y'all don't know gay men. Y'all ain't in good enough shape or pretty enough."

"Why don't you tell us what you really think?" he laughed.

"I think I just did."

COVERUP CENTRAL

"Eighteen fifty-two point one," sector dispatch came over the radio.

"Eighteen fifty-two point one, two hits."

"Ten-four, charlie-one-seven-eight responding," I replied.

I just happened to be at the front gate of the private property that the sensor was on. After I unlocked the gate and parked my truck, I went into the brush, heading south. Agent Sanchez radioed that he was at the sensor on the border road checking it for sign.

"It's good. About thirty heading straight up the wash," he said.

"Ten-four," I whispered into my mic because I expected to see them at any moment. The moon was full and there was no need for a flashlight. I took my time walking south, making sure my footfalls were quiet enough that I could hear the group coming up.

"Stop!" I heard in English. "*Alto!*"

Goddammit! I said to myself. I knew this poor Spanish came from neither an agent nor a migrant but the owners of the property. I started running south and ran into them, three men and one woman dressed in camouflage from head to toe with their pale faces painted black and green and large assault rifles at the ready.

"We got them illegals running south for you," one said.

"Yeah, I heard..."

Two shots rang out directly south of us.

"Two shots fired south of my twenty (location)," I said over the radio as I began running as fast as I could toward the sound of the shots and where I knew Sanchez was on the border road. When I got close to the clearing and the new border fence that stopped right at the arroyo, I slowed my run and pulled my new .40 caliber Berretta that I already hated. The pretend Border Patrol agents disappeared like the racist chicken shits they were.

I popped out on the border road and saw Sanchez walking back and forth with his gun in his hand, muttering something in Spanish. The driver's side door of his new Chevy Tahoe service ride was wide open and his sign-cutting light was still on. The engine was running.

"What the fuck, Sanchez? I thought you were tracking them north?" He seemed shocked to see me.

"Oh, Budd! They fucking rocked me! I had to shoot! They could have killed me!" he said franticly.

"Calm down." I had my gun pointing south. "Everyone went south?"

"Yeah."

"Anyone hit?"

"I dunno!"

"Wait, did you shoot into Mexico?"

"Yeah, but they were rocking me!"

"Why would you leave your truck running on the border road?"

Before the wall went up, we rarely if ever had people throwing rocks at us. It was common for citizens of the small town just south of this area to use the same border road we used. While technically they were on the U.S. soil, the communities along the border could use our east or west border road without fear of us arresting them. We knew the locals and they knew us. If they needed help, we helped them without question of citizenship. Kids who lived south of the manmade border had grandparents on the north side and used to move back and forth freely, especially during Christmas time. With the new wall, they were forced to drive south a mile, then go west for about thirty miles to the Tecate Port of Entry, possess a passport, which cost money, then drive back east thirty miles to see family who lived no more than a hundred yards from their house in Mexico.

When Clinton's wall went up, it destroyed any relationships we may have had with the community. Now rockings were almost a weekly occurrence. I had been rocked a few times in the same area that we knew was responsible for most of the narcotics traffic. If they needed a distraction, cartel members would pay kids to throw rocks at our trucks and break the windows. I had never been injured from a rocking, had never heard of an agent getting injured by a rock, but it was still frightening to have it happen. Usually, we sped up and got the hell out of there. I'd never seen an agent being rocked while on foot before and never by actual migrants who were crossing though there were reports of such events. No agent had ever died from a rocking. In the academy, our instructors told us to only say that we feared for our lives if we shot rock throwers. I and most agents I knew preferred to get out of the way.

"Alright, stay here. There's a supervisor on the way. I'm going south to check for bodies," I said.

"You can't! What if *federales* are there? They'll arrest you," he objected.

"Well, then I guess I'll make the papers. Try not to shoot me."

I saw no one. No bodies. No blood trail with the footprints running south, and I returned quickly to see Sanchez sitting in his truck, crying.

"What are you doing?"

"I'm going to lose my fucking job!" he wailed.

"Shut up, man. Come on, pull it together. No one was injured. Looks like it will be your lucky night," I said when the supervisor pulled up.

"Set team is on its way from sector," Supervisor Watkins said.

"What's a set team?" I had never heard of this special team even though I'd been in the Patrol for over three years.

"CIIT. Pronounced as 'set.' It's the Critical Incident Investigative Team. Every sector has them. Sometimes they're called CIT. They are like forensics for the Border Patrol. They'll come out and see if this is a good shoot or not. Sanchez, I called your union representative. He'll be here shortly. Don't say anything to anyone about what you did," he said as he traded guns with Sanchez. This was routine to keep the evidence secured.

Watkins and I stood away from Sanchez, who sat in his vehicle, crying. "Any bodies south?"

"No, sir."

"You check?"

"Yes, sir."

"Okay. Did you see anything?"

"No. Just heard the shots, and then ran down here. Says he was rocked."

"You feared for your life, son!" Watkins yelled at Sanchez, who just nodded.

The union representative pulled up and took Sanchez back to the station as the CIIT guys pulled up in unmarked cars and civilian clothes. I stood on a boulder near the opening in the fence to make sure no one from the south walked up on us. I lit a cigarette and watched the CIIT guys walking around the scene as they took photographs and talked to my supervisor. There were a few small rocks in the road, but his vehicle showed no signs of damage and neither did he. Whether he really feared for his life or not, I did not know. He was a junior agent and had just gotten off his probationary time.

"You can go ahead and leave, Agent Budd," one of the CIIT agents said.

I headed back north on foot toward my service truck when I heard breaking glass. I turned and saw CIIT agents tossing rocks onto the road near the truck. One threw another rock into the windshield. I turned around and went back to my truck, thankful that I had been wearing my bulletproof vest that night.

The next night Sanchez was back at work.

WORDS MATTER

"*De donde nació?*" **Where were you born?**

"Sinaloa, Mexico," the man standing in front of me said.

I was assigned processing that night, which meant for every migrant apprehended crossing illegally, I was to enter their biographical information and the events of their illegal crossing into the national IDENT computer system. Campo Station was also finally given the ENFORCE processing programs that made asylum or criminal paperwork much faster. I learned it quickly and was in charge of training the entire station on it.

IDENT had not yet been linked to the national criminal index system. If the person standing in front of me had a warrant or a previous criminal record, I wouldn't have known it unless I ran their full prints through the Automated Fingerprint Identification System (AFIS). This still required us to manually roll their prints and fax the card to AFIS, where the prints were run against their computer database and then confirmed by an analyst before we could determine if we had a criminal on our hands or not. Sometimes that took a few hours. Sometimes it took three or four. We couldn't do that for the hundreds of arrests our little station made each and every shift.

"*Cual es su fecha de nacimiento?*" **What is your birth date?**

"*Cinco de Mayo, mil novecientos setenta.*" **May 5, 1970.**

I was startled when my classmate Quintano slammed his hand down on the laminate countertop I was working at. My Spanish was getting better, but it did not prepare me for the rapid cursing that spewed from his mouth at the man standing before me. I looked up at the migrant for the first time and could see the fear Quintano had just put in him as his eyes began to get watery.

"What is your problem?" I yelled at my classmate.

"He's fucking lying to you, Jenn! I hate that bullshit when they lie!"

"About what? His birthday? I don't give a shit what his birthday is," I told him. In fact, many migrants had no idea what their birthdays were. It was not uncommon for them to be orphans or raised by family members who had no idea when they were born. Most would simply pick a date and stick with that. Cinco de Mayo was a common choice as it was the date the Mexican Army defeated the French in the Battle of Puebla in 1862, which was an important holiday for them. I was used to some of the Latino agents being harsher on the migrants. I didn't understand it, but I was used to it.

"Well, I am not going to sit here and listen to this!" he said, jabbing his finger into the countertop.

"Is this really worth getting that angry about? Is it?"

"Yes, it is. He's from Sinaloa, no?"

"Yeah. So what?"

"That's where I am from. My family is from Sinaloa, and he is being disrespectful by lying to us when he does that. I take that personally!" Quintano exclaimed.

"You've got to be shitting me! Really?" The migrant leaned against the wall and watched as we yelled at each other in English.

"Yes, really! My parents came here...."

"Illegally or legally?"

"Illegally back then," he confessed.

"Oh! So, your parents are toncs, and you're pissed because this guy is a tonc too then?"

"Fuck you!" he screamed as he walked out the front door slamming it behind him.

I quickly finished up processing, closed out my computer, and put Mr. Cinco de Mayo back in the cell with the rest of the group. When I walked out to the wrought iron platform to see where Quintano went, I was surprised to find him leaning against the railing waiting for me.

"That was pretty fucking racist," he said as I lit a cigarette.

"How?"

"Calling my parents toncs? That's racist as shit. You're all the same."

"What is that? You're all the same? What does that mean?"

"White agents are racist," he said without a hint of irony.

"You call these guys toncs too. What's the difference? If a tonc is Brown person who entered illegally, and you use the word for that, then you're racist too," I said.

"It's just different."

"How? Maybe you're just pissed because you realize your parents were no different than these guys. Maybe when you look at them, you see your parents."

"My parents crossed a long time ago. Those people in there are breaking the law right now. They're criminals. I mean, yeah, it was illegal back then but…shit! I don't know! I just know that whenever someone gets promoted around here, it's always a white person!"

"Well, that's true. It's also true that it's almost always a man and not a woman," I pointed out.

"Yeah, but that's because there are so few of you."

"Is it? And why do you think there are so few of us? Because the work is physical? Because we can't handle the terrain? C'mon!"

We both let out a sigh, looking out at the mountains. "So, why do you think they don't promote Latinos?" he asked.

"I'm going to be honest with you. I'm going to tell you why that really is, the truth. You won't believe me, but I promise you it's the truth. As a white woman from Alabama, I can tell you that it is because you are Brown."

"C'mon, Budd!"

"I'm serious. Why do you think they teach us to call them toncs? It ain't for other white agents or me. Hell, there are plenty of racist words we whites could call them. It's for you, for the Latinos. That's why we don't call them 'beaners' or 'spics.' That's why they teach us to call them something else. It's so you don't identify with them. So, you see yourself as different than them. So, you don't feel sorry for them. So, you think you're one of us, but I'm telling you that they will never see you as one of us. You will never be white enough, and I will never be man enough. Any promotion, any decent detail we may put in for and are selected for will never be because we earned it or because we were the most qualified. You hear the guys talk in the locker room. For me, it's because I must be sleeping with someone. For you, it's because they need to quiet the other Latinos down about not having representation. They needed to fill their quota."

"It's true that they say that about female agents," he admitted.

"And it's true that the management, the white management, does not trust the Latino agents. How many supervisors we got here now? Like close to twenty-five, maybe thirty. How many of those are Latino? One. One lonely Latino, and no women. Shit, the Patrol's got over fifty percent of y'all. Seems like we should have at least ten or more."

"Yeah, I know. So, you think if we move up, we can change it?"

"Doubtful. Look at all those who came before us. They all start out saying they would make changes and then they just fall in line."

"Fuck," he said as he walked away.

KEEP YOUR MOUTH SHUT

I pulled into the station parking lot and hopped out of my Tahoe to give it a quick wash before turning my keys in for the next shift. It was late; a few hours past the end of my swing shift by the time I was done gassing up. I locked the truck and threw my duty bag that carried my binoculars, extra ammo, tampons, and toilet paper into the back of my car before walking across the street to the station to sign out on my timecard and turn in the keys.

The night was like any other. I was covered in dirt and brush, my green shirt was soaked from sweat. I had black soot all over my face from chasing a group through burned manzanita trees that had become stiff from a fire months ago. It even punctured one of my truck tires and took me nearly an hour to change it by myself. I caught three groups in all that night. The first two groups I apprehended like usual, without anyone answering my calls for assistance until I needed transport.

Agents never talked about it, but we were all lucky that the vast majority of those we arrested were not criminals. It's the only thing that allowed one agent to arrest twenty, thirty, even a hundred people all at once. Contrary to what the agency claimed, most agents died of either natural causes or accidents while on duty. Even today, being a Border Patrol agent is one of the safest jobs in law enforcement simply because the vast amount of people they apprehend are not criminals.

I thought about the lack of backup and wondered if it would ever change as I closed my car's hatch. I had to consider that my luck might finally run out someday. I wasn't great about wearing my bulletproof vest. It was something I had never got in the habit of doing once it finally arrived. The thought that some agents would refuse to answer my calls for backup because of something they thought I did in the academy was ridiculous. Especially after I'd more than proven myself over the years. Not getting backup always took me back to being raped and how the agency had done nothing about it. I could never fully escape that memory, even though I spent a great deal of time trying.

It seemed like not having backup was happening more often though. Like the more trainees we got at Campo Station, the less help I got. Rumors were being spread that Campo's post-academy instructors Linda and Will were talking about me to the new trainees. They were married and managed to talk supervisors into putting them on the joint detail together which was an unethical choice, in my opinion. Karen called to tell me that they were hanging around Mendoza at sector and that she had seen them partying with him as well. It wasn't too much of a leap to think he had shared his version of my sexual assault with them.

Senior Patrol Agents Simpson and Anderson, the ones who'd taught me how to track groups and gave me a fair chance, came to me and said that agents were telling Linda that I had turned out to be a great tracker and I was better at catching migrants than she was. This was shit talk the guys always engaged in to make the few women at the station jealous of each other. I ignored it like so much else, but I knew that she had a queen-bee mentality. It was absurd in my mind. I could never hate someone just because I thought they were better at something than me. I never believed in rumors and never spread them because of all that had been done to me. Whatever her issue was with me, I wanted to hear it from her.

The only problem was that I never saw her. Post academy had moved down into town at the new sector headquarters in Chula Vista. Still, the lack of backup was getting worse, and I wondered if all the rumors were true. I was senior to these agents, after all. They ignored my calls, left me hanging, or tried to poach my groups, and that wasn't right. Several of the crusty agents suggested I file an EEO complaint against the couple.

As I thought about this, I looked up to see a trainee coming out of the north station gate across the street where I was headed. He stopped his old Bronco and waved for me to cross the street. I waved back and had almost made it to the other side when I heard him gun the engine and turn the truck into me. The driver's side bumper came at me, and I tried to jump out of the way. My left forearm was positioned in front of me as if I was blocking a tackle, and I felt the soft tissues tear in my left wrist and hand as it took the brunt of the grill head-on. It spun the left side of my body back as he parked the giant tire on my right foot. My body fell to the ground in what seemed like slow motion, and I saw that my foot was stuck in the standing position underneath the giant four-by-four tire. I could feel my right knee tear on the inside as my back hit the pavement and my leg extended straight out. I looked up at him as he lowered his window and spat his dip out onto the street with a smile. He was a trainee

I'd only seen a few times before. One of Linda's.

"Get the fuck off of my foot!" I yelled.

He laughed before throwing the truck in reverse and rolled back off my foot slowly. I felt the skin tear off the top of my foot along with the leather from my boots. My right leg sprang straight into the air from the relief of the pressure. He jumped out and knelt by my side. "You should keep your mouth shut." He mentioned something about how I got what I deserved before other agents came running up to where I was lying on the side of the street.

Don't you fucking cry! Don't let him see you cry! I thought to myself.

They put me in an ambulance before management decided that it would cost the station too much money. I was then placed in a supervisor's truck and raced into town. The hospital took X-rays and put my right leg in a half leg cast from my foot to mid-thigh. I had another partial arm cast for torn tendons and muscles in my left arm. It would take some time before they could tell if I'd suffered any fractures, but there'd been no clean breaks. An agent carried me up to my second-floor apartment and dumped me off. I took my pain pills and passed out.

Days went by without a word from the station until I finally called and asked what I was supposed to do. My car was still parked at the station. I couldn't drive, shop, or even go to the doctor. There was no such thing as Uber or grocery deliveries back then. Would there be an investigation? Did they want a statement? I'd seen how the agents took care of each other when shit like this happened. Naïvely, I thought I should have expected the same, but only a few of my closest friends at the station had offered.

I ended up having to call and accept help from my mother. I'll never understand what made her eager to help me then and not so many other times. She offered to drive me around to my appointments and get groceries for me. I sent her back in less than a week after she got drunk with one of my girlfriends and opined that I took after her in personality.

Months went by and my casts were replaced with soft braces; my crutches became a cane. I returned to the station on light duty and worked in the office again with Donner while I waited to be healed and cleared to return to the field. The PAIC ordered a speed bump with reflective paint right where I was run over. They all laughed and called it "Budd's speed bump." Like in the academy, there never was any investigation. It was simply deemed an accident. The trainee who ran me over wasn't fired. He never visited me, never called. I saw him off and on over the years at the station. Not once did he bother to say one single word to me.

I did my best to ignore the rumors, the talk that he did it to impress Linda. I just couldn't believe that he would do that even though I remembered what he'd said that night. I didn't want to believe it. Agents came to me and told me how they were trained by Linda and Will. They spoke of how the couple claimed I did not deserve to be an agent, how I apparently fucked my way into the Patrol, that I yelled and treated trainees like shit and that I was a fuckbag. They said Linda told them that I filed a false allegation against a classmate in the academy because I couldn't pass the physical training. They told their trainees they kept a file on me and encouraged them to contribute anything to that file with the intention of somehow firing me, although they did not have the authority to do so.

Just doing my job and keeping my head down for years didn't stop the accusations and harassment. I was sick and tired of this crap. I reckoned if I didn't stand up for myself, then nothing would change. I decided to take the advice and filed a complaint against both of them. The PAIC said I had to file EEO even though they were not my supervisors, and so I did. I never asked for any money or a transfer. I only wanted an apology and a confession about how they lied about me. I just wanted to be left alone to do my job. For this, my car was vandalized with a black magic marker and its tires were slashed while parked at the station. Supervisor Donner received a threatening letter that stated they would tell his wife we were fucking. They claimed to have reported him for having an affair with a subordinate and that he'd lose his job.

A few weeks after filing my complaint, I walked into the station to find Mendoza, the agent who raped me at the academy, working overtime on my shift. This happened off and on for months after I filed. Every time I walked in and saw his face, I felt my heart drop into my stomach. I immediately turned around and left the room, feeling dizzy and sick with fear from the flashbacks. Without fail, just seeing his face made me feel helpless and small again just like I felt that night, like I did when Mom whipped the shit out of me. My green armor and weapons were no match for this threat, and all those memories and feelings punched a hole in the mortar of my mental wall. It flooded my brain, and I felt the heat crawling up my neck and the saltwater rushing into my mouth again.

My choice was to work with the man who raped me or use my sick leave. I naturally chose to be sick and knew better than to complain about it. This frustration, this anger, festered within me and filled my dreams and thoughts for days, sometimes weeks afterward. I told no one. Not my family, my friends, my lovers. I took my anger and fear out on the trails just as I always had. Only now, I found myself taking it out on the migrants from time to time, screaming and belittling them when my patience was running thin.

Many of the trainee agents who told me about Will and Linda's scheme eventually lied once they were asked to put it on the record. They came to me privately and said they didn't want to get involved even though they had witnessed it all. Agents like these seemed worse to me than the outright corrupt agents. They were the ones that made long careers out of the Patrol, the ones who were willing to look the other way and cover for others just to cash that paycheck. They were the spineless ones who always got promoted. This culture was what kept the rape culture, the corruption, the lies, and propaganda going. The Patrol had a lot of criminal agents, but it was the ones who ignored the corruption that caused the most damage in my mind.

Enough agents did tell the truth in the end, and two years later, EEO finally decided in my favor. Linda and Will had targeted me. They had instructed trainees to harass me, to complain about me, to leave me without backup in the field. They put my life in danger over rumors. I never got my apology, never got any remedy as EEO found that because neither of them had been my direct supervisor, it did not affect my employment or my promotion ability, and therefore, their actions did not matter. I never took any money for disability, never got an apology or a confession, but agents now knew I wasn't afraid to file against them. I hoped that would make them leave me alone.

WHO NEEDS WARRANTS

My promotion to senior patrol agent came with added responsibilities like station intelligence duties, prosecutions, and assisting younger agents with casework. I had already learned and performed all these tasks as a junior agent because of Supervisor Donner's attention. That much was not new. What was different was the increase in pay and all the available details or special units that I could now apply for, like sector prosecutions, sector intelligence, joint narcotics task forces with other agencies, and undercover task forces—all of which I did, including being a field training officer.

When I walked into our daily muster before going out to the field and saw the PAIC standing at the podium, I braced for some new rule or policy that would once again limit our patrol area. Once President Clinton's wall went up, deaths of migrants increased drastically and complaints from human rights groups started coming in. Instead of admitting that the wall was pushing migrants out to the more dangerous terrain as it was intended and that this was what caused more people to die, management decided that they would limit the areas we patrolled. We could no longer go north of Highway 94, the first paved two-lane road running east/west. Most of the bodies we discovered were north of this road. If we couldn't patrol there, then we couldn't find the bodies and the numbers of deaths attributed to Clinton's Operation Gatekeeper would stop exploding. In the eyes of politicians, the problem was solved.

Our new management in Washington, D.C. didn't care about migrants getting away or dying any more than the politicians. They cared about the optics, about how it looked to the public, about getting promoted. Younger, newer agents didn't understand either. They hadn't had enough time in, had not yet experienced the finding of the dead women, men, and children. They hadn't sat for hours with them and wondered who they may have been, that those bodies were someone's mom, dad, brother, sister, aunt, uncle, someone's child. They didn't wonder who had loved them, why they had "Lupita" tattooed over their heart, who would be devastated by their loss or what made them take this dangerous journey in the first place, or how bad their lives had to have been just to consider it.

The more time that had passed, the more decomposition the bodies suffered. The natural progression of death and decay, the extreme temperatures, and the animals transformed their physical presence; I preferred to find them like that because it was selflishly easier on my soul. The less decay, the harder it was to look at them because they simply looked asleep. I wanted to shake them awake and take them home to their loved ones when they were like that.

Campo was no longer immune to the micromanagement that had engulfed the stations down in the city, and dead migrants were now just numbers that embarrassed the administration. My station had gone from over fifty agents to over two hundred. More agents meant more supervisors. The days of only one supervisor per shift were long gone. Each shift now had five or six supervisors, each with a crew of six or more agents underneath them. Each shift's supervisors were supervised by a supervisor known as a field operations supervisor. Then there was a special operations supervisor who handled all the special details outside of normal patrol activities.

The PAIC hadn't come to talk to us about dead migrants, though. The increase in manpower meant it was harder for smugglers to get their goods across, which in turn made them take greater risks. For months, we had known of a new smuggling organization working in our patrol area who intentionally drove west on the eastbound lanes of traffic late in the evening on I-8. Agents and locals had witnessed the driver enter the interstate east of our checkpoint at Buckman Springs Road, going the wrong way. The smuggler, or *coyote* as we called them, then drove west, past our checkpoint to the next exit at a high rate of speed, and then re-entered the interstate on the westbound lanes at the next exit. His only goal was to get past our checkpoint. For several nights, we watched from the checkpoint median as he sped past. Cars going eastbound in the eastbound lanes were forced to play chicken with this smuggler.

So far, no one had been injured, but agents argued to the Campo station management that it was only a matter of time. What were we going to say when the inevitable became a reality? What would the Border Patrol say when an innocent family was hit head-on and killed? What would the PAIC say when he had to admit that we knew this had been going on for weeks, that we did nothing to stop it, that we kept quiet and did not warn anyone of the potential dangers? Some agents suggested spiking the tires, but at the speed the smuggler was driving, it was likely spiking the tires would cause a crash. Management wanted to ignore it, but agents kept pushing for them to respond.

Campo's PAIC eventually relented. His plan involved using senior patrol agents to monitor the smuggler in undercover cars in an attempt to follow the loads until they arrived at their drop points or stash houses in San Diego. We would then arrest the driver and bust the stash house. I was chosen because of my knowledge of casework, and because I was experienced in vehicle pursuits. A bonus for management was that I never got into chases that went off the rails. I pushed and chased at high speeds, but I did not bump cars with my bumper, spinning them out of control or pull up alongside load vehicles and throw rocks through their windows or pull my gun on them and threaten to shoot as many other agents at Campo frequently did.

There were other senior patrol agents in the unit from Chula Vista who were more experienced with following loads in the city. My partner, Jiménez, had been an agent in north San Diego County at the Temecula checkpoint before he took a senior patrol position at Campo. I was his training agent when he first arrived, teaching him the area and the trails. As ordered by the PAIC, we dressed in regular street clothes and each was assigned an undercover car. None were outfitted with car radios, and we had to make do with our handheld walkies to communicate.

The first few nights were uneventful, and I'd started to worry that the smuggler had somehow found out what we were up to. He had always gone once it was dark and no later than midnight. He missed no more than a few days before we saw him again. On the third night, I sat underneath the interstate at the Corte Madera Ranch gate a few exits west of the checkpoint, listening to my walkie and fighting off boredom when Jiménez came over the radio, saying that the smuggler had just jumped on the eastbound lanes heading west at Buckman Springs Road. I got on the interstate and headed west at a normal rate of speed, knowing full well they would catch up and pass me.

"10-20?" I asked Jiménez for his location. "You should be here by now."

"He got off and is heading up to Julian the back way! Meet me back at your spot under the interstate," he replied, ending the tail before it got started. We were set up along Interstate 8 and had no way of safely following the load vehicle through the mountains.

He pulled up not too long after I had returned. "Well, that sucked," I said.

"Yeah, makes me think he has lookouts. Nothing for three days and then this change of route. Means we must keep moving or stay farther off the freeway. We can't rely on a helicopter being up right when the chase starts."

"Yeah, but how do we get to him in time before he's gone? We could just have the checkpoint radio us the description of the next car they use, and we wait farther down the interstate closer to town with the other guys."

"I got a better idea," he said holding up a black box.

"What's that?"

"A scanner that can pick up cell phones. In Temecula, the smugglers contact one another by cell phones and not radios. We can listen and figure out their plans and stay a step or two ahead of them. We'll be able to hear the lookouts telling them which route to take or if they are warning them about one of us up ahead."

I knocked the cherry off my cigarette butt and flicked it out the window.

"What's wrong? You look like you smelled something bad," he said.

"It's just that...it's against the law. We need a warrant to be able to listen to private communications."

"Oh, come on, Jenn. You don't think we're the only ones doing this, do you? Fuck, they listen to us! All the stations do this. Every sector does this. Agents ride around and listen to cell phone communications all the time. It's just a tool to help us level the playing field. There are agents that do this all night, all across the border. If they get busted, we just say we were listening for cartel activity south of the border and no cell phones in the U.S."

"What happens when you go to court and have to disclose that you were secretly listening to their communications? Doesn't the judge throw the whole case out?"

"Not if you never mention that you did it. They don't know what we don't tell them. We just say the car was heavily loaded, proximity to the border, our experience as immigration law enforcement officers that this normally indicates that it is a tonc load and so on like we always do. Besides, constitutional rights protecting search and seizure are limited down here on the border," he added.

I knew of less than a handful of agents who understood constitutional rights. The rules of searches and seizures, evidence, interrogations, arrests—all these things were lightly covered in the academy, but there was never any additional training after the academy in this area. The training that agents received after graduation and in the field contradicted the little legal training we had in the academy. Less than a handful of agents I worked with knew that the Constitution applied to all persons and not just citizens, that you could not legally just pull over any car with a Brown driver because you were on the border, that it was illegal for us to listen to cell phones without warrants.

When agents broke the law to get the arrest, they most often lied on the casework and stated that the driver had gotten away or absconded.

Without the driver, there was nobody to prosecute and therefore nothing to evaluate and see that they were breaking the law. If the driver was a U.S. citizen and they could not simply be returned to Mexico, agents would claim that the U.S. Attorney's Office refused to take the case even though they never even bothered to request a review of the case. Even when prosecutors were interested in the case, they were often forced to decline it because agents had broken the law in order to make the arrest. Agents refused to take responsibility for their illegal actions and for not knowing the law. Instead, they blamed the U.S. Attorney's Office, claiming they did not care about people entering our country illegally. For Border Patrol agents, it's not about casework or jail sentences. It's about pounds of dope, numbers of migrants and vehicles seized. This is still the case today.

My cases were rarely ever declined. If I didn't have the level of suspicion needed to make the stop or it was not safe, I simply did not do it. It was not worth my reputation as a federal agent to violate the law or risk anyone's life by asking someone their citizenship. It was a line that I was not willing to cross even though so many around me did.

"I don't feel comfortable doing it. Honestly, I don't even agree on having checkpoints. I've never agreed with the whole proximity to the border excuses to limit rights. Why should anyone have to be inspected for their citizenship just because they live close to the border? The Constitution doesn't say the Fourth Amendment applies to all persons except those within so many miles of a land or sea border."

"See, that right there's the problem with hiring you college-educated dweebs."

"Yeah, well, that's how I am, I guess."

"Oh, come on! They are fucking criminals! Listen!"

He turned the scanner on and turned the dial until we could clearly hear someone speaking on a cell phone in Spanish.

"You hear that? There's another load going. Scouts are everywhere. It's just leveling the playing field. It's what we have to do to catch the bad guys," he said, trying to convince me.

"You can do whatever you want, but I don't want any part of it. Besides, I cannot understand them. They are speaking too fast," I said, thankful to have discovered an excuse.

"Oh yeah, maybe you should learn Spanish better," he joked.

"Maybe you should learn English and write your own damn reports," I said, laughing.

Within a few weeks of trying to follow the loads, the unit was disbanded. They feared another massive crash, like the one that had originally shut down our ability to pursue back in 1992 when agents chased a car into San Diego, killing three innocent civilians. Whatever intelligence we may have gathered went to the California Highway Patrol who had far more experience and expertise in dangerous pursuits. It was what should have been done in the first place, but Border Patrol always had an inferiority complex about not being seen as real cops and tried to get involved when it shouldn't have, when agents didn't have the training or experience or even the legal authority to safely engage.

I was scheduled to go to the desert in Indio, California, for a month anyhow.

INDIO

Indio, California, is about an hour and a half drive north of the southern border from Calexico. It is in the flat, sandy desert where temperatures often reach over 120° during the summer months. A handful of us was detailed there for a month to provide support for the Border Patrol's two checkpoints on either side of the Salton Sea, a landlocked body of water created by diverting the Colorado River during the early 1900s to provide water for the Imperial Valley farms.

In the 1950s and 60s, developers had intentions of making it another desert spa retreat for families, like Palm Springs. Miles of paved roads that created the framework for neighborhoods still exist with street signs and cul-de-sacs, but no homes were ever built. As more water was diverted to farmland south, the Salton Sea became more toxic with higher concentrations of salt and chemicals from the farmland runoff. Fish, birds, and other wildlife began to die, as did the interest in buying property. Driving around the neighborhoods, it felt like I was looking at the remnants of a nuclear blast site. Like there'd once been homes and families, but all that was left were the roads, dirt and sand.

It was July and 110° already when Jacob and I stood in the morning hours on the banks of what looked more like a lake than a sea to me. The rot of fish and dead vegetation filled our noses. Different colored lines on the rockface surrounding the lake showed how much it had dropped in volume through the years. The notion that anyone had ever thought it would be a tourist destination seemed implausible now, absurd even. At our feet were hundreds of small dead fish staring back up at us, warning us of what was to come, telling us to leave, but we did not listen.

Jacob was the only redeeming thing about being sent on detail. There was no other agent I preferred to work with more. He was a few years junior to me and had specifically requested me as a journeyman back when he was still a trainee because he heard that I knew how to do casework, that I'd never lost a case in court, that I knew how to develop actual reasonable suspicion as opposed to relying on racial profiling. He'd wanted to be a police officer, to put criminals away, but the pay and the adventure had lured him to the Patrol as it did for many of us.

He never liked the line work of dragging, sign cutting, and hiking, but preferred to work the checkpoint and the surrounding roads. I don't think he even knew how to track. Like me, he knew when to call it quits on pursuits and did not take it personally when he had to. There would always be another load. It was Jacob and I who started to identify and put together the profiles of the smuggling organizations working in the Campo area. We knew who their leaders were, how they obtained their cars, who they used for drivers, and where they would stash the loads. Before us, agents stopped loads here and there, never developing the intelligence or profiles of the organized smuggling groups. Together, we spent a great deal of time working with the U.S. Attorney's Office, putting away smuggler after smuggler.

Indio wasn't all that bad in that we got to work together and hang out with each other every night at our spa hotel in Desert Hot Springs. Per diem pay was enough to eat well and stay at a nice hotel, where we could enjoy massages, the swimming pool, and hot tubs every night if we wanted. We were assigned the day shift and after our initial muster at the Indio station, we drove rental cars from our hotel to one of the checkpoints every day. Each week we swapped checkpoints with the other unit to try and keep the agents from being bored, but there was little need to worry about that.

Our first week there, we were assigned to the checkpoint that sat right next to the railroad tracks. Train engineers would slow down just enough that we could check the trains for any migrants that might have hopped on to evade us. Indio agents had warned us to not get too close to a fast-moving train as it could sweep us under the cars. I stood next to the tracks when the first train arrived and wondered just how fast was too fast.

"Grab a ladder and jump on!" Jacob yelled as I watched him go past me on a car. I grabbed the next car's ladder, which was above my head, and felt the weight of myself and my gun belt as I pulled myself up. It took every bit of muscle I had to get my footing before I noticed two young men sitting on the knuckle between my car and Jacob's. We were warned at the station that the knuckle mechanism that joined two cars was designed to have space so that the cars could rock back and forth as the train slowed down. This action would cause anyone sitting on them to possibly get a limb or finger pinched within the mechanism which could then sever the entire appendage. There were numerous stories of this happening to migrants.

"Jacob! Two on the knuckle!" I yelled.

We both held out our hands and yelled for them to climb back up to us on top. They quickly stood up and promptly jumped straight out past the rail cars and onto the gravel and dirt ground as we watched in fear. Another agent quickly ran over and placed both under arrest.

"They're okay. Just banged up a bit," he said over the radio.

By the time we jumped from the moving train and walked back to the checkpoint, they had already been processed and were eating crackers and drinking the colored sugar water we routinely gave them. Jacob and I were red from the sun, the heat, and the concern that these two had put us in. We sat in the airconditioned office with them and explained why they should never do that again. The color drained from their faces when they realized what could have happened from sitting on the knuckle and from jumping from the train as they did. They'd not wanted to hide with the others in the cars because the metal cargo cars or boxcars were even hotter than the outside.

We quickly developed a pattern and assigned ourselves specific tasks while conducting train checks. Near the train signal, there was a metal ladder at least a couple of stories high. Because Jacob and the others did not care to be on that skinny little metal ladder so high up, I volunteered to be the lookout. When we saw the train coming, the guys ran to the tracks while I ran to the lookout ladder, put on my black leather gloves so that I did not burn my hands, and climbed as fast as I could to the top. I hooked my left leg in the rungs so that if I lost my balance, I would not fall to the ground. As the train rolled by, I could see which cargo cars had been opened because they could not be latched from the inside and were left ajar.

"The yellow one," I said over the radio. "There's another two back here on the knuckles. There are women and children in this beet container." Ten, twenty, thirty...on and on it went. Whenever we had women and children or older men, we forced the train to stop completely before taking them off. If there were only young able-bodied men, we told them to jump from the car ladders as we did.

Occasionally, they could see us on the cars further north and would jump off the train before reaching us. Atop the ladder, I could see a group of people running through the desert, east from the tracks. Jacob and others jumped into a car as I directed them to where the group was.

"They say they're too tired to run back," Jacob responded.

"They were running when they jumped off. Make 'em run back. Ya! Ya! Get them doggies running!" I said over the radio. I watched as he made them pick up the pace and run back to his G-ride.

As we sat in the cool office processing our catch, the door flung open violently and our supervisor ran in, telling agents to get their gear and follow him. I stayed behind to finish processing the group, and everyone else took off in various cars and trucks. I could hear over the radio that Indio agents had located the sign of a group of seven that had jumped off of the train and ran west before taking an arroyo north to circumvent the checkpoint. I finished processing and closed the doors to the cells before standing at the window of our closed checkpoint, looking out west across the flat desert sand to where I knew they had all gone. I looked at the thermometer and realized it was 124°.

"I found two," Jacob said over the radio. I noted that he did not say, "I'm 10-15 with two," which was how we normally reported apprehensions over the radio.

"I found another three," someone said. The next shift came in and my supervisor said they'd meet me back at the hotel later.

Back at the hotel, I had already cooled off with a swim and shower. I was on my second Long Island iced tea when Jacob sat down next to me at the bar.

"What's up? Thought I'd see you before now."

"They died," he said as he signaled the bartender for his usual beer. "Better yet, give me what she's having."

"How many?"

"Seven, maybe. I don't know."

"Wow," I said unemotionally. "Probably already dehydrated from crossing the border, sitting in a hot train car, and then trying to run from *La Migra* across the desert. Women?"

"Yeah, but no kids. I guess it shouldn't bother me more to see the woman than the men, but it does. I'm sorry if you think that makes me sexist."

"I don't think it makes you sexist. It's our societal structure. I feel the same way. We are used to seeing women in the context of caregivers, as softer or kinder than men. Plus, you have a wife and kids, a daughter. You probably think about that when you see them."

Jacob was still drinking by the time I left. My head hit the pillow in a drunken fog that did little to ease the images of death. The following morning, I stood outside his hotel room, banging on his door. We were late and supposed to already be on the road to the checkpoint. His roommate answered the door.

"He's still drunk. Help me get him to the car," he said.

I threw Jacob's gun belt in the trunk of my rental, and we got him to the checkpoint and inside to sleep the rest of his hangover off. He appeared at primary at around noon and thanked me for helping him get to work. From that day on, this became our routine. Soon, Jacob was drinking Long Island's out of wine carafes instead of the normal bar glasses and downing five or six of them every night. I never said anything to him about his drinking, and I do not believe anyone else did. We all knew why he was drinking. There was no reason to talk about it. We only had a few days left before our detail was over anyhow.

* * *

Indio and the Salton Sea weren't willing to let us go without a parting gift. On one of our last days there, as we were almost to the checkpoint, we came across the guys from the midnight shift and the California Highway Patrol. As I rolled up and pulled to the side with my emergency lights on, an agent ran over to tell me a migrant had been run over by a semi-truck and his body was dragged down the road, leaving a large red stain. Here and there, we found parts, but not much was left, not much that was recognizable as human.

In front of the other agents, Jacob commented on how crazy it was. He laughed and joked about the smear and the pieces strewn across the highway. Back in the car, he let out a huge sigh and I could feel the weight of what we had witnessed enveloping us. He didn't say a word except to ask me to stop at a small convenience store in the middle of nowhere and pop the trunk. I did as he asked and sat waiting in the car with my window down in what was already 100°, smoking one cigarette after another. I knew by the sound that he'd thrown his gun belt in the trunk. We sat there, me smoking and him drinking beer early in the morning before shift. The man I knew as Jacob, the one I had trained and loved to work with, the guy who always had my back, was gone. Somehow, he sputtered along in his job a while longer.

I noticed that I was changing too. I hated coming to work and felt like a fraud. The agency called us heroes when we returned migrant bodies. They said we risked our lives out there to do that work, said we protected the country from people who they referred to as "criminals" and "got aways" from our fellow agents down on the border, that any one of them may have been a rapist, a drug dealer, a murderer. The only thing wrong with all that talk was that it just wasn't true, and we knew it.

I didn't feel much like a good person anymore. I certainly was not a hero. I started thinking about how much had changed in such a short time. I had helped the agency build that wall. I helped push those migrants out to the desert they now crossed. I manned those checkpoints and patrolled the border roads like I was trained to do. It didn't matter how many migrants I apprehended, how often I told myself that the next one might have a violent criminal in the group, they rarely ever did. After thousands of arrests, I estimated that I prevented less than twenty-five, maybe thirty criminals from re-entering the country. And while stopping any dangerous person was good, risking thousands of lives, seeing their bodies decay in the sun, and violating people's rights to catch those few didn't make any sense to me anymore. Not after that bloody summer.

While in Indio, I had the chance to see what many of those "got aways" did. Jacob and I leaned against my Patrol sedan and watched them in the fields sometimes. Contrary to what we'd been taught in the academy, most did not sit around, living off welfare. They weren't taking good-paying jobs from Americans. They spent their time picking strawberries or artichokes; jobs that most did not want. Day after day, bent over, picking our food in the hot desert sun for little money.

It occurred to me then that the reason we did not have a decent worker program was that it would cause wage increases and benefits demands. We enjoyed affordable food and other products in part because it was undocumented migrants doing this work, the ones who got away from me. Landowners and business owners enjoyed the cheap labor and the fact that they didn't have to pay competitive wages as well as denying them healthcare or any benefits at all. If the immigration service increased workers' permits, then these companies would have to pay fairer wages, and they would lose money.

When I returned to Campo, I tried to forget about it and put it all behind me. Time and again, though, these thoughts kept coming back to me. I was growing tired of all my excuses, and I think Jacob was too.

COMING OUT

In the summer of 1999, I decided to come out at work as a lesbian. Agents had been going to parades and community events in uniform to represent the Patrol. More and more, management asked agents to participate in these events. They paid us taxpayer money to do what most people do as unpaid volunteers—reading and tutoring kids, running Cub Scout-like groups called the Explorers, visiting hospitals and showing our appreciation for nurses or adopting a poor family for Christmas and helping pay for presents.

I believed that these public relations stunts should not have been done in uniform and that agents should not have been paid taxpayer money to do so. It felt like propaganda to me, like it was meant to get people to not hate us because we chased Mexican families through the mountains and treated them like animals. I was starting to see all the ways that we did that… the ways in which I did that, and I was beginning to think it was wrong. Maybe we needed to issue more work visas instead of trying to convince people that all migrants were criminals and all agents were heroes, but that wasn't the way the Patrol or the federal government wanted it.

When I ran into San Diego Police Chief Bejarano at a function, he suggested I join him in marching in the upcoming local Gay Pride celebration. No Border Patrol agent had ever represented the agency in uniform at the San Diego Pride Parade before. I'd come to accept that it never mattered how many migrants I apprehended or how much dope I seized, I would never overcome the rumors of my sexual assault and would always be seen by most agents as one who would not "play ball." I was tired of being accused of screwing Donner and any number of other supervisors. I also wanted to make a point of pushing the agency in an uncomfortable direction. Plus, I was a senior patrol agent now, and I was not as scared or as intimidated as I had been before. I sent a memorandum to Campo's PAIC and requested to march in Pride in uniform. I passed on Chief Bejarano's invitation to all the upper management at San Diego Sector as well.

Within a day, I found myself standing before the PAIC's desk as he berated me for my offensive memo. "You can't make us go to this fag fest!"

"It's an invitation from Chief Bejarano. No one's trying to make y'all do anything," I replied.

"What kind of shit is this? Why should the Patrol pay for you to march in this?"

"Why should the Patrol pay for O'Conner to march in the Irish Parade? Why should it pay for Johnson to attend a Martin Luther King Jr. celebration?"

"That's different!"

"No, sir. It is not."

"Yes, it is. It's a choice. Do you know I can fire you just for being gay? Are you a lesbian? The federal government doesn't recognize homosexuality as a protected group, you know."

"Yes, sir. I am. I have always been."

"Wait, I thought you were fucking Donner?"

"Sir! For the record, I have never had sex with an agent! Ever! Unless you think rape is sex!"

"You calm yourself down there, little lady! I never said such a thing." He took a long drag off his cigarette. "You can go to this, but I want you to rewrite the memo stating that you're gay," he ordered.

"Is that an order?"

"You bet your ass it is. What's wrong, Budd? Don't got the balls to do it?"

Moments later, as I sat in processing and wrote a memo that officially outed me for the Border Patrol record, Armando walked in. He'd already heard about the blow-up the boss had. Border Patrol stations spread gossip faster than sexually transmitted diseases, and the supervisors wondered out loud if I might file grievances against them simply because I was a lesbian. Not that I had any reason to file, just that I might because I was both a woman and queer.

"What day is it? I'll put in a memo and go with you," he said.

"Why would you do that?"

"Because it's only fair and I support you. I'll stand with you, Jenn."

We rarely worked the same shifts, but when I most needed it, Armando was often standing beside me. He knew it would shield me, would quiet the gossip. For him to march in Pride with me, knowing he could get hit with rumors of being gay, the harassment the guys would give him—well, I thought that was brave of him.

If someone had ever told me that he was a bad guy, that he was like so many of the other agents, I would have told them to fuck off. I would have told them all these great stories that I knew about Armando. I would have said that he was one of the good guys, trapped in a world of few opportunities for a young Latino who'd grown up on the border doing the best he could for his family.

And I would have been wrong.

* * *

I had no idea why Supervisor Jones had called me in from the field that day. I assumed it had something to do with the Explorer Program he was in charge of and that I'd been leading at the station. I never wanted to take on that responsibility, but Jones had requested me, and I respected him enough to do it. Local high school kids who joined got to meet at the station, wear blue cargo pants, boots, and Explorer polo shirts. They learned about immigration law, first aid, constitutional law, and participated in local community volunteer events. They were not allowed to do ride-a-longs or work with migrants in any way, not at least with me in charge.

"I just want to say that no one has complained yet," he started.

"About what?"

"Your gay sticker on your car."

While at Pride, I had bought a thin rainbow car window sticker and put it on the back of my brand-new Mazda sedan. It was discreet, and I was excited about not having to live a lie anymore. It never occurred to me that this would be what he wanted to speak about.

"What about it?"

"What happens if some of the Explorer kids' parents see that sticker?"

"I don't know. What happens?"

"They see that the leader of the Explorer Program is a lesbian, they'll pull their daughters out. What if they make accusations? Agents are already talking about how some of those teenage girls are pretty hot. We don't want them wondering if you are hitting on them or not," he said seriously.

"Wait. Are you asking me if I'm a pedophile?"

"No! I'm just saying their parents might wonder if you are attracted to their daughters."

"Well, Gomez is my second agent in charge of the Explorers. Did you ask him if he was attracted to the girls? Did you ask him if he was a pedophile?"

"Well, no. That's not how it works. You're the one advertising that you're gay."

"Are you saying that because I'm gay, I might try and sexually assault these girls?"

"I'm not saying it, but their parents could. No one has, but we just have to make sure..."

"Fine. I resign from the Explorer Program. Effective immediately."

"You can't do that," Jones insisted.

"Sure, I can. It's voluntary. I don't have to do this. I have never even been written up for a single violation in my entire career. I've only received excellent and outstanding ratings on all of my evaluations. Now you're saying I might be a pedophile because other agents are commenting on the looks of these young girls?"

"Just take the sticker off and it will all go away."

"No, sir."

I stormed out of the office and typed up my memorandum of resignation for the Explorers. The following day, Supervisor Jones' supervisor called me in. Special Operations Supervisor Maxwell was the number three guy in charge of the station. He was a military man, a stickler for following policy, and eager to write agents up over every little infraction.

"Why are you suddenly quitting as the lead of the Explorer Program?"

"Supervisor Jones brought it to my attention that there are rumors going around about me. Something about male agents commenting on female Explorers' looks and how attractive they are," I replied.

"Well, guys do those kinds of things. As long as you take the sticker off, I see no reason why I shouldn't rip this up."

"I'm not going to be lead if agents are going to spread rumors about me being a pedophile. Gay is not the same thing as a pedophile. You can be straight and be a pedophile. Why aren't you more concerned with them talking about how attractive little girls are?"

"Are you accusing them of improper behavior around children?"

"No. You're accusing me of it. I didn't work this hard to get into this damn agency just to lose it over rumors that you guys spread," I said angrily.

"You know what you are? You're a quitter. Just when things get a little tough, you just up and decide to quit."

"You're not serious, are you? You have no idea..."

"Stand up when you talk to me, quitter!" he barked.

I stood and stared straight at the wall in silence for what seemed a long time.

"What ever happened with you and Supervisor Donner? Was that really true? I mean, I just can't imagine that big guy on top of you. How long did that last?"

"I request to be excused. You have my resignation from the Explorer Program. I have nothing more to add."

"I thought you were tougher than that, Budd."

I left the room and the Explorer Program never explaining why I'd resigned to the kids. Maxwell blew his brains out years later.

WHO AM I?

When the sensor went off just after midnight, I knew not to bother starting my hike at the border road. As a young agent, I'd chased many groups on that same path so many times, and it always burned my thighs out climbing up and around the giant boulders. Besides, I didn't have as much strength in my right knee after I was run over in the parking lot by that trainee. I couldn't jog after work anymore like I used to.

It was a steep climb up, and I knew it would make their legs feel weak and shaky once they got to the road and started the next climb. So, I leapfrogged them and went to the top of the next mountain where the groups usually popped out. I quietly crept in with my Tahoe's headlights out and parked far enough away that I knew they could not hear me when I quietly closed my door.

In the dark, I walked the dirt turn around at the top of the mountain south toward the drop-off I knew they'd be climbing up. In my ear, I heard over the radio that a helicopter was heading my way. I didn't like using the birds because they created more chaos scattering the groups in all different directions and making dirt and foliage fly everywhere. There was also the fact that the pilots liked to hotdog it and get right above the migrants, scaring them until the women and children cried. I didn't see any reason why that was necessary and could not understand why they thought it was hilarious.

I quietly started to make my way down the path when I heard a junior agent say that he was tracking them and that the group had moved more to the east side of the mountain. I turned left and started making my way through the thick brush and rocks until I came to another path that led south. I could hear the helicopter below me but could not see it. A few more steps south and I could see a few people hiding under the brush. I turned on my flashlight and saw that it was a large group, about forty or more men and women.

"You can't hide from the big bird," I said in Spanish. "Let's go."

No one moved and I felt a sudden tightening of my chest and nervousness I'd not felt around migrants in years. I grabbed the back of the young man's shirt who was sitting right at my feet with his back toward me and again told them to get up. Again, I got no response.

I could hear the agent climbing up to us and figured I would just wait for him when I was suddenly blinded by the helicopter's spotlight. As I looked south, I realized for the first time that I was standing right on the edge of a cliff. It looked like a thirty-foot drop or more and I felt my body panic and my muscles tighten. If this young man at my feet pushed back on me or just jumped up and pushed me, I would go over the side and die right then and there.

Stephen Starch's face flashed in my mind as I recalled how he had been pushed off a cliff and died when we were junior agents. We had taken the entrance exams together in Jacksonville, Florida. He was a part of the 295th session, an educated and extremely fit man. If he could go like that, I could too.

My left hand still held the young man's collar, and in my right, I held my large, red six battery Maglite. I yelled for them to stand up again and still they defied my orders. I came down on the young man's right shoulder with my heavy light and ordered them again to stand up as the helicopter blew dust and debris all around us. I could barely hear myself yell at them again when I came down on his shoulder a second time and he cried out.

This time they all stood, and I heard the junior agent calling them up to the top where I had parked my truck. Once everyone made it to the top, I let go of his collar and went back to the edge to make sure we didn't miss anyone. My mouth filled with the familiar saltwater and my jaw tingled with pain. I spat over the side and took in a few deep breaths to calm myself before returning.

"We got all of them," I said.

"*Puta!*" the young man I'd hit said.

"What the fuck did you just call me?" I threatened.

"I called you a *puta* for hitting me with your flashlight!"

I noticed the young agent just watching as he patted down others. *You can't let this tonc talk to you like that in front of another agent,* I thought. I walked over to the young man, pulled my flashlight up to his face and said, "And I'll fucking hit you again if you call me that one more time."

I could see the anger in his face, the humiliation of being threatened by a woman, a female *Migra.*

"You know, she is a good person. She could have shot us or beaten us, but she didn't. I have been caught by her before. She is nicer than the others.

She's a good person. A good person," an old man kept repeating in Spanish.

His insistence that I was a "good person" shocked me out of my bullying, and I put my flashlight in my belt loop and took the young man aside. "I'm sorry for hitting you with my flashlight. I…I just…I shouldn't have done that. You are right. I am sorry if I hurt you." I'd done the one thing agents had said I should never do, I apologized.

He nodded and apologized for calling me a bitch.

"Are you injured?"

"No. It's okay."

"Next time, do as the agent tells you."

As the group sat waiting for the transport van to pick them up, the young agent and I stood to the side. He asked what had happened and I told him the truth. I told him how I had gotten scared and that I hit the young man with my large flashlight when I shouldn't have.

"Wow! So, you literally tonked him," he said, laughing.

"Shut up!" I said, feeling ashamed and embarrassed about my behavior. I needed to get out of the field.

HEADQUARTERS INTELLIGENCE

I was desperate to find some way to keep going in the agency. I tried to push the thoughts of quitting from my head. Maybe I could manage to stay if I had a change of scenery and learned something new. I transferred from the mountains to a commercial building with cubicles in town. Though my office was in Chula Vista at the San Diego Sector Headquarters, my area of responsibility was still out east in the mountains. As a sector intelligence agent, I was expected to use the skills and knowledge I had accumulated in my assigned areas. I would not have been of much value to the agency if they had assigned me to Imperial Beach or El Cajon station areas as I knew less about their terrain or the smuggling patterns.

Operationally, stations could differ drastically even though they were in the same sector. This was especially true for an area the size of Campo. Most patrol still occurred on foot, and we still did not have GPS capabilities back then like agents use today. It took years to learn the trails and where they led. Knowing where you were when you started hiking in the dead of night and where you'd likely end up wasn't something you could learn in any book. How old was the sign, the footprint? How many were in the group? Were they running or walking? Any women? Children? Where were they likely going? Were they being picked up on Highway 94 or Interstate 8? Would they likely hit sensors or not? Some of it was instinct, but most was experience. These were skills and knowledge a sector intelligence agent for the east mountains had to have already in their skill set before taking the position.

Like most things in the Patrol, there was little training for my new position. On my desk, I found a folder of investigations conducted by other intelligence agents that the boss, PAIC Hodges, considered to be great examples of how he wanted my reports to look. When he called me into his office and asked if I thought I could write reports as he wanted, I made sure to respond appropriately—with a little bit of confidence, but mostly deference to his ego. I knew well what was expected of me as a woman in the Patrol by then and did it easily.

The men in the Border Patrol who had fragile egos were the most dangerous. As long as I observed the appropriate amount of respect for Hodges's rank, as long as he was not close with anyone who hated me like Mendoza or the agent who ran me over, as long as he didn't ask me to "play ball," I would likely be fine. Besides, I had been warned about Hodges beforehand by others that respect was what he most craved, what he valued above all else.

It was all I could do not to laugh as I sat patiently, waiting for him to speak. I could tell he got his hair cut weekly and his nails done professionally. I hated these kinds of agents; the press officers, those in management and the like. I believed they were sycophants and administrative dweebs who were paid extra law enforcement pay because they carried a gun and a badge even though they spent most of their careers behind a desk or in front of a camera. His boots were spit-shined and his brass showed no green or grime. I imagined he spent an hour or more in the morning just to place his rank perfectly on his collar. His night school juris doctor degree was prominently displayed on the wall, and his desk sat up on a platform, which forced his guests to look up at him.

Before being dismissed to set up my work area, I assured him I would do my best and I looked forward to his guidance. Only one of the reports gave any semblance of a trained law enforcement intelligence investigation, something I had learned at my internship in Mobile with old Mr. Eddy. The others were simply racial profiling reports of vehicles whose drivers looked to be "too Mexican" to be driving such an expensive car.

I did my own investigations as I was trained to do before I joined the Patrol, as the U.S. Attorneys I knew had requested of me. I would establish my suspicion with my knowledge of the area, run numerous records checks and criminal histories and interview witnesses and victims like real investigators did. I had no leads when I walked in the door. No basket of intel waited for me. I came up with cases on my own.

* * *

Suzanna Primo was a legally admitted permanent resident, a "551" or "LAPR" (pronounced lapper) in Border Patrol slang. She ran a large smuggling organization thanks to her son, a U.S. citizen and a National City police officer down in San Diego. She preferred to smuggle in used cars bought by and still registered to Father Joe's Catholic Charities. Father Joe was not involved in the smuggling, of course. She just happened to like his auction prices and never bothered to change the registration. When we ran a license plate of a car driving through Campo and it came back to Father Joe's, it was always good. Meaning it was a load of migrants looking to get north to find work. Always.

She was a smart lady and knew that most agents racially profiled. So, she made sure her drivers were never Latinos, only whites. It was easy for her to get away with this for many years when Campo had so few agents. The Interstate 8 checkpoint was often closed simply because we did not have enough agents to staff it. Even when it was open, everyone knew they could just take the access road around the checkpoint to avoid us because we did not always have that road staffed either. It was easy money for her, and she never got her hands dirty. If you wanted to make a living smuggling, that was the best way to do it in San Diego County back then.

Her son, the cop, was responsible for finding the drivers. A homeless encampment in his patrol area known for heroin addicts was his hunting ground. Whenever he busted a white addict, he took their dope away from them, promised to inflict pain on them from the end of his baton, and then offered to let them go if they would drive a load for his mother. Desperate people forced to make desperate decisions was a resource on both sides of the border like anywhere else. Unscrupulous people and corrupt cops could see the hopelessness in others and managed to figure out ways to profit from it.

Suzanna preferred her drivers be addicted to narcotics because she knew the feds were not interested in paying for their detox, which was required if we sent them to jail. This meant that if the driver had an addiction to drugs, we simply could not press charges. We had little money back then, and the Border Patrol certainly didn't want to spend it on two months of treatment.

This meant that her drivers could then turn right around and drive another load for her within hours of being released from our custody. Using the same drivers meant less time spent training new ones. Smuggling, after all, is a business, and lower overhead or less time training meant more profit for her. There was a huge demand for undocumented labor in the farmland in central California and elsewhere that elected officials did nothing about. She was willing to meet that demand.

As more and more agents were assigned to the area, we started sharing intel with each other and the Primo patterns quickly developed. Campo's PAIC even assigned five of us to work around the clock to snag her loads. Between Bob, Jacob, Ricci, Linton, and I, we stopped and seized ten plus load cars a day, nabbing fifty to seventy migrants who crossed illegally. Dope loads and stolen vehicles were part of the mix as well. A typical day ran sixteen or so hours because of all the paperwork required. We made our own hours and answered to no one but the PAIC. We ate our lunches in our cars and smoked while we chased them. It was constant lights and sirens, bailouts, and running through the brush, up the sides of mountains until we caught them. Soon, we were able to put a real hurt on her business and others. We kicked ass. Nothing got through our area when we were on duty.

Like every effective operation in the Patrol, it was short-lived and cancelled after a month. The PAIC complained to us about our reports, saying that the groups and drugs were crossed in our area of operations. He, in turn, felt pressure from his boss at sector for so many crossings occurring in our area. The administration had told the press and public that Operation Gatekeeper, specifically the wall that now extended through our area, reduced illegal crossings. They publicly claimed it prevented migrants and dope from crossing, even when it never did.

Reports of crossings in areas where the wall was built meant President Clinton's wall was not working to deter illegal immigration as they'd claimed. So, our PAIC ordered us to say our loads were coming from Calexico, farther east where the wall had not yet reached. As agents, we cared less about the politics of the stupid wall and wanted to state the truth. We refused to lie and wanted to stand on principle; the wall did not deter crossings of migrants or drugs. It was a waste of taxpayer money. For our obstinance, all five of us found ourselves sitting on X's or stationary positions the next day. That's how Campo's PAIC got his nickname of Dirtycop from us.

More than anything, I wanted Primo's immigration status revoked. I wanted to take her green card and cut it up right in front of her smug face. The thought of an LAPR smuggling in our patrol area and easily getting away with it drove me crazy. She wasn't a citizen, and I took her lawlessness as a direct insult. Part of being an LAPR meant she had promised not to break our laws. That included immigration laws, even if most didn't think twice about breaking them.

That was the real issue for most of us, that it felt personal. The fact that most didn't think much of committing immigration crimes made us feel like less than other law enforcement agencies. The way politicians played politics with our operations and would let migrants who entered illegally get away to protect their legacies; their policies infuriated us. Yet, when Border Patrol leaders exaggerated the danger we faced or started using the guestimates of supposed "got aways" to make our points that we needed more resources, we didn't care because that benefited us. Whatever it took to get what we wanted was deemed appropriate. The general collective low self-esteem and morale that had always existed in the Patrol, in every station, in every sector came from this. I was not immune to it either.

I received praise from the other sector intelligence agents and even from PAIC Hodges himself on the report. "Good job," he wrote on the Primo file. I was ready to gather a team, draw up warrants, see the judge, do a raid. This was what I had been working towards for years, what a law enforcement officer should do. We were supposed to take down the real bad guys, protect the public, enforce the law. But there never was any of that in the Patrol, not even at sector intelligence. The report just went to a file like all the other reports.

"Your job is to develop intel that will stop toncs from crossing the border," he said. "The goal is to make Operation Gatekeeper a success, to show how the wall works and that all these agents are preventing people from crossing. This does not do that. It shows how the wall fails to do any of this and that is not what the administration or management wants."

* * *

It was not uncommon for Cindy to stop by sector and say hello to me. She always found excuses to get out of the field, and there was usually something that needed running from Campo to sector headquarters anyhow. I never bothered to ask why she was in town. It wasn't worth having to listen to her gossip.

She should have been assigned to one of the San Diego city stations instead of our station in the mountains, maybe as a press officer or some other administrative position. She wasn't a hardcore agent, didn't care much for the hiking and the getting dirty part of the job that I loved so much. She was one of the most unemotional, mean women I ever knew. Which was saying a lot, because most of the women in the Patrol fit that description, including myself.

I had long ago stopped feeling much of anything. Whether it was from my childhood or from being in the Patrol, I didn't know. I just kept pushing everything over my mental wall. I told myself things didn't affect me, that I was tough, and it was all in the past. To think about those events and my feelings about them made me feel weak. I couldn't be weak as an agent. Being an agent required toughness. I was part of the five percent of women who had made it. If I couldn't hack it, then I shouldn't have been there. I knew that I likely had it no worse or better than any other female agent. Like they said over and over, we all bled green. That was my mantra too. That's what I told myself to keep going. To think any other way felt traitorous to me.

Cindy considered me to be a friend, and for that, I tried to be kind.

We had plenty in common: both from the South, both short and skinny blondes who had put up with all the shit the Patrol threw at us. I could tell she had childhood trauma like me. It had something to do with her father I reckoned because she never mentioned him. Her choices in lovers were older, like the age I imagined her father to be. In that typical unhealthy way, we never spoke of our traumas. We preferred instead to just ignore them. Sometimes they sneaked over our walls and showed themselves in the most inappropriate ways that were regularly encouraged by the male agents—like when we drank too much, or when we yelled at the migrants, pushed them around, or treated them as less than ourselves. She was more prone to this, but I was not innocent either.

I cannot say if she ever felt guilty like I did when that happened. I don't think it ever crossed her mind. Even though she had a college degree in Spanish, she rarely ever spoke it choosing instead to make the native Spanish speaking agents translate for her. Cindy hated the migrants anyhow. She hated their very presence, their existence. "Why do you listen to their bullshit stories?" she asked me. "They lie every fucking time their dirty fucking mouths open."

Campo guys gave her the nickname "Weed Whacker" a few years after she arrived. It was a nickname they had decided on because she apparently had a large bush. When her uniform orders came in, they wrote it on the cardboard box in big black letters. If she felt shame about it, she never said it out loud. The guys sat around the station and compared notes on her body and her performance and wrote them on the bathroom walls in the station.

She slept with over twelve or so of them. Many I knew because she told me. Others I was never sure if it was just guys making it up or not. It was a game to them, a dare, and she was the station *fuckbag*, according to them; that official Border Patrol name for a female agent that slept around, the word we'd learned from our instructors at the academy. It preceded everything about her like my rape did for me. She was less of a person, less of an agent, a joke in their eyes for having a sex drive, for being human. The very fact that she had a badge was called into question because of this title. It was assumed by the men and many of the women that she had slept her way through the academy. I never cared about any of that.

"Did you hear about Wilcox?" Cindy asked.

"No. What's the gossip now?"

"Loaded van full of drugs came down the West Indian Road at shift change. He waited for it with a shotgun in his hand. Blew out the back window. Dirtycop's furious!"

"The back window, huh." She raised an eyebrow and nodded her head at me, knowing what I was getting at.

I knew PAIC Dirtycop was literally a dirty cop for years. Most station rumors were bullshit, but I began thinking that there was some truth behind a few after I worked on a narcotics detail with a couple of Drug Enforcement Administration (DEA) agents. DEA intelligence was literal intelligence, not rumors or racially tinged assumptions like I was used to from Border Patrol agents. After a couple of days of lying in wait for smugglers, their intel paid off when a small group of backpackers crossed with marijuana.

These backpackers were known as mules to us, and they were not actual drug smugglers. They were migrants forced by cartel members to carry the dope. Their choice was their life or to smuggle the dope. Sometimes they held their wives captive on the Mexican side and forced the husbands to carry the dope. They truly had no choice but to do it, but the government didn't care. I can't say that I cared back then either. They went down for it if we caught them, another statistic for the Border Patrol, another family torn apart.

I took DEA Agent Statton in my truck, and Senior Patrol Agent Jiménez took her partner Agent Williams; one Patrol agent with one DEA agent. They did not know our area, where the barbed-wire fences started and stopped, how to orient themselves by the few buildings or other landmarks out there in the middle of nowhere that we used as markers. I heard Jiménez yell something on the radio, when I heard brush breaking in the dark just north of the border. The mules, those carrying narcotics on their backs, tried to run to an abandoned trailer to our east while others ran around aimlessly to distract us.

Statton was right beside me, unsure where to go or what to do. I took off, running east through the brush. My eyes were adjusted to the dark just enough to catch a glimpse of a white ball cap as a mule ran in front of me. Instinctively, I jumped over the barbed-wire fence that I knew was in between us and landed on his back. He fell underneath me with seventy-five pounds of dope on his back. Statton was five seconds behind me. Her eyes were wide open, amazed at my catch.

"Process him," I said as I pushed him to a junior agent. He was nothing more than a conquest to me, a trophy to be bragged about, the one that didn't get away. I told myself he was a smuggler of narcotics, convinced myself that he was a danger to my community, to my country, even though it was just weed, even though I knew he was no drug smuggler. I told myself that he had a choice in the matter but that he chose wrong, and I moved on to the next smuggler just like I was trained to do. I cannot even recall what this man looked like.

Maybe she trusted me because of that night. Maybe she was just shooting in the dark, just taking a chance. Either way, Agent Statton took me aside to tell me that the DEA was there to gather intelligence on Dirtycop. They had busted some loads in town that originated in our area from Jackson's Pig Farm, a suspected drug smuggling ranch that butted up to the border wall. Its owners often drove around their property on ATVs with their children in tow, one in front and one in back in case anyone thought of shooting.

She said that a couple of their interviews came up with Dirtycop as the organizer on the north side. It all made sense when I thought about it. Our station was getting bigger and bigger. More agents, trucks, guns, a bigger checkpoint. All this made it harder not just for the migrant smugglers, but for the drug smugglers too. Things especially got tight for them once the I-8 checkpoint started staffing K-9s and the access road that went around the checkpoint.

In general, we expected that the harder we made it to smuggle drugs, the more dangerous our jobs would become. But we knew that we still had little impact on the narcotics smuggling simply because they did not try to kill us. While it was true that the majority of drugs were coming through the ports of entry with corrupt customs agents easily available to the cartels, there was still a decent trade out there in between the ports of entry. There had to be someone organizing drive times to get around the agents on the border and at our checkpoint.

My detail with the DEA agents ended and nothing seemed to come of their investigation. Dirtycop was still the PAIC, and I tucked that bit of intel away and kept it to myself like most things. I was reminded of it a few months later when he suddenly altered our shift change operations. No longer were we allowed to take the East or West Indian dirt roads south to the border wall and Jackson's Pig Farm. Now we could only take the paved road, Tierra del Sol (TDS), and we were ordered to announce over the radio our position so that the prior shift could begin their drive back to the station.

Management claimed it was to keep agents safe, to account for everyone. Grumblings and curses were heard from the crusty agents during shift muster when it was first announced. They tucked dip in their gums or held unlit smokes in their mouths, staring down the supervisor who held court. If anything, this was more of a danger to agents. To announce your location across our channel that was monitored by smugglers and Mexican *federales* was just as insane as taking the same roads shift after shift was. Habits just made it easier for the smugglers as one agent shouted out. The supervisors reminded us that orders were orders, and we quieted down, tucked our tails, did as we were told, just like we always did.

* * *

I met with Wilcox privately about the shooting and the drug van. He said that he intended to prove that the new shift change order was what allowed so many smugglers to get away. He planned to argue for two more shifts that would fill the gap caused by only having three shifts, and he wanted to announce his ideas at muster the following day even though his gun and badge had been taken from him while the corrupt Critical Incident Investigation Team (CIIT) looked for a way to make his shooting out the back window look like he had feared for his life. The CIIT unit had become better known among agents by their nickname, the Coverup Incident Investigative Team, or the Coverup Incident Team.

Wilcox was a young agent, chubby and constantly trying to prove himself to be one of the guys. He reminded me of the last kid picked for the kickball game, the one no one wanted. He'd been my trainee for a few months, and I found him to be naïve, simplistic, and unbelievably out of shape for someone who had just graduated from the academy. He lacked impulse control, and frankly, was downright dumb. "But I am digressing," he often said, no matter how many times I told him he said it wrong. He was dangerous when combined with a badge and a gun, but my recommendation that he be terminated went nowhere as the agency was more interested in filling positions than hiring good agents or holding them accountable. It was the new Patrol now, and they took anyone.

Wilcox's impression of management's operations change was that it was a simple mistake on their part. He did not realize it was intentionally done by Dirtycop. In the way that kids think of their parents, junior agents regularly thought upper management didn't know what they were doing; they did not realize management had once done our jobs with much less gear and support. Dirtycop knew exactly what he was doing, but I did not explain this to Wilcox as I believed the less he knew, the better.

"Do you think they'll fire me for shooting out the back window?" he asked.

"Why did you shoot?"

"Well, they were coming at me!"

"In reverse? It's a big area. Obviously, you stepped out of the way because you shot through the back window and not the front," I pointed out.

"Am I getting fired?"

"No. They'll fire you for disobeying an order and going down that dirt road before firing you over the shooting. You're lucky that no one was hit."

"Hey, I'm a fucking hero! I kept those drugs from getting onto the streets!"

"You still have to follow the law, dumbass."

Wilcox likely had just put a target on his back, but not for violating the shooting policy. If Dirtycop suspected that he was about to be outed, he'd take Wilcox down for this. Eventually, he was returned to regular duty as he never connected the dots with Dirtycop's intentions. A clueless body in uniform was still a body. As it was, he was just another agent violating a policy that no one would ever know about simply because no one got hurt. Aside from when he talked to me, he never came forward with any suspicions aimed at the boss. His stupidity saved his job and maybe his life.

As time went on, I gathered more intel from locals who stated that they had heard Dirtycop bragging about how he controlled the drug flow through Campo. He liked to get drunk several times a week in one of the local dive bars and threaten people with his power. California Highway Patrol officers I interviewed had numerous stories of how they pulled him over in his unmarked G-ride for drunk driving as he tried to make it back to his house. Professional courtesy was demanded by our bosses, and the CHP bosses constantly ordered their officers to simply drive him home and let him go. Other agents who drank off duty in those same bars overheard the locals talk about his involvement as well. When a Campo agent finally went to the FBI to testify about what locals told him about Dirtycop, an assistant chief from sector reportedly entered the interview room and pulled him out. He was told to keep his mouth shut.

There is a saying in law enforcement that nothing is by coincidence. If someone is openly smuggling or dealing in your area, then one of your own is dirty. The rumors, DEA intelligence, Wilcox's encounter, the fact that Dirtycop ran the assignments for each shift and that he chose who was assigned as K-9 handlers—all of it led me to him as the organizer on the northside.

If I went after him, I would have to be fully loaded with evidence. Evidence that was incontrovertible. To accuse a fellow agent was dangerous, but to say that the boss of the station was actively involved in smuggling drugs into the country, well, that was suicidal.

But that was just the type of woman I was at that point.

* * *

The West Indian Road was called such because it was on Native reservation land, and it occurred to me that Dirtycop had to be using locals to assist him. If he was organizing the smuggling in Campo, he would do it the right way and not just wing it, hoping a load here and there would get through. I knew some locals were passively involved in drug smuggling, that they took money from the smugglers and allowed their properties to be used as drop-offs from mules. It was just as likely that these locals might have been paid to act as lookouts.

I waited north of the road until shift change at the turnout across from where the Campo band of the Kumeyaay tribe were building the new casino. The giant cement foundation had just been finished. *The new smugglers' haven*, I thought to myself. I was driving an unmarked previously seized beat-up Honda hatchback from sector that I knew no one would recognize. My badge and .40 caliber Beretta were tucked under my shirt in an off-duty holster that held it closer to my body than I was used to.

Driving slowly south on the road to the West Indian, trailers dotted both sides, and every so often, there was an actual house. I could not see anyone watching me, though I felt they were, knew they had to be. I pulled over and started to walk back up the dirt road toward Highway 94, where Wilcox had shot. I could picture the scene from the reports written on the incident. The van ended up sitting sideways in the dirt road where it widened. I could feel Wilcox's panic before he realized nobody in the van was hurt and knew that panic likely came back to him once he saw that nobody was armed.

Within five minutes, I heard dispatch over my walkie confirm my suspicions. "One walking West Indian northbound near Highway 94. Blue jeans, white shirt, ball cap." Moments later San Diego Sheriff's deputies pulled up in their marked vehicles, followed by the Border Patrol. I held my hands up in case anyone did not recognize me out of uniform. Before agents could clear the dispatch call as normal traffic, Dirtycop came over the radio. "Charlie one seven eight. Charlie one. Get to eight two five." Meaning, "Budd. Dirtycop here. Get to Campo station. Now."

I took my time as I winded around Highway 94's two-lane road. I had considered this scenario before going out there. I figured other agents were likely to be involved, but I did not consider that sheriff deputies working our area would be. Being the first to show up meant they were listening to our channel, which was not normal. Who else was listening? Did this mean they were involved? Were they assisting in looking out for Dirtycop's loads? How big was this?

Slow your thoughts, breathe, I thought.

I sat in the station intelligence office in the double-wide trailer that was once the only trailer we had. Cindy looked up at me and nodded with a bit of a smile. She wasn't stupid and knew what I was doing. Other senior patrol agents worked on their computers quietly when suddenly Dirtycop came in. I knew it was him before he rounded the corner because he swung the door open so hard it banged against the metal staircase outside. As he looked at me, all the other agents got up quickly and went outside. They had a sudden collective craving for a smoke.

"You," he said as he pointed his yellow, tobacco-stained finger at me. "Who the fuck do you think you are, missy?"

He leaned over in front of me, placed his hands on either side of my chair's armrests, pinned me in, and pulled me closer as his blond hair fell forward across his sunbaked, wrinkled forehead. I turned my head slightly to the right. I hadn't smoked a cigarette in seven months, and his breath smelled like an old ashtray. I felt sick to my stomach. Maybe from the smell, or perhaps from the hot current of fear I felt crawl up my neck.

"I know exactly what you're up to. Fuck you! Fuck you and all those do-good agents just like you. Fuck all your piece-of-shit buddies." His voice was stern but measured. "Yeah, that's right. So fucking what? Everybody knows. And now you know some of the sheriff boys are helping me keep an eye out. I will fuck you, and you will spend the rest of your fucking career behind a desk if you're fucking lucky! Don't you ever get into my business again! You got no idea how many people are involved in this. I don't ever want to see you over there again!"

I nodded and he left.

It was that same kind of feeling I had after that truck I chased blew its engine or when I knew I was about to be beaten as a child. Like the feeling you get after a car crash when the adrenaline courses through you and your brain buzzes a bit. My vision became more tunneled, and it was all I could do not to puke. I went out the same door he'd come in and ran into Supervisor Donner.

"What's up with you?"

My face was probably bright red as if I'd just run a race. I told him quickly, and he insisted I wait while he had a word with Dirtycop. I no longer trusted Donner. I preferred to stay away from him rather than accept his help or friendship again. Especially with this.

I jumped in my car and headed back to my office at sector in Chula Vista.

* * *

"I hear ya got into it with Dirtycop. Sit," PAIC Hodges ordered.

I'd just walked in when he called me into his office. This time, the guest chair was against the wall and faced the other wall instead of his desk. I had to tilt my head to the left so I could see him as he spoke. Word had gotten there already. I told him my version and suggested we speak with the FBI or DEA. He stared at his calendar on his desk while he twisted the ends of his dark mustache. It felt like forever until he spoke.

"You probably just misunderstood him. These things happen." His words were calm, almost soothing.

"Wait. What?"

"Yeah, sounds like a misunderstanding to me."

I jumped to my feet as I felt another adrenaline rush. "That's the kind of shit I'm talking about, sir!"

"You sit down, young lady! Don't you curse in front of me!" And I knew that it was bullshit, cause ain't no Border Patrol agent ever not cursed.

It felt like I was in an alternate reality. I knew by then that the Border Patrol was extremely corrupt. It didn't take that long to figure out that some of the agents I worked with on a daily basis were committing more serious, violent crimes than the majority of the people I arrested every damn day. It's why I went back and forth about leaving the agency so many times. Prostitution, drugs, alcohol, stealing, bribery, rape, assault—it was everywhere, and hardly anyone was ever fired or even so much as disciplined for it. It had gotten so bad with the feverous push to hire as many agents as possible under Operation Gatekeeper that I honestly felt safer when I hiked the mountains alone in the middle of the night than I did at the station with so many corrupt agents. My world of who I trusted was getting smaller and smaller.

"This is the type of stuff I'm talking about," I said more calmly as I sat back down. "The corruption in this agency is through the roof and we have to do something about it, sir. We are talking about the head of a station smuggling narcotics. Agents have died trying to stop smugglers. He's the head of a station doing this. My station. No, I did not misunderstand him, sir."

"Look, I get why you're upset. You're afraid. It's understandable. I tell you what, we at sector will create a position for you. Say, a supervisory position. So, you will get a raise out of it, a nice promotion. We'll make it competitive. Everyone will put in for it, but it will be given to you, and no one will know. That way, you never have to go to Campo again, and you'll be safe."

I'd heard of this before. Agents called it "promote to shut up." A few years back, when the agency began to bring in the new supervisory agents to Campo, many of them were "promotions to shut up" situations. Several of these new supervisors were from the San Diego city stations bordering Tijuana: Brownfield, Chula Vista, and Imperial Beach. As agents, they claimed management ordered them to lie about the number of apprehensions they got. If they caught a group of twenty, they were ordered to write down ten. This was done to make it appear that Operation Gatekeeper and the wall worked when it really didn't.

Most of these agents came forward with their allegations to the OIG (Office of Inspector General). After a lengthy investigation, many of these same agents suddenly changed their testimony and no longer claimed they were told to lie and that they had simply misunderstood their orders. These agents were then promoted to supervisory positions. More than one of them admitted this to me after they'd transferred to Campo. Agents who got their promotions especially early were most often "promoted to shut up." They had seen or been a part of something illegal or corrupt. It was the only explanation for why some supervisors seemed to be promoted years before other agents with more experience. In the end, the investigation found no wrongdoing by the management of those stations and found that the agents simply misunderstood their orders. There was no retaliation against those agents who took the "promotions to shut up."

Knowing all of this, I tried to maintain my composure. I told PAIC Hodges I wasn't his woman for that. I did not believe taking a promotion for silence was ethical, and it violated an oath that I had taken to receive my badge. In my nearly six years as an agent, there were many times where I had to enforce a law I did not agree with, but I still enforced the law because I was sworn to do so, because I took an oath. To look the other way on this drug smuggling operation would violate my core values, even if it was just marijuana. I could not do it, and I drew a line in the sand.

"Go home. Give it some thought," he ordered.

I had no idea what I was going to do. As I drove home, I became more angry than scared. Being in the Patrol was always so fucking hard for so many unnecessary reasons. Was this just another one of those times? I spent years studying law, years taking shit from other agents, and bowing down to rank who didn't deserve it. I was a real-life badass Border Patrol agent from Campo, for God's sake. It was one of the most revered stations in the Patrol for how physically demanding it was. I hiked like the guys, shot better than most, was the queen of vehicle stops, knew my law inside and out, and never once lost a case in court. I was on special narcotics teams, was a field training agent, a sector prosecutions agent, a station intelligence officer, on special interdiction teams. And now this? This Serpico bullshit was going to take me down?

I had expected to be interviewed by the FBI or DEA. I thought I was going to be protected by my agency, by my PAIC at sector intelligence. I should've been applauded for taking down a high-ranking corrupt agent, for stopping the flow of illegal drugs into our country, for following my oath and serving my country, for following our motto of "Honor First." They should have given me an accommodation, or at least a stupid plaque.

My mind did what it always did; I doubted myself, my own eyes, as the agency wanted me to do. Maybe it wasn't as big of a deal as I thought. After all, everything in that job was so traumatic, so high risk. It all blended together after a few years. Normal days became boring without a car crash, a dead body, or a dangerous vehicle chase. Danger had a different meaning to me after all those years. Maybe it was all in my head. Maybe I was blowing it out of proportion. Maybe I could act like it never happened and just move on.

The message on my home answering machine said I was to work a midnight shift. I'd just walked in from working ten hours during day shift and would now have to put on a uniform and drive an hour out to Campo and work again in five hours. There was no need to call and see if it was a mistake. There was no mandatory overtime any longer. Illegal crossings had been declining in our sector. Fewer and fewer people crossed illegally to find jobs, and many shifts ended with zero arrests even though the agency was forever claiming we were understaffed.

There was no legitimate reason for me to work that night. Besides, I was assigned to sector headquarters, which meant plain clothes and unmarked vehicles. The station knew this. They knew I had just left sector. I pictured PAIC Hodges on the phone with PAIC Dirtycop, laughing it up, telling him I wouldn't go for the promotion, saying that I couldn't be trusted, that he should be careful with me, that they should've gotten rid of me long ago.

I made sure to pack extra ammunition and magazines for my sidearm. My uniform was a bit tighter from being out of the mountains for months. It no longer felt comfortable to me, no longer felt like it would protect me. I found myself being more concerned about my weight than what I was about to walk into, and quietly admonished myself for being so vain. My Red Wing fire boots were still covered in the dirt from my last time in the field. I tested my batteries for my walkie and threw the spare in the bag. Binoculars, flexi cuffs, sensor list, collapsible steel baton—check, check, check.

I made sure to put on my bulletproof vest that usually sat in my closet.

I kissed my future wife goodbye, not knowing if I'd make it home. Sandi and I had only been together about seven months, and I was not willing to tell her about all of it. I tried not to think about it on the long drive.

There was no way to prepare for something like this.

* * *

There must have been twenty-five agents working that night. I recognized few of them. So many had moved on to other agencies or had been arrested. Others had committed suicide or become alcoholics or were now addicted to drugs. Many like me were just plain disgusted with the job and the corruption. Our attrition rate had doubled because of the rape culture, the corruption, the racism. "Honor First" was a joke. I barely remembered their names; they came and went so often. Campo felt disjointed, and its history, any small bit of pride, was quickly being erased. There was little cohesion amongst the ranks. Few from the old Patrol were left to tell them how it was before, how it should be. Most of the room had less than two years of experience.

These junior agents had clean, pressed, rough duty or field uniforms. The green had yet to be bled out from the many washings and the harsh sun. The stain of the sweat and salt on my uniform did not exist on theirs. Their boots shined like new, and their brass reflected the cheap fluorescent lighting found in all government buildings. Their forearms lacked the scratches and scabs I used to carry from when I regularly pushed through the thick brush. No sweat stains or black ash rimmed their caps. I noticed several trainees wearing the same cowboy hat I had on. It was insulting.

"Budd, zone four, scope. Jackson's Pig Farm," blurted FOS (Field Operations Supervisor) Cahill as he spit into his coffee cup. I knew Larry personally, had known him for years. We'd done that detail for a month in Indio together back when he was just a supervisor. The one with all the trains and dead bodies. I spent a whole month with him and Jacob, just drinking and talking shit until the wee hours of the morning so we didn't have nightmares. He'd seemed like a good friend back then, less than a year ago.

I waited until after muster to question my position. It was a simple matter of respect not to give him shit in front of others. To put a scope on the pig farm was dangerous as it was too close to the wall to be preoccupied with staring at a video monitor. Besides, little could be seen from there. With our night vision scopes, the closer you were to the action, the harder it was to see. A group could cross right in front of me, and I would not be able to focus on them. Plus, I knew there had to be a tunnel under the wall that went to the farm. They'd busted a large truck hauling over twelve hundred pounds of weed not that long ago. A tunnel was the only thing that made sense. It must have been a bad day for Dirtycop.

"Because the fucking boss said so," Larry blurted at me as I stood in his office doorway. His attitude and anger toward me for asking a question about my position was uncalled for and not like him at all, but I didn't have time to go at him about it. Confused, I grabbed my keys and headed out as ordered.

I assumed Dirtycop would try and get me on defying an order and write me up with a bad evaluation. So, I didn't want to be late reporting to my position. Maybe they'd give me a day off to try and teach me a lesson. I wouldn't give them a chance, though. It may have been dangerous and a trainee position, an X, or a stationary position with a scope, but I would do it because it was an order. I would sit on that X and see nothing all night if they wanted. I even went down the paved road and announced my location for the off-going shift just as Dirtycop had ordered.

At least the new scopes were automatically set up in the bed of the trucks, and I no longer had to lift the heavy camera onto the tripod like I did as a trainee. More money meant nicer trucks, fancier equipment. Our work was now something corporations made billions from. The only condition on moving with this newer style was that the camera mast had to be lowered before driving so as not to damage it. My zone supervisor swung by two or three times in the first half of the shift to make sure I had not moved. I was not used to this kind of micro-management. It further convinced me they were looking to write me up.

As expected, little was going on; all was quiet save for a few coyotes in the distance. In my time away, I'd forgotten how the SDG&E power lines hummed loudly at night as the dew fell all around, and how peaceful it was. I missed my alone time and hiking through the mountains. I'd forgotten the unique smell of the desert mountains and how clean and clear the air was. I suppose I was fortunate to have joined the Patrol when I did. I knew the border from before the wall and after, and I missed the before. Campo didn't feel like a community anymore. It felt like a large jail, and we were the guards.

All four zones and the checkpoint were slow. I stared at the green scope screen as the glow of rabbits and cows moved all around me. It was about 3:00 a.m. when I heard the first burst of shots. I looked up at the wall no more than thirty yards in front of me, and I saw the muzzle flashes as they came from a small hole cut in the old solid landing pad wall. At the same time, I caught in my peripheral vision just outside my driver's side door the ricochets of the bullets off a group of rocks. I could tell it was a fully automatic rifle of some sort as it reminded me of the quarterly training we had with M-16 and M-4 rifles.

I never considered firing back. I'd already contemplated this scenario many times in my career when I used to work this area as a junior agent and had concluded I would never fire south into Mexico unless necessary. That is unless I had a clear target, unless I had no choice.

There were houses just south of that wall. Kids that I'd watched grow up over the years still lived there. I used to let them play on the north side before the wall went up. When it was slow, I played soccer with them. What the hell would I be aiming at, anyhow? A small hole? No. Chances were that my bullets would kill an innocent person or bounce off the steel and come back at me. Plus, I was seriously out-gunned. My Beretta was no match for whatever this was. My best option was to get the hell out of there.

I quickly threw my truck in reverse and made a three-point turn to face north. Steering with my left, my right hand instinctively grabbed the mic. "Shots fired! Shots fired! Pig farm!" There was no time to drop the mast and with every turn, I could feel the heavy camera in the bed of the truck as it pulled and twisted with each stop and turn. I sped north with my lights out and kicked up a cloud of dirt behind me as the shots continued.

"Anyone in zone four, shots fired at Jackson's Pig Farm!"

No one responded.

I called my zone supervisor. "Charlie twenty-seven. Charlie one seven eight. Shots fired!"

Silence.

"Eight two five, Charlie one seven eight. Shots are being fired at me! I need assistance!" I said to the station.

I heard the static click of a mic being keyed, but no one responded.

I radioed San Diego Sector Dispatch. "Eight twenty, Charlie one seven eight. Shots fired! I need backup."

I pulled into a dirt turnout several hundred yards north of the fence and slid to a stop. I knew I would be safe as long as they didn't come north. I repeated my calls for backup with the same response, nothing. As I lowered the camera with the click of a button, my mind raced, trying to understand what had just happened. Had they put me there knowing the drug smugglers would shoot at me to move me off? Was this really intentional? A setup? I realized just then I needed to check myself, check whether I'd been hit and maybe didn't know it because of all the adrenaline surging in me. I could not see nor feel a thing except my heart racing.

I noticed a pair of headlights coming down TDS just east of me. They were coming toward me and were about a half-mile away. I grabbed my spare clips already filled with .40 caliber hollow points, shoved them in my jacket pockets, and pulled my gun, holding it on the door frame, pointed at the road I had just come down.

I'd decided I wouldn't run. I aimed at the driver's side as it slowed and came down the dirt road. They turned out the headlights and crept up to my position. I heard the high-pitched sound of brush scraping the sides of the truck just before I saw that it was a white, unmarked Ford Expedition; the kind I knew to be used by high-ranking agents. I quickly lowered my gun below the door frame but kept it pointed towards the driver, my finger on the trigger. My eyes darted from the front to the back, as I looked for who was in the giant car.

"I heard over the radio that you we're getting shot at, and no one responded. So, I thought I'd come out to see if you're okay," PAIC Dirtycop said with a smile.

We stared at each other for a few minutes in silence. He held a lit Camel cigarette in his right hand and his left forearm rested on the window frame. I removed my finger from the trigger but kept my gun on him. My mind raced, trying to accept what I did not want to. I knew what I was facing now. Dirtycop was a nine to five, day shift, pencil pusher. He didn't go into the field anymore, didn't work the night shifts and was usually passed out by now at home.

"Have you learned your lesson? They might not miss next time," he said calmly.

I holstered my gun and drove away without saying a word.

"I need sick leave," was all I said to FOS Cahill when I turned my keys in. Now I understood his outburst at me. He had been ordered to put me there and had likely questioned it because of my seniority and rank, because he knew it was not safe. He still did it though, and I knew I had misjudged him to be a friend.

I was numb the hour-long drive home. No emotion, no fear, no real thoughts about what had happened. It was that habit I always thought of as a skill when I was young; in times of trauma, my emotions turn off, I dissociate from it all. I didn't want to think about it, and so, I didn't. I drove that route home so many times in the last six years that I had no recollection of doing it when I suddenly realized I was pulling into the driveway.

I was home. Safe.

QUITTER

The United States Border Patrol was not something I could just up and quit. Like many other law enforcement agencies, it took a great deal of sacrifice and strength to get into it in the first place. Every time I thought about leaving, I questioned what it all had been for if I was willing to just get up and leave. I stayed after being raped, after the harassment, after the lack of backup, after watching so many agents who took the same oath as I did be arrested and after seeing even more get away with their crimes during those years. I had a good government job. It paid well and had great benefits. I could be outside if I wanted and was paid to hike all day. If I never made another arrest, no one cared.

Promotion-wise, I had gone as far as I could go without making the transition into management. The brass pushed me to take the promotion test and put in for supervisory jobs, but I always refused. Whenever PAIC Dirtycop ordered me to take it, I filled in the bubble sheet without even looking at the questions. Sometimes I only filled in the first bubble through the entire test. Other times I made the bubbles read "AC/DC" or "fuck you" if you turned the sheet sideways. On the off-chance that I would pass, I purposely ignored my internal resume that we all had to maintain for promotions. When he ordered me to be an acting supervisor, I wore the captain's bars on my collar, but I refused to make it permanent.

To me, going into management had always meant the end of "Honor First," but now I knew there was none of that to be found anywhere in the Patrol. I had searched everywhere for it just to stay an agent. I couldn't pretend anymore. I watched as my classmates and friends took those management jobs. They always went in claiming they would change the Patrol, clean it up, and get rid of the coverups. As the years went by, they got married and had kids. Taking a stand naturally became more of a threat to their home, their lives, and their loved ones. Soon they realized that if they did leave, they would have a hard time finding a job that paid as well. The skills they developed in the Patrol did not transfer to other jobs, not even other law enforcement jobs and they became stuck. Those in management ended up chained to a desk, beat down, forced to do things they never thought they would do. Either that or they gladly engaged in the corruption themselves. They had gone to the dark side as we said, forever lost in mounds of redundant paperwork that did nothing to protect the country, nothing that was honorable.

Corruption had become the norm, and I often found myself thinking of all the things I saw agents get away with. I could tell many crazy stories from my service, and it would fill volumes even though I only served about six years. Like how I constantly put in to be considered for the horse patrol but was never selected. They didn't care that I had a great deal of experience as a rider, that I taught people how to ride as a teenager in Alabama. It seemed only male agents were selected for the Dulzura stables in San Diego's East County back then. They kept insisting there were simply more qualified male agents than me. When they gave the detail to a few who'd never been on a horse, the supervisor insisted he wanted agents with no bad habits to break. They always had an excuse, but said I was ridiculous if I thought it was because I was a woman.

One day while working in Campo, we realized that we had not seen the horse patrol guys in weeks, months even. They usually patrolled in the valleys just east of the Tecate Port of Entry and I often helped them with their groups when I was assigned there. Calls went out to the stables, but they went unanswered by Campo Supervisor Manning, who was on detail as the head management in the Dulzura stables. It wasn't until our assistant chief drove out there to see what the hell was going on that we all learned about the pornographic movie being filmed, about how Supervisor Manning's brother was a porn director and was paying him to use the U.S. Border Patrol stables to make a film. The entire Dulzura horse patrol staff spent their shifts watching them make porn instead of patrolling the border. That explained why female agents were always turned down.

For his crime, Manning was removed from the horse patrol and sent back to Campo. He was still a supervisor, of course. When I saw him walk back into the supervisors' office, he was unable to make eye contact with me. He brushed past me on his way to his desk as if nothing had happened. I still had to follow his orders, still had to be reviewed by him. No charges were ever filed, and the management covered it up. He ended up retiring with full pay and benefits.

I could talk about the times I witnessed agents being led out of the station in handcuffs because they stole government property and sold it, or how they were found out to have committed crimes before they even entered the Patrol. I could write about the many times agents pulled their Border Patrol trucks and vans right up to the wall in Tecate and stuffed it full of dope or migrants and then drove through the checkpoints as they waved at their fellow agents who never stopped them.

I could talk about how cartels bribed agents to wave them through the checkpoints, how smugglers gave depositions in the federal attorneys' offices and admitted under oath to me that they would use a single female driver to flash her tits as the signal for the agents at my I-8 checkpoint to let them go. I could write about how agents routinely took bundles of dope for their personal use or to sell to others, how some K-9 handlers became addicted to the heroin they seized, how many of our dogs failed the tests, and how no one knew agents regularly falsified the training records when subpoenaed for court. I could talk for hours about how agents went to the same doctor because he would write them a letter stating they had a small percentage of disability from an injury caused on duty. Never too big to get them terminated, but big enough to get them a cool ten or twenty thousand dollars even though they suffered no lasting disability.

The time had come when putting on my green armor, my gun and baton, my badge and cowboy hat could no longer protect me. In my time as an agent, that armor had meshed with my personal wall, but it was crumbling around me faster than I could rebuild it. The truth that I could no longer ignore was that it never really did protect me. The truth was that my wall only protected me from those who wanted to get close to me, those who wanted to help me, from my own wife and friends. The truth was that the wall of green gave me a false sense of security, made me lose my sympathy, my compassion, my humanity and prevented me from seeing the dangers I faced from other agents and helped me excuse their behavior and my own. The truth was that the green uniform and badge was a lie, a false image that had little to do with "Honor First" and nothing to do with justice.

Putting on that uniform used to feel like the floating I did as a child to survive, like it made me into a different kind of person who could compartmentalize my emotions and thoughts. I forgot all about the tornados in my head when I ran through the mountains, when I hunted people down, when I tracked them like animals. The smell of their sweat and desperation in the desert air, mixed with my own, seemed almost addictive to me back then. The late-night car chases on the two-lane country roads when I yanked people out by their shirts and threw them to the ground. The fear in their eyes at the end of my baton: *shut up, sit down, get in line.* Would I let them go? *No.* Would I let them turn around? *No.* Why? *It's the law.*

I'd stopped listening to migrants' sad stories years ago. To listen, to sit quietly in their space as I once did as a young agent was too uncomfortable for me now that I knew the truth, now that I accepted it. Their miserable tales of drug cartels, corrupt *federales*, starving children, homelessness, rape, murder, of how some of my fellow agents abused them—I was tired of hearing about it all because there was nothing I could do about any of it, because I could no longer ignore the fact that the laws and policies that I enforced were partly responsible for their misery, because Operation Gatekeeper was killing them and we knew it. I knew it. Our government knew it and did nothing. Our wall, our deterrence policies, were forcing desperate families to cross in dangerous terrain that we knew would kill thousands of human beings. INS Commissioner Doris Meissner was wrong. They did not stop crossing, because they could not stop crossing. They had no choice. Operation Gatekeeper was called a success. Death was always a known outcome for the government and the Border Patrol. To suggest that they did not know is laughable.

To sit and listen as I once did always brought me closer to seeing the people I hunted as humans, and that made it difficult to do my job. I hardened my bitch face even more to tell them not to even try and talk with me. If they missed the signal, I was not shy of ordering them to shut their mouths. More so, my whiteness told them who I was. My skin color had generations of power behind it. I knew it and they knew it. That was the power my skin color and green armor had. I used it to stay in my job.

I did not listen anymore, could not make myself be vulnerable and feel sympathy for them anymore because I personally had no more room. I could finally see, had accepted the truth about the Border Patrol. I had joined a racist, corrupt, woman-hating law enforcement agency that, to me, resembled an organized crime family. They backed each other to the end. They covered their crimes with their secret and illegal CIIT units, forced female agents and yes, even male agents, to endure their rape games and harassment. They murdered, stole, abused, beat and no one cared as long as they didn't get caught. For the record, the motto Border Patrol agents follow is not "Honor First." It's actually, "Deny, deny, deny, counter allegate, deny."

I had no more room for any of it. Everything, it seemed, was falling apart. I had to get the fuck out of there.

Neither PAIC Hodges nor Dirtycop said a word to me. At Campo, behind my back, Dirtycop told anyone who would listen that he suspected me of either dealing in drugs or being on them. Criminals always project their crimes onto others, and they tried to destroy my reputation of being a good agent. Honestly, I think that made me more upset and angrier than anything they had ever done to me.

Contrary to what the agency told the public, agents were not routinely or randomly tested for drugs. I had only been tested once at my initial hiring. The only time agents were "randomly" called for testing was when they were troublemakers. Rat out someone for sexually assaulting migrants, you could expect a drug test. Argue with your supervisor, drug test.

When I whistle blew, that got my name added to the list at the last minute in handwritten pen with no social security number attached. I passed, of course, but when Dirtycop ordered me to qualify with my gun before resigning, I refused and turned my gun in on the day I was to shoot. I would not stand on a firing line with a bunch of other agents who had hung me out to dry, who didn't answer my calls for backup. I did not want to fall victim to the latest "accidental" discharge of a weapon at quals.

I spent the last few months in the Patrol sitting at my desk at San Diego Sector Headquarters Intelligence. I was no longer allowed to run records checks or see intelligence briefings. There was little to do but play solitaire on the computer. Agents from Campo stopped by from time to time, to express their disbelief that I was leaving. "I can't imagine you not being an agent," many said. Truthfully, neither could I.

I made sure to visit Supervisor Donner one last time at the station. "I think you're making the biggest mistake of your life," he said. "Take the promotion. You'll be a PAIC before you know it." He always seemed to think that he knew what was best for me when he never knew me at all. Looking the other way was not my way, never had been.

"Did you ever stop people when they spread those rumors about us having an affair? Did you ever set them straight?"

"Honestly, I liked the fact that guys thought this old, fat guy could catch a young, hottie like you. Why would I want to deny it?" He chuckled.

"Because it fucking followed me everywhere! Because it wasn't true! They said I only passed because of you. Every detail I got was rumored to be because we were screwing. Agents didn't back me in the field. I sat in a meeting with a special operations supervisor and before I left, he wanted to know if we were really screwing. And you couldn't be bothered to say anything because you got off on it?"

"I'm sorry. I guess I never thought about it from your point of view."

"Yeah, I guess you didn't."

* * *

Before leaving Campo Station that last time, Special Operations Supervisor Kitchner pulled me aside. We went out to the area where I'd long ago met the Mexican lawyer who questioned me on my actions, on enforcing racist and unjust laws. Kitchner left his walkie in the car, which told me he was going to tell me something he didn't want anyone else to know.

We walked out to the overlook of the giant canyon, the one I'd begged the group not to go down.

"I know what went down," he started. He was now the third-highest rank at the station, and I admired him for his calmness and honesty. He was one of the few in senior management who I trusted and had confided in over the years.

"Everything?"

"Yeah, and you're doing the right thing, Jenn. He's as dirty as they get."

"How long have you known?"

"For a while," he replied.

"How do you stay here? How do you work right next to him, knowing he is breaking the law? I mean, agents can die because of the shit he's doing."

"I got a wife and three daughters who are about to go to college. I'm in my mid-forties, too fat to go through another academy with a different agency. All I have is a high school diploma. I got nothing. I can't earn over a hundred thousand a year with benefits anywhere else. You…you have a degree. A good one from a good university. Get out of here. Don't look back. If you stay any longer, you'll get stuck. You'll be fine."

"I can't believe I'm leaving the Patrol. I fought so hard to get in and to stay."

"Yeah, I know, but this is how it always is. Sector, D.C., they'd rather not know about agents like him than admit they exist. There are better things out there. Things that won't demand you lose your morals and ethics over."

* * *

My final words to the Border Patrol were recorded on my exit interview. I wrote on the government form that nobody would likely read about how the agency was hopelessly corrupt, that management was fraught with immoral and unethical agents. I said that I could not, that I would not be a part of it any longer. As I handed my credentials and badge over, I felt a twinge of fear in my chest. I desperately wanted to grab it back, to change my mind, think about it some more. It scared me to walk away from it. My greatest fear in life was not being able to take care of myself, to need someone else, to be dependent on another. Not having a job felt like a death sentence, and the fear was deeply embedded in my mind.

When I pulled away from San Diego Sector for the last time, I had to pull over to the side of the road. I sobbed with my face in my hands as an incredibly powerful feeling came over me. I desperately wanted to know that this was the right decision. I was angry, felt like my career had been stolen from me. I felt like the Border Patrol was all a lie. I was mad because I knew that I was doing the right and moral thing, and yet somehow, that knowledge didn't make any of it any better or easier. Walking out the door didn't suddenly make everything right. If anything, it confused my thoughts, my emotions even more.

I felt as if I was running away again because I was. To others, I told a story of how I stood up for what was right, that I'd done the right thing and made the ethical choice. The problem was that I didn't feel any of that. I had no pride in walking away from the Border Patrol. I could not hold my head up high for putting my foot down. I did not know why.

I hated myself.

PART II

San Diego, California, Sandi and Jenn's "legal" wedding, June 21, 2008

GOOD FOR NOTHING

My green uniforms still hung in the closet. My work boots, cowboy hat, and gun belts were there too. I had to return my gun, my radio, my baton, and my senior patrol agent badge. My armor, the green wall that I mistakenly believed protected me, was nothing without the badge and the gun. Deep down, I started to feel like I was nothing too.

Everything I'd worked so hard for, the things I'd once been so proud of, were gone now. Those things that my family, my instructors told me I'd never achieve, I did. I had been one of the few, one of only five percent of women who survived the academy and the desolate mountains. I had endured it all: rape, harassment, isolation, intimidation, threats, bullying, being run over—and I still did my job. I did it well. I hiked and tracked groups of people in the middle of the night for hours, and I did it alone. I braved the snow and the heat, the snakes and the mountain lions, the smugglers and the crooked agents, and I was still alive.

It took years to stop behaving and feeling like an agent. I frequently found myself staring at the ground whenever I walked through dirt parking lots or hiked for recreation. I couldn't stop looking for their sign, their footprints. Everywhere I went, I continued to scan around me for people who might be undocumented before remembering that it didn't matter anymore, that it wasn't my problem because I no longer had that authority. I missed the weight of my gun belt with all its extra ammo and steel baton. My right elbow searched for places to rest now that my gun was gone. It felt as if I had graduated the Patrol, left with no one to chase or arrest, no one to harass or question. I felt exposed and naked, and I wondered if someday, when I least expected it, my traumatic past was going to catch up to me.

I wanted the chief to call me up and say that they'd been wrong, that they didn't want corrupt agents within their ranks, that they were going to turn Dirtycop over to the DEA or FBI. I wanted them to apologize for allowing Mendoza to remain an agent and ask me how best to address their rape culture problem. I wanted them to say that they still needed me and that I'd done the honorable and noble thing by turning Mendoza and Dirtycop in, that they'd been mistaken to look the other way, that they would try and live up to "Honor First." But the only calls that ever came were from Assistant U.S. Attorneys finishing up my old cases, getting last bits of information from me.

Agents I'd worked with came by my house every week. Supervisor Donner brought a plaque, thanking me for my service that some of them had made. I was touched that they'd even thought of it because I knew it was usually reserved for those who retired and not those who'd quit. Apparently, it was quite a big deal as Dirtycop did not want me to receive anything. He even went so far as to steal it and lock it in his office. Donner and a few others broke in and retrieved it.

"You were never given a fair shot. All that shit you went through, the parts that I contributed to—well, you still were one of the finest agents the station ever had, Jenn," he said. "Me and the guys who knew you wanted you to know that."

Without my gun and badge, my former colleagues felt uninhibited to tell me all the things they did while on duty, the things they'd been too afraid to say to me before. Unbeknownst to me, they were doing a lot of drugs while patrolling the border. Sometimes they took a few bundles of marijuana from their busts. Other times, they bought cocaine or heroin from the K-9 guys who held back a few bags of whatever it was they were looking for. We talked and laughed for hours about all the horrible things they'd done. I kept my shock and disgust hidden.

"I can't believe you smoke weed," I said to Jose after we finished off a joint he'd made from a large bag he'd bought from a K-9 agent at my old checkpoint.

"Yeah, well, what do you think the guys will say when I tell them Agent Budd was smoking bud?"

"That's former Senior Patrol Agent Budd!" We laughed.

"They'll never believe me. You were always straight as an arrow."

"I have no problem with weed. It should be legal. As a cop, I'd rather deal with potheads than alcoholics any day. I just never thought it was worth it to get busted and fired for smoking it."

"You know they don't test unless they're trying to get rid of us. I just stay nice and quiet. I do what they tell me to do. If I don't cause problems, they won't give me any problems. You caused problems," he said.

In a way, their stories helped me to remember why it was that I'd quit in the first place. The rampant drug use, the dating of women they'd just apprehended, the car chases that they lied about that ended in deaths or serious injuries, the parties on duty they had with the racist civilian border militias that were now everywhere, the coverups and denials—it still made me sick to think about it, and things only got worse after 9/11. My former coworkers said they were free to pursue anyone regardless of how dangerous it was. In their own words: "All we have to say is that it was a matter of national security. They could be terrorists," they joked.

I was ashamed to admit I'd ever worn that uniform.

The agency had started to align itself with these new anti-immigrant groups like The Federation of Americans for Immigration Reform that claimed their mission was to support legal immigration and national security. The Border Patrol Union started speaking at their annual conferences and had links on their website to these racist and xenophobic websites. To me, they just seemed to be a newer, more educated version of the old Klan I knew of from the South. It wasn't long before I stopped returning my former colleagues' calls and asked them not to come by anymore. Knowing all their little secrets made me feel worse about having worked for the agency, which made me feel worse about myself.

* * *

I was surprised when Jacob called. My best Border Patrol buddy hadn't called or stopped by in months. It was just past 11:00 p.m., and I'd already been asleep for over an hour.

"What's going on? Are you okay?"

"I just, uh, I just need you to come out here. Sarah is in Florida with the kids. I'm all alone and I got no painkillers for my back pain. I'm going crazy with the pain," he said breathlessly.

"I don't have any painkillers. Your doc not giving you any more?" Jacob had been in a car accident and suffered a serious back injury. It was long before the country would come to see the dangers of opioid addiction that he was experiencing now. He was still a serious alcoholic as well, which is likely why I loved him so.

"If I could just get some beer or something, that would help."

"So, go get some at the market in Live Oak Springs," I said. He lived in Campo, an hour from my house in El Cajon at the time.

"My car is broken down and all the guys are working or on vacation. Please, just this one last time."

It was after midnight by the time I pulled up to his house. He opened the door before I could even knock, grabbed the twelve-pack I brought and tore it open with one hand, popped the top, and chugged the entire beer immediately while still holding the case against his chest with his other hand. I stared at him in silence as he opened his second beer.

"Thanks," he gasped between gulps. "I just can't stand the pain."

I'd seen this growing up. Seen it with Mom and the many women I was so often attracted to. I was not an alcoholic, but so many around me were. And though I told myself that I hated it, I still found myself attracted to them.

"Jacob, I can't keep doing this."

"What happened to the green line? What happened to having each other's backs? Remember Indio and the car chases and the trains? Remember the late nights drinking Long Island ice teas out of wine carafes? Remember how you used to help me get dressed and get me to the checkpoint so I didn't get busted? How I backed you up whenever you needed it?"

"Yeah, I do. I remember all of it. I love you man. I really do, but I'm not an agent anymore. I can't keep driving out here. I can't bring you alcohol or anything else. You gotta get this under control. You have to get out of the Patrol and get sober."

"There ain't nothing else I can do and make this kind of money! Look at you! You're working for your latest girlfriend and making minimum wage! Look at the mighty Agent Budd now!"

He was becoming a mean drunk.

"I got my dignity at least. I'm not complaining about how awful the Patrol is anymore and just taking shit like all y'all. I'd rather be poor than be a part of something as corrupt as the Patrol! Remember when we used to talk about what a joke the agency was? All the bullshit and corruption? About how we would get out?"

"You won't hear from me again! I'll never ask for help from you again! Don't worry about me no more!" he yelled at me as I jumped back into my car.

I never saw nor heard from him again. The Patrol eventually let him go because he could not sober up.

* * *

Sandi and I had only been dating eight months and living together less when I resigned in protest. I wasn't sure yet if she was the one. I just knew that she was different from all the other women I had dated. She wasn't interested in me because of my nice car or my uniform. She seemed emotionally available, kind, and deeply honest. Still, I was not ready or willing to talk about my past with her or anyone else.

I didn't know what I was doing or where I was going at the time. I just couldn't stay in the Patrol any longer. I had only taken the job at her custom cabinet-making shop because she needed someone, and I had nowhere else to go. Maybe I would go through another academy with a different agency or back to get my juris doctor. I had no idea or intentions except to get away from the Border Patrol and away from my past.

In the beginning, I didn't know a thing about woodworking and spent most of my time cleaning the shop and filling nail holes with putty or wax crayons. It was monotonous and paid only minimum wage with no benefits. I'd lost my status when I gave up that badge. I had no authority, no power, no presence without it. People no longer stopped to thank me for my service or asked for my help. I missed the mountains, the four-wheeling, the smell of the brush, and the solitude of my former job.

My entire life had been fight or flight: from the violence and abuse of my family to the violence and abuse of the Border Patrol. I thought I was an expert in recognizing the threats to my safety: the slamming of cabinet doors, the sound of my dog hitting a wall and yelping, the cries of my brother or sister, watching the number of drinks Mom had, the times I found myself alone with a male agent whom I did not know well enough, the silence over the radio when I called for backup, recognizing those who believed I'd made false allegations against my attacker, listening for the sound of brush breaking as a dope smuggler walked towards my hidden position in the middle of the night, watching the reactions of groups of men I apprehended and who realized I was alone, wondering if they might try to take my life, judging whether the car pulling up to my primary position on the checkpoint would try and hit me as they gunned the engine without stopping…

That was my life, always on alert, and now I was in a large warehouse cutting and sanding wood to make into cabinets and furniture. The people around me did not threaten me. There was no danger of being beaten with a belt, of being called a bitch or worthless, of being raped. They didn't judge me as less than, ostracize, ignore, threaten, or talk about me behind my back. I had no cause to worry. There was no need to put my walls up and patch them continuously to keep myself safe. My mind knew this, but my body, my soul, did not.

I was like a dry drunk who never did any of the emotional work after quitting drinking. I was still reacting, still behaving as if I was operating in my past life. I searched for danger and anticipated threats when they were not actually there. Small things Sandi did or said to me were often met with outbursts of anger and arguments that went nowhere because they were about nothing. When I realized my awfulness and how I treated her, I got worse and yelled even more or jumped into my car and left as my father had with my mother.

I did not know what to do with all that anger. There was no place for me to put it any longer. I couldn't take it to work with me anymore and let it loose on the trails in the mountains or take it out on those I policed. All of it sat in my head and my heart, living within the tissues and cells of my body, waiting to burst. I was not proud of it. I knew I had anger issues, that our relationship would die like so many others had done before her if I did not learn how to get things under control, if I did not address my problems, and if I kept throwing them on the other side of my mental wall.

I went to therapy, got on antidepressants because that is what they told me was my problem. I learned that I didn't have to yell every time I was angry. I started to understand for the first time that anger and love were not the only emotions I could have. The aggression I was once rewarded for in the Patrol was not normal, not accepted outside of that environment. I made progress from time to time, until my anger built up again and it started all over. I couldn't understand how it was that my childhood and the Patrol had shaped me and my perceptions. I did not want to even admit that it had that much control over me. To do so seemed like a cop-out to me, as if I were blaming my parents or the agency for my problems. It felt like I was not taking responsibility for my own actions if I even went down that road.

Yes, I had a bad childhood. It was filled with mental illness, brutality, and cruelty, but I still graduated from college at the top of my class. I still got through that damn academy. I managed to become a senior patrol agent in an organization that detested women and did everything in its power to stop me. I believed that my accomplishments alone should have been proof enough that I had survived, that I had thrived and overcome. I'd made it. Despite everything, I'd made something out of myself. I was a fucking federal agent. I was strong and just. This alone proved that I was not affected by my abuse.

Didn't it?

I spent a lot of time talking about my childhood with my shrinks. I told them everything about it. When they asked how it made me feel to grow up always being afraid, I answered them honestly. I was fine. Nothing was wrong. It was unfortunate, but I had let it go long ago. I loved my parents, especially my mother. Her anger and violence were because she had suffered as a child, and I had forgiven her for it long ago. Yes, she drank, but what harm was there in that?

As for my wife, Sandi simply didn't understand someone like me. She hadn't lived my life, didn't know how much danger was out in the world and how it hid around every corner. She'd never been in law enforcement. She'd not seen or experienced what I had.

I was fortunate she had so much patience and loved me, even with my walls standing between us.

HIDING

As the years rolled along, I watched the Border Patrol from afar. My former employer was absorbed into the mammoth Department of Homeland Security after the terrorist attacks of 9/11. The individual agencies that had been known as Customs and the Immigration Inspectors were merged into one agency called Customs and Border Protection (CBP). Border Patrol was placed within CBP, but still maintained its autonomy. Although Customs and the Inspectors changed their uniforms to dark blue, Border Patrol insisted on keeping the green uniform. The name plates were different and many of the faces I no longer recognized, but the behaviors, the culture of impunity stayed the same.

Actually, it became worse simply because they could excuse their actions by claiming it was in the interest of national security, and no politician was willing to hold law enforcement accountable after 9/11. To do so meant that they were attacking the heroes who'd risked their lives that day running into the Twin Towers just before they collapsed. Cops of all forms were placed on an unreachable pedestal, even immigration agents.

By 2010, I'd been a custom woodworker longer than I'd been an agent. I was considered a master at the craft, but I didn't dream about wood grain, sap, and knots. I didn't sit in those quiet moments, staring up at the stars I used to use as guides and wonder if a client was properly taking care of her dining table or if she remembered how I'd shown her to adjust her door hinges. I didn't dream of making an elaborate kitchen or joining wood to make a cool coffee table.

My dreams were still most often filled with the Patrol. I tossed and turned whenever I saw myself back in uniform, smaller and stronger as I'd been back then. Running through the mountains at night with my large flashlight in my left hand, my right hand free in case I needed to use my baton or gun. I could smell the sage and other high-desert plants that made me sneeze. I could almost feel the scratches of the brush on my arms and face as I climbed upward on the dirt trail following their footprints, stopping from time to time to listen for them. When I woke, I always knew it had been a Patrol dream even if I couldn't clearly remember it. Adrenaline filled my body and left me with anxiety and desperation that made my heart pound. It was a feeling I once loved, a feeling I'd once craved, and now, it seemed to haunt me.

After leaving the Border Patrol, I hid out in Sandi's big woodworking shop and told myself I was content amongst the hum of the machines and sawdust. I avoided my family of birth and tried to learn how to let go of the hurt by their lack of interest in me. I couldn't deal with my mother's constant drunk calls claiming Dad was beating her, or her threats of ending her life. I told her if she called again claiming such things, I would be forced to call the police. When my little sister told me that Mom told her and others that I was once arrested in college, I cut ties with all of them: my mother for making up such nonsense, my sister for believing it and my father for saying nothing. The more I pushed them to address Mom's behavior, the alcoholism and the lies, the more they hated me.

I'd come to understand that there'd be no escaping my memories. They would likely always take up space in my mind and in my heart, shadowing everything I did, everything I experienced. They were like foggy lenses attached to my eyes through which I would forever experience the world around me. I had lost both my biological family and my green family. They were all I had, all I thought I'd ever wanted. Neither was perfect by any means, but what families were? I had accomplished much in my short life, yet I still felt like a failure, as if something was terribly wrong with me because I'd lost them both. I believed that I did not matter to anyone, not even to myself. I couldn't be what they wanted, what I thought I wanted, and so, I decided to stop trying.

I found a new family in my life with Sandi. She'd become more than a partner and was now my wife. Our small group of chosen friends became my family, even though I still longed for my old ones. I couldn't stop thinking about them, about what I once wanted so desperately to be and how I'd failed. Their constant tests of devotion kept moving the goal posts further and further away. The scars and grooves the Patrol had worn in me were as deep as the ones my mother had given me. They were as much a part of me as my tattoos. I missed them in all their atrociousness.

Mentally, I was running in circles, barely hanging on sometimes, barreling downhill with no brakes, moving from one fire to the next just trying to survive my past. I'd come to realize that when chaos wasn't present, I craved it because it was all I'd ever known life to be. It felt as if something was missing when there was no chaos, no fighting to survive, no hurdles to jump. When it didn't exist in my work, it felt like it was not fulfilling enough. When it was absent in my relationships, I thought it meant I was falling out of love. Without chaos, I had no cause to be. I could not recognize what safety was, what love was.

After all the years I spent along the wall to protect my country, I was still constantly building walls and patching them inside myself. Whether in my mind or on the border, these walls were supposed to keep me safe. But if that was the case, why was I in so much pain? Why was I standing in the middle of a warehouse, building fine furniture and cabinets while I constantly rummaged around in my past? Why had I become so angry? Why did I not feel safe? What was I so afraid of?

I spent time and money on therapists and psychologists, on books trying to find some peace, to save my marriage, to understand myself, to find me. Yoga, meditation, mindfulness—they all made little difference. I wasn't naïve enough to think none of it had affected me. I was fucked up, and I knew it. I just couldn't understand how to get past my past. The good memories of my childhood with my family, the ones that I pretended were my only memories, those that I often spoke of when asked about my childhood had become impossible to find. Even when I managed, they quickly slipped through my mental fingers only to become lost in the pile of painful memories and negative thoughts that now clouded my mind and my body.

When I dared to glance behind me at my past, all I ever saw was a wasteland of things that couldn't be fixed or explained. There were projects started and left behind, unfinished or discarded, friendships and girlfriends thrown to the curb because they dared to get too close to my wall that I was always mending, because they expected me to be someone I couldn't be, because they thought they could fix me, help me.

My past, my thoughts of my past prevented me from experiencing and enjoying life in the present. Year after year, different therapists said that I must go back and talk about it, that I must put it all out there for them to see and sift through, like a dumpster fire that never ended, no matter how much water I doused it with. They said that talking about it would create room in my heart and mind, that I would never heal if I didn't get over my shame, that I could never move on to a healthy life if I didn't explore it, if I didn't tell my secrets. I felt so broken, so contaminated, so dead.

Again, and again, I tried. And when I had told them everything that I'd been willing to tell them, all that I could let out, they said I was distant from it, that I spoke of it as if it happened to someone else, nervously laughed about it to keep it at arm's length. All that was true, but not because I didn't want to get past it, not because I was trying to hide anything from them, not because I didn't want to heal. This pushing away of feelings had been my way of surviving since I was six years old, and I could not figure out how to un-ride that bike, no matter how hard I tried. The more time I spent thinking on it, the more sensitive and distressed I became. The more I explored my feelings about what I'd been through in my life, feelings I'd not allowed myself to experience back then because they were too painful, the more depressed and confused I became.

My mental wall was the one thing in my life that I had meticulously tended to, filling the cracks when they came, patching the holes with anything I could find. My memories may have been a wasteland full of dead trees, rocks, weeds, and junk, but my wall that surrounded it was pristine and kept most of the memories held down away from my heart, my soul. Out of sight, out of mind was the idea.

Only now I felt my wall was falling faster than I could mend it. Kind words of understanding or a simple touch of a hand now made me recoil in shame and guilt that I did not understand. My defenses were killing me, they said. My wall didn't protect me at all; it had only given me a false sense of security, made me miss the real threats to my safety. If I wanted to heal, I'd have to go through all that pain again, pay for it now, experience it as I should have done. Partly, I thought that they were full of it, just a bunch of psyche bullshit they spouted to collect their co-pays. It sounded like that self-help crap that only made sense for weak-minded people, but not for me. I was strong. I was a Border Patrol agent, a senior patrol agent, a senior patrol intelligence agent. At least I had been.

They might as well have told me I needed to start speaking in Russian; it would have been just as easy. I did not speak the language of feelings, nor did I care to study it. To focus on myself and how I felt seemed selfish to me, and it made me feel guilty to spend the time and money on it. I was brought up to consider others' feelings, not my own. I certainly did not recognize my own emotions about my rape or even believe that I had them.

I just wanted to move on.

UNTETHERED

Whenever I tried to explore that pain, all I heard on that broken record in my mind was my mother's voice, because it'd been the first voice I'd ever heard. It was the voice that always meant the most to me. The one I'd wished to hear from the most. The one I'd wished to be praised by, but she'd only say I was conceited, narcissistic. "What about my feelings?" I could hear her say. She was right, I reckoned, and for this, I began to hate myself as a child.

Being raised in this relentless environment made my mind, my memories of my childhood, feel like a constant cyclone of confusion. As an adult trying to understand it all and how it had affected me often caused me to find myself sanding the same piece of wood over and over or standing in the finishing booth, spray gun in hand, respirator on my face, lost in thought. When my wife would inevitably walk up behind me and tap me on my shoulder, it startled me and made me jump. I became frightened by her touch as it suddenly brought me back to the living. It didn't take long for these daymares or dissociations, as my shrink called them, to cause me problems at work. Saw blades and sharp tools have a way of demanding your attention, should you fail to give it to them.

I cannot say that my wife was at all surprised when she came out of the bathroom one day to see me holding my left hand together as blood ran through my fingers and onto the floor. I found myself in the emergency room, in shock, with a severed index tendon, cut down to the bone. I had spaced out again, dissociated again. This time I'd been using a biscuit saw cutter. Nor was she surprised when I rammed the forklift into the racks weeks later, causing assembled drawer boxes to rain down all around me. Frozen in the seat, I could only stare straight ahead, ashamed of my mistake. My mind flashed back on those moments of my childhood, the times when I made mistakes that made Mom so mad that I wished she would just beat me instead of berating me.

Just like the physical border wall, my mental walls took massive amounts of energy and time to construct and keep up. They both could become unstable and fall without constant vigilance and tending. They both gave the illusion of providing security by keeping the unwanted, whether memories or people, on the other side. But out of sight was not out of mind and it meant that whatever was on the other side could always break through, which was a different sort of trauma and fear that never went away. It was all simply a matter of time as my walls started to crumble, and I would be forced to deal with what I had created.

I often described it as wearing my nerves on the outside of my body. I became sensitive to sound, touch, and smell. I wanted to go to sleep for a few hours, days, maybe even weeks. I asked my doctor to put me in a medically induced coma for a month or two. She laughed, thinking I was joking. I laughed too, ashamed that I had been serious. Post-Traumatic Stress Disorder the doctors said. I didn't believe them. I hadn't been to war or killed anyone. I thought I had become fragile, weak…pathetic.

There was no relief from that diagnosis, no way around it. I could not forgive myself or let myself have some time, some space from my self-hatred. I did not know how to do that. And so, it became one more thing wrong with me, one more thing to be disappointed in. I believed I had a mental disease and felt destined to be crazy like my mother. I tried this pill and that one, but none worked and only seemed to make me fatter. None of them could take away the tornado in my head; none could make me safe.

* * *

Somewhere around 2010 or 2011, my mother called me. I braced myself for the news that someone had died or that she had come to unreasonably believe she had some new uncurable disease. As it turned out, my father had the beginning signs of prostate cancer. I can't say I was too surprised by this. Pop had died my senior year of high school from it, and I knew that increased Dad's chances of developing it. Though it was one of the more easily curable cancers if caught early enough, Pop had disliked doctors so much that he let it go on far too long. He looked like a concentration camp victim in the end. I still recall kissing him on his forehead one last time. Thankfully, Dad had done his due diligence and gotten yearly checkups.

Her call came during a time when I was trying to reunite with them. I had felt that pull that sometimes caused me to go back into that environment, back into the alcoholic family. Maybe it was because Sandi was having her own sobriety issues, and in that sick sort of way, maybe it made me miss my childhood, miss what had been so familiar and normal to me.

Although a relationship with my family always meant I would be forced to ignore the past, not only to forgive them but forget it all, I thought I was strong enough to do just that. Besides, they were in their sixties, slowing down and becoming physically weaker. Whenever my sister sent pictures of them holding my nieces, it pained me not to be a part of that.

Mom said that she could no longer drive even in emergency circumstances. It scared her too much, and my father's new car was too fast and had oodles of new-fangled buttons that she didn't understand. Like most things about her, I chose not to question it and just accepted it. Decades of sitting on that couch, binge-watching CNN and drinking had made her agoraphobic. If my father did not take her to the store, the doctor, out to eat...well, then my sister had to. More often than not, it just didn't happen as my sister was always busy juggling work with two kids and a husband. My brother lived in some other state, coming to visit rarely, they said. I had not spoken to him since I was in college. He referred to me as the "faggot" of the family.

I jumped at the chance to demonstrate my love for her and immediately booked a ticket to San Antonio. It excited me to think of seeing them, to have my mom to myself as I used to when I was little. I imagined us staying up late, eating popcorn, watching the news, talking about the old times, the good times only, of course, going through the photo albums and reliving the those memories together. It never really mattered how battered and bruised I was from her love; I always wanted more.

I took care of her just as I had before. I drove Dad to the hospital like she asked. I drove her to and from the hospital and held her now wrinkled hand while we waited to hear that the operation was successful. Then I dutifully drove her to the grocery store so she could buy four gallons of chardonnay. It was cheaper that way, she said. I smiled when she said it because her alcohol-drenched brain still thought I would buy the excuse.

Standing there in the middle of the aisle among the vast array of pork products only a Texas grocery store could offer, I felt strangely comforted by her lies. It was our family tradition. I felt as if I was in a play that I'd been acting in for decades. The lines were the same ones I'd been saying since the '70s and '80s back in Alabama. I knew my cues, and my preordained responses sort of spilled from my mouth automatically without much resistance because that was my job, my part, my assigned role in our family.

Every movement, every facial expression, every emotion to every action had been performed many times before. When we got home, she would ask me to carry in the heavy jugs and open one for her. She would have her wine glass ready with a few ice cubes in it. "I cut down on how much I drink by putting ice cubes in it," she would say on cue with perfect delivery. She would then stroll over to the couch and turn CNN on, sit with one leg tucked underneath her, and pick at her toenails because she no longer smoked. The set had changed, the props were different, but it was the same play.

I could see this clearly for the first time. All those years away, without contact and purposefully refusing to participate in their lives allowed me to see it for what it was and not what I'd wished it to be. It was like she was trapped in some sort of time loop, repeating the same behaviors over and over with the same people and the same outcomes. Wherever the Budd family went, we performed this play. We all had our roles, our lines. We knew the outcome. Nothing ever changed. Different eras and different houses in different cities, but always the same dialogue, the same feelings, the same drunken tirades. It was comforting in a grossly dysfunctional way.

She was on her fourth or fifth glass of wine when I decided to gather my strength and go off-script. I thought it would be my last chance. "Mom, you know when I was in elementary school, when you used to whip the tar out of me?" She nodded. "Mom, that was really, really bad. I mean…Mom, that was horribly brutal. Do you know that?"

"I know, but you have to understand that it was your father's fault."

"What do you mean?"

"Your father was always having affairs," she said, slurring, and I noticed how thick her southern accent had become since I'd been away. "He was always fuckin' around. Screwin' this woman and that one. Always havin' affairs." Her eyes seemed to glaze over and sort of look past me even though I was sitting right next to her on their couch.

She went on. "Constantly out fuckin' anything with a hole. He was always cheatin' on me. Since I's pregnant with you. Fuckin' around. Those young girls who worked the cash registers, my friend whose husband worked with him, Nicki, yeah, Nicki. That bitch! The last one was a friend too. Always fuckin' having affairs."

"Are you saying that the reason you beat me like that was that Dad was cheating on you?"

"He was always cheatin' on me! It made me mad. I just wanted him to come home, you know. He should've been sendin' me flowers and singin' songs to me about how much he loved me."

"Why didn't you just leave him?"

"I had nowhere to go, and I loved him. Still do," she admitted with a crooked smile.

"Do you understand that his cheating did not make it okay for you to beat me like that? Or to threaten to kill yourself in front of me?"

"He was cheatin' on me! He cheated on me. He was always cheatin' on me. Cheatin' on me. Cheatin' on me. Cheatin' on me. Your dad cheated on me," she said with her head hanging low.

Her repetitive speech told me she was close to passing out. When I'd had enough of watching her jerk herself awake, I gently took her hand and led her to her bedroom. She was already in her pajamas, and I helped her get into bed one last time. She was asleep before I could even say goodnight, muttering about Dad cheating. I turned the television off and cleaned up before heading to the guest room.

That night, I laid in the dark just staring at the ceiling fan as it slowly spun. I didn't feel sorry for her, like I had when I was young. I empathized with her. She was still that seventeen-year-old girl looking to escape her own trauma, whatever that may have been. I could picture her with her bouffant 1960s style hairstyle and dress staring up into my father's Polaroid camera. The face of a young and desperate woman trying to find a way out and putting all her money on my father. It was a gamble, not unlike the one I had taken on the Border Patrol. She knew as much about him as I did about the Patrol. We'd both traded one trauma for another, unknowingly.

She'd built her walls that were just as tall and strong as mine. My wall was made of green and came with a badge and a gun. Hers was made of alcohol and drugs. She needed that alcohol to dissociate from her pain and no longer care. As a child my mind forced me to go other places in times of physical and emotional violence. As an adult, I fed my dissociation with dead bodies, car chases, midnight manhunts. When it all became too much, she took her frustrations and violence out on me. I took mine out on migrants and then on my wife. My mother isolated herself, thinking it would protect her. I ran far away, isolating myself in the high desert mountains of Campo. Different means, same results.

I could see in her face that young woman still waiting for my dad to come home. How long had it been? Over forty years, at least. Waiting for him to come home from work, to tell her how his day was. She dreamed of how she would bring him his pipe and sit him in his lounge chair to watch the news as she prepared his meal. Only, he rarely came home. She had to wait an awfully long time. In retirement, he had become all hers. He'd given up his other women finally because Mom had inherited enough for him to retire. It was her one ace she kept in her sleeve, and it had worked. He was trapped and they were finally together, but it was not as blissful as she had imagined it.

They still fought each other in their old age. She chased him around the house, repeating all his transgressions to make him ashamed. He ducked and ran from room to room just trying to get away from her rage. All that anger of hers that I'd known so well, he now experienced. The moments of their painful past swirled in her brain and often resulted in outbursts and violent fights with my father. One night, she threw a kitchen knife at him from across the room. It landed firmly in his thigh, digging too deep to remedy at home. They told the doctors it'd been an accident. Likely because no one wanted to be the ones to put a senior woman in jail, they stitched my father up and sent them home. My sister often called saying he had a new black eye. He claimed they were the result of a low-hanging tree limb here or an unseen cabinet door there. He had taken my place and become her punching bag.

There was a part of me that understood why he always left. I had done the same thing, after all. I escaped to college and migrated all the way across the country, crossing state border after state border just to get away from her. It was simply easier than addressing the problem. He would learn to sense the change in her as I had, learn to discern when he said something that triggered her fury and resentment. Just before her anger broke out, he would feverishly look for things to appease her: another glass of wine, an unsolicited compliment, could sometimes prevent the storm.

As I laid with tears streaming down from the corner of my eyes, I could see him in those moments. I could picture and feel his trauma, his fear and exasperation growing in their new house. It dripped down the walls and pooled in the corners and covered everything. It was the same stench that had existed in every house I'd ever lived in with her. It permeated everything. I could hear the slamming of a kitchen cabinet door, how she yelled his name from the other room, the sound of my dog being kicked or thrown down the hallway. The heat on the back of my neck and saltwater flowed into my mouth as I ran to the guest bath to puke.

A few days later, I left them in their personal hell. I walked out the front door for the last time. I could not fix this, and it was not my responsibility to do so.

FIFTY-ONE FIFTY

It was February 8, 2015, and I was tired. I felt exhausted from everything, from surviving, from life. That meant it was a normal day for me. Sandi and I had struggled through the recession in 2009 like every other small business around us. We'd used up all our savings, dumped our investments only to receive little after taxes and penalties. We restructured her business, and worked day and night to keep it afloat. I was never so thankful that she'd been sober and worked on herself for years prior to that. She had become stronger and healthier than I'd ever known her to be. She had become a partner worthy of someone so much more than me.

We were just beginning to recover financially. The thought of having to tell me that we did not have as much money in savings as I believed frightened her. Sandi had seen what financial hardship did to me, how it took me back to my childhood, and how it threatened our relationship and the trust we'd worked so hard to build. Feeling like I couldn't trust her again, something broke in me.

That night felt like the end of us, of Jenn and Sandi, of "the girls" as our friends called us. It felt as if something had been drained out of me; perhaps it was the willingness to try any longer. I remember it as an extreme sense of isolation, like being the lone survivor in a war, and it terrified me. I stood in our kitchen staring at the floor; it seemed as if the real world fell away from me, that it had somehow disappeared down below me as I stood on a small piece of it, looking down into nothingness. I could stretch out my arms and bend down to try and touch it, but it was just out of my reach. That last invisible string that tied me to Sandi was gone now. I was done.

I knew what the answer to this feeling was, and I decided it was time. I'd had enough pain and fear in my life, and I wanted to leave this world. There was nothing left in me to do or say. I'd let it go on entirely too long anyhow. The feeling washed over me like a warm bath. I sensed the change; knew I was ready. I calmly told her I was going for a drive. I kissed Piglet, my favorite dog, goodbye and apologized to her for what I intended to do, for not being able to care for her any longer. I left.

Going crazy wasn't like everyone said, like I'd seen it depicted in the movies. I didn't feel crazy when it happened. I didn't run around in circles, screaming my head off. If anything, I felt more in control than I'd ever been. It felt good, like I'd finally found the answer I'd always been searching for, like the tornado in my head had suddenly stopped and there right in front of me was the solution. It was a remedy from a diseased mind of course, but still, it felt like a genuine ah-ha sort of moment. And because an ailing mind feels quite indecisive and chaotic, the focus required to end my own life felt somewhat empowering to me. It was the last decision I'd ever make, and it felt like it was mine alone to make it even if I was no longer myself, whatever that had ever been. Deceptively, it presented itself as the key to the door where the answer to my problems awaited me.

* * *

It was about ten at night when I pulled my white Hyundai Tucson into one of our three warehouse bays and parked between the table saw and the big thirteen-foot panel saw. I yanked on the long chain that rolled the heavy metal door down one last time and heard the familiar bang as it hit the concrete floor when I kicked the bar at the bottom to lock it. I did not want my wife to drive through the parking lot and see my car there. I didn't want her to try and stop me.

I sat in the dark at the desk where we'd worked side-by-side for fourteen years. For a while, I searched myself for any hints of doubt about what I intended to do. I looked at all the things we'd collected over the years: pictures of dogs we'd rescued, quotations that inspired us, things that made us laugh were all covered in a thin layer of sawdust.

Thoughts of suicide came and went for me in my life. I'd always been happy that I'd let things pass, that I let my emotions calm down before going too far. I told myself to think about all the things I would have missed if I'd gone through with it at a younger age: college, the Border Patrol, loves lost and found, Sandi, fur babies, reinventing myself and becoming a master woodworker, friends and family, vacations. I decided that I was good with it, that I'd seen enough for my time. I felt I'd achieved all I could in this life.

I had it in my head that the best place to do it was in the rafters. So, I climbed the ladder up behind our spray booth with a bottle of rum and a bottle of five hundred ibuprofen pills that I had just bought from Albertsons. I'd thought I heard it did the trick rather well and only somewhat painfully. I needed the physical pain to take away the emotional agony just this one last time. Sitting amongst the old sawdust that had drifted up there over the years, I took gulps of rum, trying to get my courage about me. For the first time, it dawned on me what folks meant by "liquid courage." I thought about how stupid people were when they said that suicide was the easy way out. None of it was easy. The road to that point had been difficult and agonizing.

I called Sandi just then, wanting to see if hearing her voice would make me climb back down from there and sleep it off in the office, if it would make me go home and crawl back in bed with her under our quilts and feel her warmth, but it didn't. In between fistfuls of ibuprofen, I tried to sound in control, and I tried not to worry her. I told her that I had gone to a friend's house, and that I would see her in the morning. I was still a good bullshitter. No, nothing was wrong, just needed some time alone, I told her.

It's funny the things that pop into a suicidal mind in the midst of the deed. *How did I know that ibuprofen would kill me? Why did I think that?* Like looking up what time the movie started or ordering a pizza, I Googled it on my smartphone to be sure. No, I'd been wrong. An overdose would cause kidney damage, but not likely kill me. I laughed at my sudden concern about possible kidney damage in the midst of trying to kill myself. I laughed out loud.

Alone in the rafters with the sawdust, I suddenly felt a sharp pain in my stomach. I tried to slide down the ladder as I puked rum and pink pills all over myself. Laughing and puking, puking and laughing. I'd become a human Pez dispenser; my body was rejecting the poison I'd ingested. It was trying to protect itself from me, which made me laugh even harder.

Sitting on the edge of an assembly table, I reasoned that if my kidneys were shot, there surely was no reason to stick around. We had health insurance but there'd be no way we could have afforded constant dialysis. Honestly, I don't think I could have handled the shame of that.

I thought of all the times I'd said to myself that if I ever did it, I'd make sure I didn't come back. That I didn't want to just think or talk about it like Mom had done when I was young. That I didn't want Sandi to think I was doing it to get attention. I did not want to hurt her over and over by putting her through that experience of having a suicidal loved one. This one-time event would be painful to her, but at least it would just be this once, I told myself. She hadn't signed up for this type of crazy. No one ever did. It wasn't fair to her, and she was young enough to remarry.

I wiped away the bits of pink pills stuck to my shirt, thinking that I'd never get the stain out as I flipped the switch that sent electricity to our giant table saw located at the rear of the shop. I cannot say how long I'd stood there, how long I leaned against my car watching the ten-inch steel blade spin. *Don't be a chicken shit. Do it. Mom was right, you're dying alone, no one loving you. Just get it done with. How many times do you need to hear it before you accept it?* And I remember holding my hands over my ears as if it would stop the sound of her voice.

I only know it hurt unlike anything I'd ever felt before because I remember that I screamed, "Mother fucker!" Stepping back from the table, I did not look at it, but took a deep breath and then offered my right arm to the saw when it pulled me in quickly. I could feel the warm blood leaving my body. Leaning against the back door of my car, I slid down to the concrete floor now covered in red sawdust. The blood poured out like a punctured bladder, covering my shirt and my shorts.

I stared at my left arm, held it up and flexed it by making a fist and watched as the muscles and white tendons moved back and forth, the few left that had not been damaged that was. The blade had gone from my palms, through those little bones in my wrists and halfway down my forearms, splaying them wide open. It did not frighten me, because it did not seem real to me. As the blood drained, it took my mental and physical pain with it just as I had hoped it would.

When the cold set in, I desperately tried to get into the back seat of my car to lay down. My legs no longer seemed to work, no longer had the strength to lift me. Kneeling at the back door, I tried to open it, not understanding why my hands did not work as I commanded them. When I finally got it open, I didn't have the strength to pull myself inside and I collapsed on the floor. I laid on my right side, my right arm outstretched and watched as the blood pooled around my body.

I thought then that I needed to rest for a moment, and I'd try again. I found myself at peace as my heart rate slowed. It would all be okay. No regret existed in that moment. No second thoughts. Nothing that was forgotten or left undone. There was no more pain, no more bitterness, no more anger. No more thoughts. No more flashbacks of violence and rape. My mother's voice had gone silent. The tornado that had become my mind was finally gone. It had been a troubled, painful life but it was the best I could do.

And I thought I was happy at that moment.

* * *

Her screams were what woke me up. I opened my left eye. "It's not that big of a deal. I just need some more sleep," I mumbled at her. She was talking to someone on her phone, but I could not hear anyone answer back. I heard her say the shop address and that I was conscious.

"What happened?"

"I'm very cold," was all I could get out. The blackness came and went. I woke again when she put a heavy, blue moving blanket on me and then again when the fire rescue guys arrived. I felt them tug on my shirt collar and slide me to the back door just as I had been trained to do so many years ago.

Blackness.

"Can you hear me?"

"Yeah." I could not feel anything except that my butt muscles were clenched.

Blackness.

I could see the cheap panels in the hanging ceiling of what I believed to be a hospital. We were moving fast. A light. Panels. A light. We stopped.

Blackness.

"Are you allergic to any medicines?"

"Yes."

"Which ones?"

"Does it matter?"

Blackness.

I felt cold metal in between my breasts. They cut my bra and it felt like my tits exploded out.

Blackness.

* * *

If the afterlife is what we think it should be, what we believe and hope it to be, then I suppose that's why I only saw darkness. I am not a God-fearing woman, do not believe in the stories that many give their lives to, that they judge others by. If there was such a thing as an afterlife, it was beyond my ability to imagine it. If anything, I thought of it as a floating sense into nothingness though even that seems too much to me. I thought there was just nothing at all. No consciousness, no sense of existence.

When I came to, I saw nothing. I felt and heard nothing. I knew who I was, who I'd been. That is to say, I felt like me. For a moment, I thought I might have been in one of those sensory deprivation tanks as I could not feel my body. No feeling or recognition of my toes or legs, not my arms nor my fingers. Not even my head seemed to exist. Perhaps not even my brain though I did not know how to distinguish that from thought. If I had thought, and I did, I assumed I must have a brain, a head. In that darkness, I could not find any light to go to. I did not come upon my favored grandma or lost friends or any pets at that moment. And I remember thinking that this nothingness, this blackness, was quite calming. I felt at peace to have it, was thankful for it. If I could have, I would have stayed there as long as was possible. No stimulus. Nothing. It was fantastic.

I heard her voice just then at barely a whisper. "Honey, you're going to be okay." And I knew then that I had not died as I'd hoped. The dark nothingness was merely drug-induced and not some afterlife existence, some spiritual awareness of my soul that had been lost so long ago. It was actual consciousness but without awareness and feeling of my body.

"I love you and I'm here," Sandi said.

It was then that I felt the tears pour out of what I suddenly realized were the corners of my blue eyes. They streamed down to what I recognized were my ears and hairline. I could not open my eyes. Something was in my mouth, in my throat...deep inside. So much that I thought I'd choke, suffocate. I wondered if my head was all that existed from my attempted suicide, and this thought brought panic to my mind. The thought that I may be stuck the rest of my life in whatever way I existed now overwhelmed me. In that darkness with my thoughts, my memories seemed more terrifying to me than anything I'd ever faced in my life. The irony of trying to end my life so I did not have those thoughts, and then to be left with only being able to think and not move was not lost on me. *Calm down, breathe, calm down,* I told myself. She continued talking as she stroked what I suddenly realized was my forehead. I laid there on what I assumed was a hospital bed, and I sobbed in that ugly way I had done as a child.

"The one thing I don't get is how she did both arms at one time," the surgeon said to Sandi. He worked over six hours putting me back together, connecting tendons, nerves, eight pins to hold my wrists together, two pins in my right ring finger to save it. He tried to sew my skin back together with hundreds of stitches, paying special attention to the tattoos that covered my arms, trying to align them again and again. It was a kind gesture that I think about whenever I look at the scars running down my arms today.

"She didn't do them together. She did them one at a time." He thought that was not possible. Surely, no one could do such a thing and then turn right around and do it again. "She is a very stubborn and strong woman," Sandi said.

I was in the intensive care unit for a week, I believe. I woke up to different voices, different faces each time. Machines beeped at different intervals, nurses ran in and out, volunteers sat in my room reading books to keep a constant eye on me. They said it took four and a half bags of blood to replace what I'd lost. It seemed like a different room, different people all the time. And every time I opened my eyes, it required a moment to realize where I was, who I was, and what I'd done.

God had blessed me, many said. I shooed the Catholic priest out of my room when I woke to find him praying for me. The loss of all that blood and vomiting had prevented the ibuprofen from getting to my kidneys and causing permanent, irreversible damage. Collapsing on the cold, concrete floor for hours had lowered my body's temperature enough to slow the blood loss. Whatever blood was left in me had pooled in my organs that needed it the most: my heart, my brain, my lungs.

And I remembered then that Sandi had walked into the shop that morning, turned on the lights and saw me there, laying in a pond of blood. Her screams echoed in my brain, and I realized what I'd done to her. I heard her calling for an ambulance, remembered how she covered me with the shop blanket before the firefighters dragged me out. I recognized that I'd traumatized her, that I'd been selfish and not thought for one second about where I did it or that she'd be the one to find me. I knew then that I had lost my mind, as people say. I may have been many things, but I was not inconsiderate of her feelings. I had never intended to hurt her in that way.

The head psychiatrist at Sharp Memorial Hospital, Dr. Christopher Morache, asked if I regretted my attempt. No, I still didn't. Regret for hurting my wife, for failing, for all the money she was spending on me... yeah, I had plenty of that. I knew what I was doing and why. I had always known it would come to that moment. It just took me much longer to get there than I thought it would have. Forty-four years to give in to thoughts that had been present in my brain since I was a child. It was always an option for me. A get-out-of-jail-free card. A gift Mom had given me, introduced me to. In between the drugs and few moments of consciousness, my thoughts would drift back to her time and again.

"I think there's more to it," the doctor said. I was in the psych ward or, as my wife called it, the spa. I did not have to do much for myself there. They cooked and cleaned, brought my meds in little paper cups with a paper glass of water to keep my mind soft and my psychosis quiet. "I think you're bipolar II. Meaning more depressed than manic."

"Sounds about right," I told him, disinterested and feeling more like my mother with every label. As a child, I often wished that I would wake up in a good mood. My moods seemed random to me. I could not understand the connection to my mother's moods, how much mine were dependent on hers. As an adult, the constant need to be vigilant, to watch for dangerous temperaments that I'd learned as a kid stayed with me. I'd thought it was a great skill for the work I did in the Patrol, but not so much for relationships or woodworking. My depression had finally taken over my life. I could not outrun it anymore.

"You definitely have PTSD. Your wife told me about your anxiety and flashbacks. The staff says you violently jerk yourself awake several times a night. Are you dreaming?"

"I don't know." That was the truth.

"What about the Patrol?"

"What about it?"

"Any traumatic experiences there?"

"No, the Patrol was just the Patrol."

"That's not what your wife says."

I had told Sandi about much of it over our many years together. She'd been the only one I'd talk to about it. Now she was telling my secrets to this man sitting before me, telling him that I'd thought I was joining a federal law enforcement agency much like the FBI or Marshals, that I'd come to believe that some of the agents I worked with were the real criminals, that I'd grown tired of arresting families or single guys from Mexico looking for work, that I'd started to believe it wasn't about honor at all, but about selective enforcement, about racism, about the ends justifying the means, about getting away with murder, about impunity. I told her about how rarely we ever apprehended an actual criminal, how corrupt management was, how it didn't matter how hard I worked, how far I hiked, how many apprehensions I got, because I still didn't belong.

I told her about how being a female agent meant constant sexual harassment, that the management condoned it, encouraged it, and often times were the ones doing it. I talked about how women who complained were ostracized, humiliated, and further harassed as I had been and how the systems meant to investigate those things only kept the truth from the public and even the victims. I'd told her about how the union attorneys who defended the abuser were the same ones that victims had to use. How the system was manipulated for the benefit of the assaulters.

She knew about my friends and colleagues in the Patrol who had killed themselves and often feared that someday I would be among them, just another number added to the column. The one upper management ignored, refused to recognize, refused to include in their officer memorials. She'd heard the stories about how Dave drank himself crazy and set himself on fire, when Bob had blown his brains out with his service weapon, when Mitch sat in the carpool parking lot along I-8 and took a bottle of pills. She watched as Jacob became addicted to pain killers and alcohol and heard those late-night calls when he begged me to drive out to Campo and buy him beer. She watched as Ricci and Linton stood in our living room and drew their loaded weapons in a quick draw contest, fully loaded with beer and bullets.

My memories, my feelings, about being an agent I shared only with Sandi while lying in our bed late at night not able to sleep, not wanting to dream. Now, she had ratted me out; dimed me out as we said in the Patrol. She didn't know everything though. I still kept my rape to myself. It was the most terrible, the most shameful to me. To admit it would have given it strength, made it real again, and I'd spent far too many years pushing it away to revive it. Why should I give it life through my voice? It was done and gone. There was nothing to do about it anyhow.

* * *

I cried that first night in the psych ward. Not because I was in pain or because I had not succeeded in killing myself, but because I was sitting in a mental ward with all the other crazies. Yeah, what I did was crazy. I knew that. I just didn't think I was that crazy, considering all that I'd lived through in my life.

"Am I fifty-one fifty?" I asked Dr. Morache.

"You graduated to a step above. I signed papers to keep you here longer than the normal three-day hold from a fifty-one fifty." Fifty-one fifty is law enforcement talk for a crazy person. They were the people that agents laughed at. The ones who tended to cross near the ports of entry, and the ones agents treated horribly. Now, I was one of them.

My days were filled with group meetings where people talked about their problems. There was the guy who talked endlessly about all the famous people he knew, like Beyonce and Jay Z, and how they were going to visit him, which always prompted the doctors to demand he shut up or leave. John was schizophrenic and had been self-medicating with meth because he believed the drugs doctors gave him were controlling his mind. We got along easily. Mostly because I didn't mind when he woke me up in the middle of the night to tell me that some bad guys were coming to take his car and kill him. He said I could protect him because I used to be a cop. I didn't bother to correct him and walked him back to his room each time telling him I'd take care of them. Old Sarah seemed to be suffering more from dementia. She was happiest when her son with the giant swastika tattoo on his neck came to visit. There were several young women there that reminded me of Ally Sheedy's character in *The Breakfast Club*, dressed in black and angry at the world.

I had little to say. It was bad enough that I was stuck in this spa with no end in sight. I certainly didn't identify with these people. They couldn't possibly understand my life or the reasons why I had chosen to end it. Still, I did as I was told simply because I knew that I would be released sooner if I did.

Then perhaps I could finish the job.

"The antidepressants your past psychiatrists prescribed to you are known to cause suicidal ideation in people with bipolar, especially bipolar

II. Did you know that?"

"I didn't even know I was bipolar."

"Bipolar II. There's a difference. Your manic episodes likely look more like highly productive episodes."

And suddenly so much of my life made sense. I thought of those times when I was younger and could read a large book in a single sitting, how I could easily spend twelve, thirteen, fourteen hours hiking after one group, or working on one case only to run five or ten miles after getting home, or how I took excessive amounts of time applying the finish to one of our handmade kitchens to the point of eating up all of our profit, or when I worked for over twenty hours straight to get a job out while Sandi was in the hospital. Those were my manic moments, my highly energized and productive moments. Those were the moments that I showed how dedicated and hardworking I was, or so I thought.

I felt more like I was becoming my mother as each day passed. How was it that she still used alcohol and prescription drugs to treat her mental illness, and I was the one sitting here in the spa? How was it that I was the one stuck in this place? Was it because I admitted my confusion, my anger? Was it because I'd spent years going to different therapists and psychiatrists? They never once bothered to test me for bipolar. I did all the shit they told me to do, and yet here I sat. I was the crazy one.

* * *

Every shift in the psych ward brought me a new aide who sat at my door to watch me. "Why did you do this to yourself?" they whispered. I never answered, not caring that my silence made them uncomfortable. On day two or three, the aide was not like all the others. She sat next to me on my bed, put clean socks on my feet and started talking. I sat there in my hospital gown, staring straight ahead with both arms still wrapped and splinted as I tried to clear the drug fog from my head.

"I am so glad you are awake," she said with a thick accent that told me Spanish was her first language.

"Well, that makes one of us."

"No, don't talk like that. There is much to live for. There's God…"

"Oh, no, no, no. Don't start with that God shit," I told her.

"Okay. Well, how about your husband?"

"I don't have a husband, I …"

"Well, that's okay too. At least you can be thankful you are not one of those…mmmm…how do you say, women who likes other women. Those women are disgusting. I mean, they make me sick…yuck…bleh!"

As she made puke faces and gestures and went on and on about how horribly disgusting lesbians were, I couldn't help but picture how Sandi's face would look when I told her about this. I could see tears streaming down her face as she laughed so hard it turned into that cartoon Muttley sort of giggle. We both grew up in families and eras that required us to hide our sexuality, to be ashamed of it. And though we saw younger gay couples proudly out in conservative areas of San Diego more and more, we still maintained caution in certain places because of how we were raised.

Sitting in a psych ward after my suicide attempt didn't seem like it should have been one of those places where I should have to hide my sexuality. I was tired of hiding all my shame. My gay shame, having an alcoholic mother shame, victim of child abuse shame, rape shame, sexual harassment shame, shame from untrue rumors that so many agents had spread about me, shame about being in an agency that was so blatantly corrupt and racist, shame, shame, shame…

"Nurse, this woman cannot be my aide today. I need you to find another person or no one at all," I said.

"She's the only one we have available."

The aide threw her arms around my neck and tried to pull my head down to her shoulder to soothe me. "Oh no, my friend. Shhhh, it will be okay."

"Get your fucking hands off of me." I pulled away with my body because I could not use my hands or arms and explained to my nurse why the aide needed to leave. "I don't want her fired but she needs to understand that homophobia is not okay. Not ever, but especially not when I'm going through this."

I was at the lowest point in my life, but I decided to stand up for myself, to say I was not willing to stay in that situation and deny who I was just to make someone more comfortable. I wasn't willing to be ashamed anymore, and that felt great.

* * *

I only left the spa to go next door for therapy on my hands and arms for a few hours every other day. It was difficult for me to walk the hundred yards or so because of all the blood I'd lost. Weak and exhausted all the time, I most often hopped in a golf cart for the short ride. I was thankful the drivers never asked me what happened.

Therapy most often consisted of picking up a little block and putting it back down. Again, and again. Some days they dipped my hands in a warm paraffin wax bath, which helped as any kind of cold or touch sent my nerves into overdrive. I had tons of opioids in my system to deal with the muscle and tendon pain, but nothing stopped the nerve pain.

When they unwrapped the bandages, I did not recognize my own hands. Large Frankenstein-ish stitches ran down the inside of my forearms to the middle of my palms. The muscles in my forearms and hands that I had developed from years of shooting guns and cabinet making were gone. I could only feel two fingers and a thumb on my right hand. The outer index tendon on my left hand had snapped causing it to push against my middle finger. My right ring finger had two permanent pins in it to hold it together. Both of my wrists were still locked with four or five pins in each that held them straight so the little bones could grow back and replace the eight-inch gap created by the saw blade. Two months later, I had another surgery to remove them all. My hands were red and swollen with dark black spots of blood crusted around where the hundreds of stitches had been.

There were few things I could do anymore. I'd once shot large guns and played classical guitar. I cooked and cleaned, petted and bathed our dogs, played basketball and volleyball in my younger years, put on makeup and loved my wife. I wrote letters, built kitchens and tables, drove across the country, rode horses, and climbed trees. I turned the pages in many books and could open jars and vacuum the carpet and mop the tile. Now I needed help with the most basic of things: eating, bathing, combing my hair, brushing my teeth.

It was humiliating.

I was surprised each day when Sandi came through that door. What I had done to her was unforgivable. I hadn't even had the decency to finish the fucking job. She had every reason to leave, to simply not show up, to move on with her life. A huge part of me wished she would give up on me, divorce me, because I did not feel worthy of her. No one would have blamed her if she did. I did not want her to see me in my shame, in my grossness. My pathetic failed attempt was now her burden, and I did not think that was fair.

She'd saved my life, and I could not decide if I loved her or hated her for it. She helped me stand and guided me to the bathroom, towing my IV stand behind us to take my first shower since my attempt. Sandi washed my long hair as I held my arms up because they were wrapped in plastic with rubber bands at my elbows to keep them dry. We both cried when we saw all the blood curl around the drain. The nurses had been surprised to see that I was a blonde and not a redhead.

As the weeks passed, I noticed how hard my wife worked to keep our business going, to provide for us, for me. Even with all the drugs in my system, I could see how she loved me in that way I had always wanted to be loved. She loved the good Jenn that was still deep down in me somewhere. She could see the Jenn who used to save earthworms as they washed into the streets after the rains, the one who loved to adopt the old and abused dogs, the daughter who still missed her parents, the citizen who still thought highly of her country regardless of the blender it had put her through, the Jenn who had endless amounts of sympathy for others but none for herself.

She also loved the beaten and ugly Jenn, the scared and desperate one that carried over forty years of physical and mental scars, the one who blew up all too often from anger and frustration. She stuck around even when it spilled over onto her, when I could not completely trust her though I desperately wanted to, when I could not believe her when she said that she loved me, when I could not trust in her because every little good thing felt just as dangerous as the bad things. I'd caused her many deep wounds and yet, she showed up every single day. I had no choice but to let her help me, let her love me. I hated every minute of it because I did not feel that I deserved it.

It was not lost on me how many people in that hospital were willing to devote their lives to helping me. Most didn't pry; they did not ask why I'd done it. When I talked, they listened and never judged. I watched and listened as others told their truths. Slowly, I started to feel safe, like I could speak my truth. As the doses of antipsychotics became smaller, as my mind began to clear, I discovered that there was something to be said for being so vulnerable, for being forced to ask for help, for tearing down one's walls. It was uncomfortable and irritating at first, but it was my only option. I had to accept their help, and ask for it at times from complete strangers. I was forced to give up my pride, my privilege, my vanity, my fear, and genuinely ask for and learn how to receive help.

When she told me that her name was Dr. Amber, I wanted to get up and leave. She was attractive, young, and stylish in her black leather jacket. Dr. Amber? Really?

"Tell me why you did this," she said.

"I was tired of living."

"What is the earliest childhood trauma you remember?"

* * *

My brother wasn't around, likely fishing with Pop at the lake or at a Boy Scouts meeting. I, as usual, stayed home and played with my dog, a red dachshund named Daisy. Mom had started locking us outside during the day when Dad was not home, telling us to drink water from the hose if we were thirsty, as if she could not stand to look at us anymore. I spent the time digging in the yard or riding my pink bike with butterflies on the banana seat.

She had to let me in that humid summer day because the weather had suddenly turned bad. Black clouds rolled, and the wind whipped up as the storm got closer. I ran fast to put my bike in our old metal shed in the back yard. I opened the door as fast as I could and threw my bike in before the cave crickets that lived in there had a chance to jump in my hair and make me scream.

She'd fallen asleep on the couch in the den again, the room that Dad had lined with that dark, faux wood paneling that was all the rage in the mid-1970s. I'd known not to make noise when she was sleeping, but I was a loud and boyish child who preferred to play with trucks and rough house with my brother instead of playing with dolls and Easy Bake Ovens. I let the screen door slam behind me.

She didn't say anything, just kicked Daisy into the wall and made her yelp in that high pitch cry that always broke my heart. She grabbed me by my shirt and carried me into her bedroom; my feet kicking underneath me. I heard myself then, yelling like my dog, only in my own voice, not human-sounding, not words, but guttural moans and cries that no child should ever utter. I did not feel like myself then, like a little girl, that is. I felt even more helpless like I thought my little dog must have felt. I wanted to get away and curl up into a tight ball like Daisy. Desperately, I looked around for something to hang onto, the door frame, the chair, a doorknob.

She stripped me down naked, threw me onto her bed, and began whipping my back, my butt and legs with one of my father's leather belts she'd doubled up. I cannot think of any time in my life that I was ever so confused and scared. I was not able to form a sentence or word, not able to ask her to stop, plead for forgiveness for whatever it was that I'd done wrong. The sound of the leather belt against my pale, freckled skin dug deep into my brain.

I can still feel it, how it stung as it bit into me like a thousand yellow jackets. I can see her face as it turned bright red and the white, foamy spittle that fell out of her mouth. I can see her swing with all the might she had in her small body, that belt held up high over her head. I thought she was not my mother then, for I did not recognize this woman. My screams and tears did nothing to soften her or slow her rage. I was only six years old and thought I might die.

Hours later, after she had calmed down, she called me to the living room. As I sat up in my bed, I felt my shirt pull on the puss and blood that had already dried to it. My eyes were raw and red from crying. I stood away from her, there in the doorway, afraid of my own mother for the first time. She motioned for me to sit on her lap. I can still feel the left side of my body against her chest, her face nuzzled against mine and her warm breath in my left ear as she held me with both arms rocking us back and forth.

"I am sorry for what I did to you," she sobbed.

I did not know what to say to her.

"I don't understand why I got so mad and hit you like that. I think it's because my father hit me once. My childhood was much worse than yours, you know. My parents hated me, honey."

She had returned, become the mother I knew, so soft and caring. The one who stayed up late with me whenever I was sick. The one who'd consoled me when my great-grandfather suddenly passed away. The one who let me stand on the kitchen chairs and help her make sugary treats. The one who'd taught me how to do the stroll and the mashed potato. She was the mother I loved more than anything, and I could not help but feel sorry for her. I knew she could not help herself sometimes. I had seen her kick and throw the dog across the room before. I'd seen her become angry with my father and hit him with her fists over things I did not understand, but I had never had this part of her attack me.

"Do you forgive me?"

"Yes," was all I could muster.

"Do you love me?"

"Yes."

"Say you love me," she pleaded and held me tighter.

"I love you."

"You need to do as I say. Be quiet when I'm sleeping. You need to be a good girl for Mommy. Don't tell your daddy about this, or your grandparents. If you tell them, you'll never see them again. You hear?"

"Yes."

I laid in my bed with Daisy after that, not knowing if something was wrong with my momma, trying to understand the things that changed in her. There was no thought about how it felt to have my mother do this to me, whether she was wrong or right for doing it. No thought on what that first time did to whatever small bond we may have had. It was something too big, too traumatic for me to understand at such a young age, and so, I turned my thoughts inward.

I got on my knees every night after that and prayed to keep her from doing it again, and asked God to make her happy and healthy. I prayed that I would be a better kid, that I would not push her to be so mad. And I remember that I felt sorry for what her parents had done to her, though I didn't exactly know what that was. I only knew that they lived far away in Seattle, Washington. She always said they were mean people, and I knew that when they called, Mom would always end up crying and fighting with Dad, screaming into the phone at her parents and slamming the receiver down. She'd lock herself in her room at some point, and Dad would then drive us across town to Grandma Budd's to get us away from her.

More than anything, I felt bad for her. Bad that she'd apparently gone through such a terrible childhood, and I wondered why anyone would do such a thing to my momma. I wanted to protect her, take away her pain, find her justice, make it all right for her, but I didn't know how. I didn't know why my dad stayed away so much, why she kept losing babies, why she slept so much and so hard at times.

No matter how much I tried to be good, it seemed she was upset with me more and more. Upset because my brother and I played too loud, because I brought a caterpillar into the house, because I drank the last of the Kool-Aid, because she could see my eraser marks on my homework. "Do it again," she yelled as she threw my notebook down. Whenever I got tangles in my long, blond hair, she no longer had the patience to work them out gently like before but yanked the hair right from my scalp, ripping the skin, leaving it bloody and beating me about my head with that hard, plastic, pink brush of hers.

The whippings came more often as time went on. My brother was forced to join me every now and then. One to him, one to me. I no longer cried or yelled from the pain. That part of me had died, it seemed, the part that was concerned for my own physical well-being. Instead, I stared into the corner of the room where nothing hung on the white wall. I wanted to avoid his blue eyes that stared back at me as she made us lay on her bed, on our stomachs, bent at the waist with our feet hanging over, bare butts exposed. It bothered me to see him cry. His eyes were no different than mine, like I was looking into the mirror, and his screams reminded me of that first time. He was always so soft, so weak. Prone to crying, not able to take pain as I could, and I wished I could make things better for him even though he was older than me by over a year.

I could not save him, could not so much as saved Daisy back then. This was when I learned I could dissociate, go elsewhere in my mind while she beat me. I thought I had a gift, a superpower that no one else had. If I focused my mind on other things, I tolerated the pain better. It wasn't that I didn't feel it or that I didn't know what was going on. I simply did not react to it.

I often thought of what it would be like to live at Grandma and Pop's all the time. Thought I might like to be a stewardess on a ship like the *Love*

Boat someday. I was sure the actress who played Julie on that show would have been a good mother, and I wondered what that would be like to have a mom not whip the tar out of me. I wanted to get a motorcycle when I was older, wear a leather jacket like Fonzie because he was cool. Maybe I would join the army like Pop and see the world. They let women in, and they could even be officers now. What if I just went away to boarding school like the girls on *The Facts of Life*, but then I remembered we were poor. No, that was not very likely. Maybe I would move up north and live with a friend like Lavern and Shirley, work in a factory. I could go to Chicago and see Grandma's favorite baseball team play. These were my thoughts as the belt snapped with every swing.

Eventually, she'd collapse into the chair in the corner of her bedroom after having worn herself out, and it'd be over. She'd point to our bedrooms, unable to speak. Her hair looked like a bird's nest that had fallen out of a tree. I stayed in my room afterwards, continuing to daydream about anything to avoid the present pain. I hoped my backside would heal quickly so I could go spend the weekend with Grandma and Pop. If they ever saw my back, Mom would not let me go back. I pretended it never happened and tucked it away behind that brick wall my mind had unknowingly begun to construct.

She no longer called me in to apologize. There were no more forced kisses, no more "I love you" demands. I didn't think she was sorry anymore, and I knew my indifference about it angered her. She thought that I did not care because I no longer cried, that it showed that I was not concerned about her feelings, that I only cared about myself. Sometimes she begged me to tell her that I loved her again, because I did not say it anymore.

"You will grow old and alone because you do not feel," she said.

I supposed she was right about that, but still, I would not cry. It did not matter if my brother begged me to cry so she would stop, it did not matter how hard she whipped me, how deep my skin split. I would not break because there was nothing left to break in that part of me. I had put up a wall to my feelings, sealed off my heart and soul because it was safer that way.

* * *

When I was done telling my story, I expected Dr. Amber to say that I had to take responsibility for my problems, that I shouldn't blame others. But all she said was that no child should ever have to live like that. She told me that it was not my fault, that my shame was not mine but my mother's and that I could let it go. I was left speechless for a moment because no one had ever told me that before. I did not know it was even possible.

"I don't know how."

"Picture little Jenn in your mind. Picture your mother beating little Jenn. What do you want to do?"

"Save her. Take her away," I said quietly.

"You're a caretaker. You were the adult in the family. You took care of your mother and your siblings. That's why you joined the Border Patrol. But who took care of Jenn?"

"No one," I confessed. "Not even me."

There was something about visualizing myself as a child and seeing that young Jenn outside of me. I would have never treated that little child like my mother did. I would have saved that child and helped her see how none of that was her fault, no matter what her drunk-ass mother had told her. I would have told her that she was important to me and she mattered, she was pretty and smart, she could have become anything she wanted, and supported her. I would have told her she didn't deserve to be called a bitch and slapped and punched and whipped and kicked and spit upon as I had been.

Going it alone, not trusting anyone but myself, the dissociation—I'd once considered all of it a gift, survival techniques that I naturally had in me. These coping skills served me well for many years and carried me through some horribly traumatic and violent times in my life, but they had also gotten me into this place. They were what had allowed me to lay both my arms down on a table saw. I was sitting in a psyche ward with bandages from my fingertips to my elbows because I built those walls, because I threw all those painful memories over the side and tried to bury them, because I had so much violence done to me in my past. I kept trying to push it all away, not think about it, trying desperately to not feel the pain of it.

When things were quiet, when the doctors had gone home and dinner was over, I stared out the window into the center courtyard at the grass and trees as the sun set over San Diego. For all my efforts to not be like my mother, I had ended up just like her. I was crazy, mentally ill, angry, and sometimes verbally abusive. The way my mother used to make me walk on eggshells was now how I made Sandi feel. I was no better than Mom. Now I was about to become even more like her in that I would not be able to work at the shop anymore. I could no longer earn a living or carry my own weight.

At that moment it dawned on me that I didn't have to be like her. That I could choose to be different. I didn't have to keep that wall up. Didn't have to keep making the same choices I'd always made. I could choose a different path. I could ask for help and take it graciously. I could stop hiding it all, stop fighting it. I could trust my wife, trust these doctors and nurses and my therapists. I could do the work and admit my pain. These were the things that my mother never did. That could be the difference between her and me, and just maybe it would help me get past the memories, the pain, and the shame.

I wanted to quit many a time. I wanted to walk out of those classes that they made me take about bipolar moods and negative thinking. I wanted to stop taking the medications that often changed because my depression and mood swings were still occurring. It felt like everything I did and said was wrong. The difference was that I now knew the problem I faced wasn't with anyone else, but with me. I was the problem. I likely wouldn't get out of the hospital anyhow unless I worked hard to make some changes. So, I went to every group meeting, talked openly to the doctors and therapists, shocked them, watched as their jaws dropped. I asked for assistance when I needed it, and slowly, I learned to accept it without beating myself up every single time, with a little less shame each time.

When I finally left the hospital and my outpatient classes were completed months later, I was referred to Dr. Marla Vencil as a therapist. Her type of no-nonsense, accountable therapy felt like a great fit for my personality. I wasn't looking to blame others for my problems, but I also knew that much of my mental health issues had been contributed to by others.

Yes, I had been horribly abused as a child, in that *Mommy Dearest* sort of way that still prevents me from ever watching that movie. I had terrible examples of what love was and what healthy relationships should look like. Those things were done to me. They were not fair, not just. My childhood abuse led to poor decisions like joining the Border Patrol and ignoring all the signs, all the red flags that were plain as day. Being raped and the constant harassment, the systemic abuse the agency dished out towards female agents that I suffered was frankly normal for me, and so I stayed when most would have left. I'd simply left one abusive family for another.

My walls and all my running did not prevent me from becoming an abuser myself. This was perhaps the hardest revelation I had to contend with. I had been cruel and abusive to my wife and others at times. My past did not excuse me from my anger, from my abusive behavior. My constant fear of becoming like my mother, the bad parts of her, had come to pass. It didn't matter how hard I tried to be different, or in how many ways I was different than her. I still managed to become an abuser too. I had to accept responsibility for this.

Within a few years, my medications changed to one small dose of a new antidepressant that had an immediate positive effect on me. I still had ups and downs, but they were less severe. I could recognize the moods as a part of who I was and no longer tried to ignore or deny them. I admitted when I was angry, sad, or depressed. I understood when I became overwhelmed or had flashbacks from my PTSD and when I needed to take a step back. Most importantly, I could tell Sandi where I was mentally, how I was feeling, and I did so without guilt or shame. When I needed time alone, I took time alone. When I found myself becoming irritated with her, I told her so and we talked about it. When I was scared, I let her comfort me.

I was fortunate to have her. She never wavered and stood by me each and every day. Whenever I felt like giving in, I reminded myself how lucky I was to have her, how many people like me had no one, how privileged I was to have found a good partner. When I became scared and doubted my trust in her, I reminded myself of all the things she'd done for me, the times she was there and when she didn't have to be but had chosen to be. I could recognize the good things, could see them now instead of focusing on only the negative and the past.

In time, I learned that needing help and asking for it did not make me weak or put me in danger like I had feared. Vulnerability, the mental exercise of tearing down my walls, created a level of trust that I had never experienced with my wife and with others. I stopped feeling ashamed for needing help, asking for it, and wanting it. It was a conscious decision to try and do the opposite of what I'd been doing my entire life. It was a choice to behave differently from my mother. This was how I tore down parts of my wall. Every time I took my medication, I chipped away at the mortar I'd placed so long ago. Every time I met with Dr. Vencil and spoke the truth, I was choosing to trust and refusing to live in shame.

When Dr. Vencil suggested that I try writing, she advised I focus on my time in the Border Patrol more since I still did not care to talk about it. The only problem with that was that I could not physically write. I could not so much as hold a pen or type on my laptop. Voice recognition with a few taps on the keys with the middle finger of my right hand and the pinky of my left was how I started. I spent hours writing until my hands and fingers cramped so badly that they became stuck in weird positions, frozen in cramped pain until Sandi gently massaged it away.

In the beginning, I believed that I didn't have many feelings about the Patrol. This was partly because I was on drugs that numbed my emotions, partly because I did not understand how to feel, but mostly it was because that part of my wall was still solidly there.

Yes, the Border Patrol had been traumatic, but not for the reasons most people thought. I expected the car crashes and fights, the drug runners, the human smugglers, and the bodies I would find, but I never expected the trauma to come from my colleagues, the agency, and institution itself. I never expected to arrest families, women, and children who were not criminals but simply needed help to survive. I didn't expect that my rape was more than an anomaly, but part of a large rape culture instigated and protected by generations of agents. I didn't realize that I'd joined a criminal organization disguised as a federal law enforcement agency. I didn't expect to become a member of a deeply racist agency. I didn't know any of it until it was too late, until I lost myself and my soul became untethered.

Huntsville, Alabama, 1975

San Diego, California, post academy graduation, 1996

Campo, California, 75th Anniversary badge, 1999

San Diego Pride, first Border Patrol agent
to march in Pride in uniform, 1999

Campo, California, Acting Supervisory Border Patrol Agent, 2000

Washington, D.C., Andrea Guerrero and Representative Joaquin Castro (D-TX), 2019

Right: Juarez, Chihuahua, Mexico
Dr. Reverend William Barber
at a migrant shelter, 2019

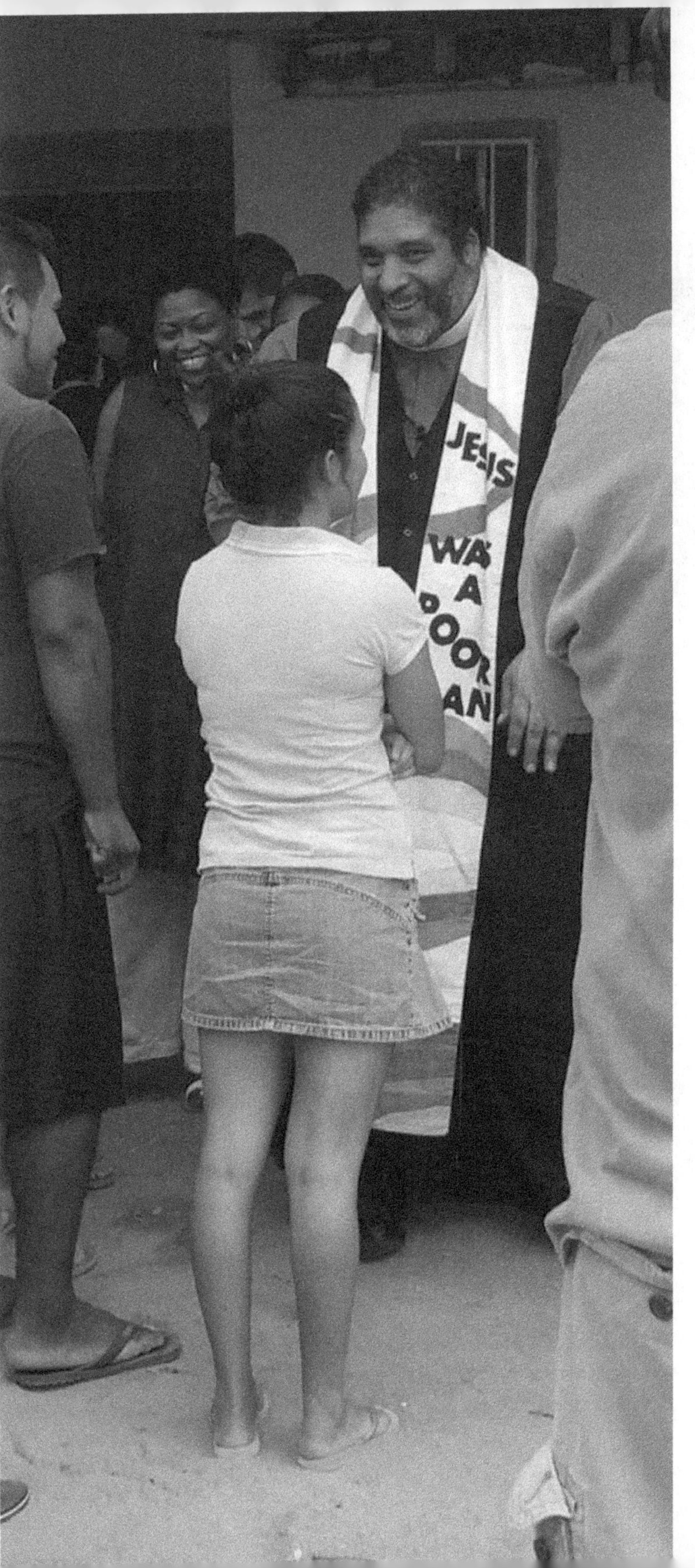
JESUS
WAS
A

El Paso, Texas, Moral Mondays protest with Reverend Ryan Eller, 2019

Nogales, Chihuahua, Mexico with AnaMaria Vasquez of Border Victim's Network and Dona Taide Elena, grandmother to Jose Antonio Elena Rodriguez, who was shot and killed by Border Patrol agent Lonnie Swartz as he walked down the sidewalk in Mexico, July 2021; Photo by John Kurc

Ciudad Jaurez, Sonora, Mexico, migrant shelter, 2021; Photo by John Kurc

Green Valley Samaritans, Green Valley, Arizona, 2021

Calexico, California border wall, 2021; Photo by James Cordero

Campo, railroad tunnel leading to Mexico

San Diego, California, with Robert Vivar of Unified Deported Veterans of Tijuana after he was repatriated to the U.S., 2021

Record of Deportable/Inadmissible Alien

U.S. Department of Homeland Security

MEXICO

05/28/1999

EDC/CAO

PB

Tecate, CA 05/28/1999 2127

JOE A. JOHNSON

PWA Mexico

TRAVEL/

AT ENTRY

See Narrative

See Narrative

None Claimed

Left Index Print

Right Index Print

FATHER NAME AND ADDRESS:

MOTHER NAME AND ADDRESS:

JENNIFER B. BUDD
SENIOR PATROL AGENT

TO FILE
SECTOR
STATION

JENNIFER B. BUDD

May 28, 1999 at 2136

Voluntary Return

MICHAEL J. SYZDEK

Form I-213

Anastacio Hernandez-Rojas I-213, 1999

Campo, California, racist memorial from border militia group in support of the Border Patrol, 2021

Old Campo station is now a processing center. Migrants refer to these as "hieleras" or "ice boxes" because agents keep the temperature inside at an uncomfortably cold setting. This crosswalk was installed after I was run over intentionally by the other agent, 2021

PART III

Campo, California, returning to my old patrol area with water for migrants, 2021

LISTENING

It had been two years since my attempted suicide. My childhood memories did not haunt me as much as they once had. When my past did come to mind, I had more of a calm sadness, a compassion for the little girl I'd once been. I had developed some sympathy for myself, and even a bit for those who were mentally and physically brutal to me.

This new journey I was on, the healing of my soul, coincided with the election of Donald Trump. When he descended the escalators to announce his candidacy by characterizing migrants as criminals and thugs, I was in the middle of exploring my actions as a Border Patrol agent. The press called his racist rants "dog whistles." To a woman who'd grown up in Alabama, as a former Border Patrol agent, it was a clear call to arms for all those who hated immigrants and people of color. He said the hateful words that I knew so many whites said in private; the talk they only used when mixed company wasn't around. Whites called it political correctness, which was our politically correct term for when whites wanted to use the n-word but felt others would shame us for it.

When Trump called for a Muslim ban, my former employer did not hesitate to enforce it, although it clearly violated the Constitution. To exclude any person based solely on their religion was and still is plainly against the law. I was not shocked by this ban. I expected it. I was ashamed of it but not surprised. Not a single agent, new or old, came out publicly and refused to follow a blatantly illegal order. I was embarrassed that I'd ever worn that uniform and disgusted with myself for ever believing their lies. I thought about how I judged my parents for not participating during the civil rights protests of the 1960s and how so many people never said a word when Nazis began rounding up Jews before and during World War II. I thought about that night when I apprehended Pedro and we talked about just and unjust laws.

It had never occurred to me that our immigration laws would be applied more harshly, in a targeted way to those with Black and Brown skin. I should have known the history of the Border Patrol, our country's history regarding the southern border and the racism that it was built upon. I should have learned in school and at the academy that many of the first Border Patrol agents were Ku Klux Klan members and others were the sons of confederate generals bitter about losing the Civil War and those they enslaved. I should have been aware that they often lynched Mexicans and shot Chinese migrants, that they claimed migrants carried disease and forced men and women crossing the border to strip naked and be deloused with chemicals. I should have known that the political leaders who wrote our immigration laws, the laws that I had enforced, were devout segregationists and white supremacists. I should have known that the agency I worked for, the uniform I once proudly wore, had deep roots in white supremacy.

I knew none of that until I began researching and educating myself in 2015. Increasingly, I acknowledged how the white supremacy system that was created long ago still afforded me the privilege of not knowing, the privilege of ignorance. Once in the Patrol, once I became an agent and heard the racist terms and witnessed the brutality aimed at migrants of color, once I understood that the laws and policies that I enforced were racist, once I became comfortable with racist names, once I hit a young man on his shoulder with my flashlight—I became a white supremacist too. I contributed to that system. I was a part of that system. I was responsible for it.

I had many reasons for what I did. I can try and justify my actions as I used to: I needed the job, I was escaping a violent and dysfunctional family, I was a gay woman in Alabama, I didn't make the rules or the laws; it was just a job. Those are all excuses. Those are the excuses the white supremacist system gives us who are white. They help us explain away our racist actions and thoughts. They help us justify our brutality and ignore our responsibilities as human beings to one another.

I was not brave enough to stand up against what I witnessed. Worse than that, I did not just sit on the sidelines. I chose to wear the green uniform, to enforce laws based on racism and white supremacy. And when I learned what it was, when I saw the truth, I made justifications and chose to stay for six years.

Now, I consciously and intentionally choose to listen to those who I harmed, who my agency harmed, who my government harmed. I have found that as a white woman, if I go for too long without hearing and facing the racism of my former agency, I fall back into my old patterns of wanting to believe what the Border Patrol says, of giving them the benefit of the doubt. I believe that this is the result of living in a culture designed and built for me as a white person. Sometimes, my first thought when I hear about a horrible Border Patrol encounter is to doubt it. Many times, they seem ridiculous, and then I remember how ridiculous the Game of Smiles sounds. Yet, I know that the Border Patrol rape game exists even today.

I wanted to be different and not follow the easy, well-worn path designed for people of my skin color. I wanted to be that person that practiced what she preached. I wanted to become the type of person who stood up even when she was afraid and spoke the truth when no one else around her did.

* * *

In February 2017, the San Diego Islamic Center had invited local leaders to speak about what the new Trump Muslim ban would mean for our local Muslim community and what they should expect. I sat listening to Christian Ramirez, a local activist for immigrant rights, speak about what it was like to be Brown in San Diego County. That's when I forgot all about why I came to the mosque in the first place, and my disgust was turned inward toward my past. I looked down at the linoleum floor as I listened to every question he asked, every word he spoke. He didn't know who I was, who I'd been. He wasn't speaking to me directly, but it felt like it.

"Do you know what it is like to take your child to Disneyland, and to be stopped every single time by the Border Patrol agents at the northern checkpoints?" the speaker asked. "Where are you going? What are you doing? Where were you born? Do you know how it feels when my son asks me what I did to make the Border Patrol policeman pull me over and search my vehicle for drugs? How do I explain to him why they keep asking if I'm a United States citizen? Why won't they believe me when I say I have no drugs in my car? Do you know why they still question me when all their record checks on me come back with nothing? Or how about when they separate me from my son and try and get him to say that I'm not really his daddy? Do you know how it feels as people drive past, looking at you, wondering what crime you've committed? None of this is because I did anything wrong. It's because I had the nerve to take my son to Disneyland like so many other Americans, and I happen to be Brown. It's because of the color of my skin that I always get put into secondary for further inspection. I am an American," he proudly declared.

As I listened, I realized for the first time that I never had truly listened to someone with this experience. I had never contemplated what it must be like to be Brown or Black on the southern border and be forced to drive through an immigration checkpoint. I had never wondered what the person I stopped and asked for further inspection thought about my questions and why I posed them. I'd never even been stopped at an immigration checkpoint, and that wasn't because I was in uniform. I'd gone through checkpoints plenty of times in street clothes, through different checkpoints filled with agents who did not know me from any other driver. My pale complexion and blond hair always get me waved through. Not so much as "Hello," or a "State your citizenship, ma'am" has ever been aimed at me, and I knew that if it had been, I would have been pissed off about it.

Everything he said was true. Everything.

When he finished speaking, I introduced myself and shook his hand asking him to be gentle with mine. The swelling had diminished greatly, and I had lost most of the muscle that surrounded and protected the nerves and bones in my hands. I lived in constant pain. A firm handshake could leave me in severe pain for days.

"If you ever want to speak with an ex-agent, give me a call."

His eyes widened with surprise, and we set a date to meet at his office. As I drove home that night, I wondered what possessed me to do that, to offer to meet him. What did I have to say to him anyhow? *Guess what I used to do? Let me tell you about all the people I caught, all the families I hunted down in the middle of the night, how I used to call them the t-word, how I stopped listening to their stories because it eventually made it difficult for me to do my job and made me feel bad about myself. Let me tell you how hard it was to be a female agent.*

A Google search told me that Christian was the human rights director at Alliance San Diego, a local grassroots organization that worked toward equality and justice for all residents in the area. They were involved in immigration rights, healthcare, homelessness, voting, education—anything that made the community a better place to live. His office was modest and filled with pictures and banners from various protests, events from the border, the San Diego City Council, and Washington, D.C. I noticed a picture of his beautiful son on his desk.

We sat at a round table, just the two of us. Even though I'd learned how corrupt and beyond redemption my former agency was, I still held many of the false beliefs about immigrant activists that the Border Patrol had taught me. There was still that distrust of the other, that part of myself that I did not like to admit to that made me feel uncomfortable. It was the racist bit of myself that I preferred to ignore, the part I often claimed did not exist, the side of me that I found unlimited ways to justify. Like most white people I knew, I didn't think I was a racist because I didn't wear a hood or burn a cross on someone's lawn or use the n-word.

"Tell me about your time in the Patrol," he said. "Whatever you feel comfortable talking about," he said.

He was genuine, sincere, and listened to me intently when I told him vaguely of my time there, why I had left and how I had been treated as most women in the Patrol are. I mentioned my sexual assault, when I was run over by another agent and shot at by another, how I tried to whistle-blow, and had my life threatened and nearly lost it again from PTSD. I don't think I can ever forget the look of sorrow in his eyes for the few things I was willing to share with him that day.

"I am sorry for the trauma you endured in the Patrol. Most do not realize how traumatizing being an agent can be, especially a female agent."

Christian's words confused me. I did not expect this reaction from him, this kindness. I was more prepared for comments of how horrible the Border Patrol was, how we were all racists and a bunch of thugs. I expected he would tell me how his people wished us all dead and how every agent was a piece of shit, a *pinche Migra*, how agents raped and routinely beat migrants, how we were never held accountable by the law, how we treated them like animals, how I should have been ashamed of my past and what I did, how I deserved no sympathy and had been dealt some small piece of justice with my suicide attempt and subsequent disability for having been a part of an organization that had terrorized his community for generations.

I expected a fight, wanted it even. I was accustomed to feeling cornered and forced to defend myself for acts I was ashamed of. Fighting and hiding my shame was what I was used to doing, what I was comfortable with, but he gave me none of that. He had effectively disarmed me and my old talking points were now moot. I wanted to say, "Oh, but I wasn't as bad as the others," or "I was just following orders," but the journey I'd begun now allowed me to accept his kindness. I chose not to second-guess it and took it for what it was. I chose to trust him in a way I was never able to trust my fellow agents. His empathy helped me see there was no reason to fight.

Christian's words inspired me to want to change more, rethink things in that moment, and choose a different path. I did some of those awful things. Yes, it was true. I wore that green uniform, said those racist things, defended Border Patrol policies and laws, knowing that they had only driven thousands of people to their deaths. I hunted migrants like criminals. I spoke about them as if they were animals and sometimes locked them away in holding cells where I would not have left my dogs. I chased them down and pushed them to the ground, dumped their belongings in the trash, and yelled at them to shut up and sit down.

Only now, I thought it was time I admitted it. It was time I took responsibility for it. My healing didn't just involve my pain or the pain I'd inflicted on my loved ones. I needed to look at the pain I'd caused migrants. This was what I felt was missing from my recovery and from my life. Maybe, just maybe this would be the answer to healing my soul.

"What you said the other night, at the mosque, about what it is to be you, to be Brown and go through a checkpoint? I'm ashamed to say that I never considered it from the other side," I confessed to him. I felt like I'd placed my heart on the table in front of him and waited for him to snatch it. He nodded as if to say that he knew what I was doing and left it sitting there.

"I always told myself that it was just part of the law. That being on the southern border where most people illegally crossing were Brown simply dictated that we would stop predominately Brown people. I worked the I-8 checkpoint a lot, you know. When it was slow, I checked everyone. If it was busy, I checked every third car. I was trying to prevent that habit of racially profiling. I thought that it somehow made me different than the rest. That the stink off all the bad things the agency and its agents did would somehow not cling to me if I did things like that. I realize now how foolish I'd been. I think that I've got a lot of work to do."

Six years of wearing that uniform amounted to what seemed a small portion of my life. The thought that it could have had so much influence on me now seemed ridiculous. My unease with Christian, how uncomfortable I felt listening to his story, the difficulty I had in talking about the Patrol, the fact that I told my old colleagues many years ago not to come around anymore, that I couldn't bear to see a Border Patrol truck go by, that I constantly had dreams and nightmares of being in that uniform—it all meant something more. There was a more important lesson to those six years that I had not been willing to acknowledge before.

I realized the discomfort was what I needed, and I found myself drawn to spend more time with it.

* * *

I agreed to attend when Christian invited me to listen to Maria Puga speak at a local event called the "Black and Brown Communities Unite!" I had never heard of this woman. Obviously, I was not a person of color, but he assured me that I needed to come and listen. The event was intended as a way for members of the Black and Brown communities to speak about how local law enforcement affected their everyday lives, and what they should be thinking about with this new administration that was so blatantly racist and anti-immigrant. I looked around the Malcolm X Library and noted no uniformed law enforcement in attendance. From my days in intelligence, I knew they would know about the event, and that they would likely have undercover agents in the audience.

Something told me I needed to be there in that space, that it would be an important and life-altering part of this new journey I was on. I saw the pain in her face before she spoke, how it lined her smile and forehead. It was easy to see that she had endured some sort of trauma, though I did not know exactly what. It seemed like an eternity before she picked up the microphone; each moment that passed built anxiety in me until she spoke in her native tongue, and I heard the monotone translation in my ear a few seconds behind.

As I listened to the words, I closed my eyes and pictured it as she spoke. I saw the Chula Vista station she spoke of, could hear it, and smell the stench that was a Border Patrol processing center. The handcuffs and the badges, the batons and the trucks, the creaking of my old leather boots and belt all came back to me. I knew of the area she referred to at the San Ysidro Port of Entry called Whiskey Two, because we agents often had agents on duty open the door for us whenever we went south on our personal time with friends. I pictured the bridge above the gate, the many people who walked back and forth across that man-made border line I used to defend.

I listened as she described how over a dozen Border Patrol and CBP agents beat her husband to death while he was handcuffed behind his back.

I thought of all the times I knew of when agents yelled out for people to stop resisting in case anyone was filming them as they beat up migrants. When really, they were not resisting at all. I thought of how they sat around after work and told their tales, how they tried to one-up each other with their brutality, and how they laughed at the violence they imposed. I thought of how some agents liked to pepper spray people for any little thing, how others liked to tase them, how some preferred their batons while many others liked to throw them around like dolls. Out in the middle of nowhere, where no one could see us, we could do as we pleased. We knew full well no one would believe the migrants even if they were brave enough to complain. And though I was not one of those agents and had even reported some that were, I knew they existed and that they did not ever get disciplined for such actions because the Border Patrol had figured out how to rig the system long ago with their illegal and secret Coverup Incident Teams or CITS.

Later that evening when I went home, as my wife slept, I looked for articles on Anastacio Hernandez-Rojas. I watched the videos of his beating on YouTube. It was a Rodney King type of incident had that occurred in May 2010. Maria's husband was clearly handcuffed behind his back while agents kicked, punched, and stomped the shit out of him. I felt nauseous at the sight of them beating this man to death. It was like watching my mother beat my brother, like if you witnessed your father raping someone. I felt it in my gut that I was somehow a part of it, in some way connected to it, even though it had happened nine years after I resigned.

What could Anastacio have done to deserve this treatment? Why didn't anyone stand up and tell the others to stop? Why hadn't anyone said that the man had been beaten enough? Border Patrol's official account came from the San Diego sector's then Acting Chief Rodney Scott. The agency hit the press far and wide with accounts of Anastacio being "combative." They said he refused commands and attacked the agents, even though that was not possible with his hands behind his back as he laid in the fetal position on the ground. Maybe he was high; maybe he was crazy, they suggested. Later they stated he had meth in his system. This, I knew, was an old Border Patrol trick. They made it seem like he was an out-of-control drug user who deserved what he got, even though none of the arresting agents said he behaved like he was under the influence.

It had taken fifteen hours before the San Diego Police Department was notified of the beating. Their homicide detectives only learned about it when a local reporter called and asked what was going on at the port. Border Patrol never bothered to call and report it. This was against policy, and a signal to me that the Patrol may have actively covered something up.

The agency has no legal authority to investigate assaults and deaths. This meant the police department should have been called immediately by a supervisor. I knew how the agency used time delays to their benefit, of how they often used their CIT[1] at sector headquarters to hide evidence of agents' crimes, how they allowed agents who were involved plenty of time to get their stories straight before they spoke with the San Diego Police Department so that all their reports and testimonies would be identical. I remembered witnessing the CIT team in action as an agent and learned the truth of what they were when I was assigned to sector intelligence.

CIT units were and still are the agency's cleanup crew. Those permanently assigned there are hand-selected by the sector chiefs for their willingness to fix things for the agency. The agency comes first. Always. If that means throwing rocks onto the scene where they claim rocks had been thrown to justify an agent firing their weapon, then they do it. If it means getting rid of witnesses by threatening them, they do it. I had seen it with my own eyes as an agent.

I also knew how the area called Whiskey Two was full of cameras the day Anastacio was killed and that the orders to CIT would have been to stall the investigators, and that they would eventually claim that the video

[1] San Diego sector's team was called the Critical Incident Investigative Team (CIIT), but most sectors used the term Critical Incident Team (CIT).

was lost or somehow taped over. The Border Patrol CIT routinely inserted themselves into investigations with the guise of assisting the investigating agency. Their actual purpose was to gather intel on what investigators knew, to find out what evidence they had on agents. Then they shared it with management in an effort to develop a game plan on how to deal with the fallout and minimize criminal and civil liability against the agency.

As with so many other investigations, the San Diego CIT did just enough so that nothing happened to any of the agents involved. It was their collective word against Anastacio's autopsy report that showed he had died of a heart attack brought on by the repeated tasings. Even though the report stated that his death was a homicide, the Department of Justice ultimately argued that it could not be determined if Anastacio had a heart attack from the tasings or from the supposed drugs in his system. None of the videos nor the witness testimonies of all those on the bridge that night were honored; only the testimony of agents was considered trustworthy. It was a well-designed system, built with an insurmountable advantage given to an agency that had always been out of control and filled with corrupt agents. I was sure that the investigation likely had no references to the CIT team as the unit was secret. There was likely little that could have been done to bring justice to the family.

I used to bleed green. When one of us died needlessly, I felt it to my core. Now I had watched several of my brethren unnecessarily beat a man to death and lie about it. My core, my soul, felt this death equally. I wanted to help this man's family seek the justice they deserved, but I did not know how yet.

Speaking Up

On June 18, 2018, *ProPublica* published an article about the Border Patrol separating children from their asylum-seeking parents. Journalist Ginger Thompson had somehow obtained a recording of those children in custody. Plain as day, you could hear them crying, "Mami, Papa!" Then a clear, adult voice was heard in Spanish, "Well, we have an orchestra here. What's missing is a conductor."

I could not believe what I saw and heard. The first thing that came to my mind was pictures of French-Jewish children in Drancy, France, in 1941 and 1942, when the Nazis and French police separated French-Jewish children from their parents. It was done not simply to be cruel, but also to make the adults comply with their orders. It was a common tactic used by Nazis all over Europe, separate the children first and parents would do anything they were told to try to save their kids. It was how dozens of soldiers were able to contain hundreds of people that could have surely overrun them had they wanted to, had it not been for their children. The adults got on those trains because they were told that their children would be following right behind them and that soldiers would not hurt them if they obeyed their commands. Eventually, they did all go to the same place; only it was to concentration camps like Auschwitz.

I normally cringed when comparisons were made between the Border Patrol and Nazis. The label had a way of shutting out discussion, turning people off, or making them reluctant to talk about immigration without backing into their ideological corners. I hadn't heard of or seen any concentration camps when I was an agent. And though I now disagreed with many of the Patrol's policies, I did not think calling them Nazis was appropriate or respectful to those who had suffered at the hands of Nazis during the Holocaust. It felt blasphemous to make the comparison. Obviously, I had a personal reason as well. Such a comparison was also a judgment of my behavior that I was still not willing to make.

Nevertheless, I could not shake this thought of Drancy or the cries of those children in custody of my former employer. Would I have refused that order? Would I have walked away at the first separation, the first time a child looked up at me with tears in her eyes as I pulled her from her mother? As a young agent, would I have recognized the systemic trauma I would be putting those kids through? Would I have gone to the press and given inside information? What if the agents did not understand the historical significance? That was not an unreasonable question. I remembered how uneducated many of them had been even back when I served, and the standards for employment had been significantly higher back then than they were now.

I thought back to that first night when I apprehended a family and how I told my mother that I felt like a Nazi, how I pushed those feelings aside time and again. I wore the green uniform with a badge and a gun, with the might of the U.S. government behind me. It was so easy to excuse it all. Perhaps that was the point; that racism, that being racist and enforcing racist policies, was easy for those of us who were white and for those seeking the privilege of being "white enough."

It was easy because our leaders had set up a system that forced migrants to cross in horribly dangerous terrain. Along with deterrence policies like walls, a small army of agents, and militarization of our borders, Congress had quietly started to make it more difficult for migrant workers to cross legally. They did this with the knowledge that migrants, especially those seeking asylum would still come because they had no choice. Within a few years of Operation Gatekeeper, the government knew for a fact that deterrence policies did not stem the flow of migrants and that our policies were funneling thousands of people into the dangerous areas, resulting in their deaths.

Instead of doing what was right and acknowledging the brutality and failure of deterrence policies, administration after administration simply doubled down on it. They then told us, the agents enforcing these cruel and inhumane policies, that we were the heroes, the just, the righteous, simply for rescuing them after we had put them in danger in the first place. If you were the kind of agent who couldn't see, or refused to see, the connection or the bigger picture, it was easy.

Today's agents had it even easier. Back when I was an agent, we didn't get the medals they now give them for rescuing migrants. We didn't have special tactical names or special gear to rescue people. We just did it. In the late 1990s, management turned the agency into a first responder patrol. But it was less about rescuing migrants and more about getting good press and making the agents feel great about their jobs without looking at the reasons why migrants ended up needing to be rescued in the first place. The new rescue teams called BORSTAR did not rescue everyone after all. They were particular about which calls they answered. If it was more than three days, they assumed they were dead and didn't even bother. And if we didn't find them, if their bodies were found by citizens or other law enforcement, then they weren't counted. Dead migrants added to the death totals that shamed the Patrol and made activists mad.

Agents now train to rescue migrants from the dangerous waters, deserts, and mountains that our immigration policies push them to cross. They fly around in Blackhawk helicopters and drive speed boats to save migrants from all the catastrophes that their policies create. Every sector chief now has a Facebook, Twitter, and Instagram account, where they post each day's rescues. These rescues give the agents something to be proud of, something they point to assuring the public that they aren't as brutal as immigration rights activists and migrants say they are. Rescues give them the ability to falsely claim they are humanitarians and ignore all the other ways in which they are not. Our immigration policies create the need for rescues that those agents are then rewarded for doing.

When Sebastian Murdock of *Huff Post* called to ask if I had anything to say about child separation, I took the opportunity to address agents that may not have understood what they were doing. I wanted to inform them of the historical similarities people would surely make. I told them to lay down their guns and badges, that separating families seeking asylum was immoral and unjust. That it was a line too far in immigration enforcement. I believed that separation would not only bring shame and judgment upon the agency, but that the agents would be seen as personally responsible as well. When the reporter asked how I felt about having worn that uniform, about having been one of them, I paused and became flushed with shame and regret.

Crossing the border illegally was now charged as a criminal offense and not just as an administrative one as it had been in my day. This change in enforcement of statute 8 USC 1325 was done by the George W. Bush Administration after 9/11. Border officials claimed crossing illegally needed to be criminalized to protect the country from terrorists, although none of the 9/11 terrorists had entered the country through the southern border. The general belief was that it would not be used for common migrants seeking employment or asylum. Besides, asylum seekers were already protected by the 1980 Refugee Act signed by former President Jimmy Carter that stated all illegal entries by asylum seekers should not be considered in their cases because they were fleeing for their lives and that families should be kept together out of detention whenever possible. The only problem was that the act said they "should not" instead of it "could not" be used against them.

What all of this meant was that the CBP and Border Patrol could technically, legally treat asylum seekers as criminals, that they could imprison them like drug dealers and rapists and remove their children from their custody, that they could fill private detention space with families asking for help, all on the taxpayers' dime. What had once been a culture of crossing to find work, an accepted part of the border experience, border culture, or even a humanitarian cause was now framed as a national security issue and that made it big business.

Just like those parents in Drancy all those years ago, asylum-seeking parents wouldn't fight back for fear of never seeing their children again. The Border Patrol knew this. CBP knew this. Just as they had made it easy to justify the wall, militarization, pushing migrants to their deaths, our government made it easy for agents to justify family separation of Black and Brown asylum seekers.

It wasn't as if I thought child separation would stop because I called out the Border Patrol. It had been over seventeen years since I resigned in protest. If anything, I wanted to say something simply because I could, because I stayed so quiet about all the other things in the past, because I'd been on the wrong side of history. I had learned the hard way how keeping my mouth shut had nearly killed me. I hoped that if one agent heard my words, they might question their actions and step down. I wanted to use my privilege for something other than protecting myself. I'd hoped to be that person who did the right thing instead of going along to get along. I didn't want to do the easy thing as I had done so many times before when it came to immigration policies and immigrant rights. I wanted to start living my core values, and so, I spoke.

* * *

When Christian Ramirez left Alliance San Diego to run for a position on San Diego's City Council, I was passed on to Hiram Soto. A Tijuana native prone to wearing flat caps, Hiram was the communication director and worked on the Southern Border Community Coalition (SBCC) that Alliance San Diego ran. Sometimes we met in his office, other times at a restaurant for lunch, but mostly we talked on the phone.

It was Hiram who suggested I write an open letter to my former colleagues about the Trump policies they enforced, how it would affect them personally, and what they could expect if they continued down the path of just following orders. When it was published, the Border Patrol responded by following the SBCC newsletter and started keeping tabs on me.

Dear former colleagues at the U.S. Border Patrol,

I know that you've been working long hours with families seeking safety and protection at our nation's borders. I remember what those shifts were like when I worked at the Campo, California station: people from many different countries, some sick and injured, children and babies that needed special care, lack of resources and a management that often seems more against you than with you.

I assume that like me, you joined the U.S. Border Patrol for many reasons: to serve and protect your country, to pay off that college tuition and to provide for your family or just to have a stable job. Maybe some of you were like me and had no idea what the Border Patrol did; perhaps the only thing you knew about the southern border was what you learned in the academy. If this is the case, you would not be all that different from many Americans who have no idea that the southern border is one of the most vibrant regions of the country, home to more than 15 million people who live in peace and harmony with their neighbors to the south. They consider their communities places of hope and opportunity and are tired of politicians using their communities to promote their careers.

Today, we are living the consequences of our decades-long obsession with our deadly enforcement-only policies, and you, my dear former colleagues, are the tip of the spear. You are the enablers of a deportation force responsible for separating families, terrorizing communities and responsible for enforcing policies that have killed thousands of people, including six children since November who died in U.S. custody.

I mean, you didn't really sign up to put babies in cages and babysit them...am I right? You didn't really wake up one day and decide you thought sending people who were escaping violence and terror to concentration camps was a good thing...did you? That's not why you went through federal law enforcement training, and not why you carry a badge and a gun. When you raised your right hand and swore to uphold the Constitution and the laws and treaties of the United States, you meant it just as I did. And I know that you know those laws and rights apply to immigrants, whether legally present or not.

You also know, as all Border Patrol agents know, that with the coming summer months comes more death. You see it every year without fail. Every agent, from trainee to Chief Provost herself, knows that metering asylum seekers will force desperate families to make desperate choices and cross in the dangerous deserts, mountains and rivers in an attempt to turn themselves over to you for processing their asylum claims. You also know that claiming asylum is not a crime, that crossing without inspection is not to be considered in their claim. That the very act of resorting to this proves how credible their fear is and that is why they are crossing.

When you participate in pushing asylum seekers away from the ports and out to the dangerous terrain in between, your actions are likely to lead to many deaths just as my actions did. Whether they die in your custody or not, when you enforce such a blatantly harmful policies, you share in that responsibility for their deaths just as you deem the smugglers do when they tell groups where to cross. Following management's verbal orders to stay out of those areas where you know bodies are likely located or releasing someone from custody just before they expire does not negate your responsibility either.

Yes, I know about the games management plays.

When a Supervisory Border Patrol Agent (SBPA) orders you to put 250 human beings into a cell meant to hold 75 with only one toilet, you know you are violating policy and endangering the health of those under your care. When your Field Operations Supervisor (FOS) demands you throw away all the belongings and medicine of those in your custody, you are aware that some men, women and children may die because of your actions. When the Patrol Agent In Charge (PAIC) of your station orders you to dump contaminated water used to clean the holding cells into the city's drinking water, you know that you are breaking the law. And when the President of the United States orders you to put asylum seekers on a bus to be shipped to concentration camps on military bases so that they will be hidden from the public and the press...well, let's be honest...you know this is not going to end well.

Need I go on?

As you know, to be a law enforcement officer in any capacity means you must be both a humanitarian and an enforcer of the law. That's the trust the public puts in you, and a challenge you accepted. So, I get why you're stressed out. I understand why you might be fighting more with your spouse and your kids are mad at you for never being around. I know that even when you sleep, the images and things you are ordered to do creep into your dreams. They weigh on many of you because not all policies currently being ordered are written, not all orders being given by management are legal. And you damn well know that in the end, management will blame you. You know that unwritten policies and orders are their way of protecting themselves while making you take the fall.

Whether or not you are ever legally held accountable for following the illegal, verbal orders of a superior is only one issue you will be faced with as the years pass. Trust me on this. How do you think your family will see you? How do you think your community will view your actions? What do you imagine your relationship with your children to be like after you develop post-traumatic stress disorder from the things you are currently doing and seeing? "Just following orders" won't hack it when this is all over.

Look around. How many of your fellow agents have already quit? How many are having issues with drugs and alcohol? Are cheating on their spouses? Are on their second or third divorce? How many of your fellow agents have killed themselves or threatened to do so?

Yes, I know.

As I see it, if you intend to follow your oath, you are left with two choices: either resign in protest as I did many years ago or demand changes from management and your union. You swore to uphold the Constitution and the laws and treaties of the United States. Keep that oath. You have a union. Demand they back you when you come forward with being ordered to violate those laws. Let them know you will pull your dues if they don't. Make them hold your managers accountable for ordering you to violate people's rights. Demand that all orders must be written and signed. Let them know that this is a humanitarian crisis created by this administration and that you have no intention of being held responsible for it. You are needed for those few that are smuggling drugs and committing crimes, not for families seeking asylum as that is not a crime.

That is what being a law enforcement officer is about. It is not enforcement at whatever cost. It is a delicate balance of governance that is needed at the border.

It is what Honor First actually means.

I was not so naïve as to think that Hiram or anyone else at Alliance did not have an agenda with me. The Border Patrol is notoriously secret about everything. This secrecy they demand from agents isn't limited to how operations are managed or where sensors are located, the things that are literal national security issues. It encompasses everything from what agents are taught in the academy to what is said inside the stations and done out in the field. The press is the enemy just as much as immigrant rights groups are the enemy. Only those with official permission, the high-ranking agents or the PIOs (Press Information Officers) are allowed to speak to the media and other outsiders.

Everyday Border Patrol lingo and culture is confusing to outsiders, even to those like Hiram, who know a great deal about the organization. The only things people outside of the agency know are what the agency wants them to know, but official statistics and press releases do not tell the whole tale of the agency and how it works. It is merely the picture they want people to have of themselves: riding horses, ATV's and helicopters, busting drug smugglers, arresting dangerous felons, and rescuing migrants.

Tales of heroism are spread widely to anyone willing to publish them. Local reporters who are willing to not question their highly polished statements that leave out any details of agent wrongdoing get the most access and act as a cog in the agency's ever-expanding propaganda wheel. Fox News, Breitbart, The Daily Caller, Newsmax are all counted on to spread their propaganda and disinformation nationally, and often I see it even in the mainstream press like CNN, the *Washington Post* and the *New York Times.*

Since 9/11, the Border Patrol has spent every year using the tragedy to justify the expansion of their budgets and power. While Congress increased their budget and allowed the chiefs to buy new toys, hire more agents, and further militarize the border, they consistently failed to increase oversight. More and more agents came on board but with the same poor hiring practices. Corruption increased so quickly that by 2012, nearly one agent was arrested every day for crimes like drug smuggling, murder, rape, bribery, and others, according to James Wong, President Obama's Deputy Commissioner of CBP Internal Affairs.

Instead of cleaning up the agency, management spent millions of taxpayer dollars to produce films, place opinion articles in national media outlets, and create all sorts of community relationships to craft a perception of honesty and morality that does not exist within the agency. This included sending agents to elementary and middle schools to participate in reading programs and Explorer junior agent programs, hoping to indoctrinate the youth in their ideology. They spent little money on changing their toxic culture and tons of taxpayer money on hiding it with slick propaganda.

I watched as the chiefs claimed year after year that the border was out of control even though the number of illegal crossings was lower than it had been since the 1970s. In 1995 and 1996, when I was an agent, less than six thousand agents were stationed on the southern border. We averaged over one and a half million apprehensions each year, which made me wonder what today's agents did all day with such low apprehension numbers. Even with nearly twenty thousand agents, the Border Patrol was averaging about three to four hundred thousand apprehensions per year before the Trump Administration. The fact was that fewer and fewer people crossed illegally, but all anyone ever heard from the agency was their propaganda of how out of control and dangerous the border was. Even today, under the Biden Administration, with the number of migrants crossing illegally at a twenty-year high, fiscal year 2021 had roughly the same amount. With nearly three times as many agents and resouces today the agency should be able to handle three million apprehensions a year.

So, when Trump came along with his not-so-original idea to build a wall, I was not surprised to see the Border Patrol Union state that they were against spending more money on such a project. We have had a wall on parts of the southern border since the Carter years, and while the border wall did cut down on much of the drive-through traffic, it did little to stop anyone from crossing illegally on foot. What the wall did do was push desperate people out to the dangerous terrain where thousands died. It has been estimated that over ten thousand migrants have died trying to cross the mountains and deserts I used to patrol. That's over ten thousand men, women, and children. Over ten thousand wives, husbands, sons, daughters have died out there and many still remain where they fell, yet to be found.

Walls have never stopped people from crossing our southern border illegally. Agents knew this when Trump suggested it. The union only changed their tune when they realized Trump was going to win the Republican nomination and that he was virulently anti-immigrant, which meant he was super pro-Border Patrol. The insecurity and low self-esteem of not being seen as regular cops that I recognized so long ago were still present in the agency, and they would back any politician if they praised them and called them heroes. Trump gave them his support once they pushed for his wall, and the Border Patrol Union subsequently erased from their website any mentions of how ill-conceived and wasteful they thought Trump's wall was.

This kind of insight was what I could offer to human rights workers, but more than anything, I no longer wanted to be silent on what I knew. I wanted to tell the truth, and I had a lot of secrets to tell. I could see what was coming for immigrants and the immigration agencies. I knew the agencies were prepared for this. I knew the kind of power this president would have over them. I also knew that the demographics of those who crossed illegally now had changed from the mostly single males of my days in uniform to families with children seeking asylum.

This is what compelled me to start talking with Hiram, to share everything I knew about my former agency.

WE DEPORT OUR VETERANS

I wanted to see the injustice for myself. I wanted to go to Tijuana and come back able to say that it was not true, that lies were being told. That maybe it had all been a mistake, an error, even though I knew it was true.

If you wear a law enforcement uniform, you can't get through a day in America without hearing: "Thank you for your service." It is said on the news, in the stores, at sporting events, in casual conversation. Ever since 9/11, it has become the defining quote for an entire generation. Perhaps code to let people know where you stand politically.

I do not care for it. Not because I don't appreciate police, military, or first responders, but because it feels hollow to me. Like uttering the words is some sort of magic spell that makes it okay to send our fellow Americans to the Middle East for some reason that doesn't make sense. It also pust all those in uniform on a pedestal without ever considering that underneath those badges are people with all the faults and weaknesses of everyone else.

As I crossed the border at the El Chaparral pedestrian crossing of the San Ysidro Port of Entry, I saw Robert Vivar waiting for me. He was easy to spot with his Unified Deported Veterans shirt that pictured a soldier in silhouette carrying a wounded soldier off the field with the red, white, and blue prominently displayed. He still loved his country even after it threw him away so many years ago. As we walked, he started to talk about a variety of different projects they were working on to repatriate veterans, but I had to interrupt him.

"I'm sorry, Robert, but I need a lesson on how and why this happens. Honestly, I knew nothing about this until recently. I know that people think I know everything there is to know about immigration, but I don't. Is it alright if we start there?"

We stepped into the little office not even a hundred yards from the port. Pictures of veterans in their uniforms lined the walls. Some from Vietnam,

World War II, Korea, various Middle Eastern wars, Navy, Marines, Army, Air Force. He explained that he was not a veteran himself, but that he had been deported for a drug possession offense when he was a young man. He became the co-director of Unified Deported Veterans to honor his son, who still served in the U.S. military. I could tell he was a devoted father, that he considered himself an American regardless of what the government said or where he was living and that he was the type of Christian who practiced in deeds and not just words.

We talked about how these deported veterans had served in combat with honor, how they were unable to finish their citizenship paperwork due to the trauma and stress they endured because of their service. They were veterans who came back with PTSD and found themselves self-medicating with drugs or alcohol. Some were arrested for theft, domestic violence, drug possession—typical crimes found among their American citizen brethren that they served beside. The only difference was that these vets were not citizens, and they had not finished their paperwork to become one before they committed a crime. Once arrested for a felony, especially for a drug or violent felony, immigration put a hold on their release from prison and deported them.

"How does the military feel about this? Seems like they would be on your side because of their service."

"Some are, but many say that they knew the rules when they signed up. The military itself stays clear of it. They won't back us. But they served their time just like those vets who are citizens. They got a second chance," he replied.

"So, you're saying that this is a double sentence then. Deported vets are paying again for the same crime?"

"Yeah. I do not deny that some deported vets have issues."

"I would imagine so."

"Like some are just fucked up still. There are few services down here for PTSD and some vets are still using drugs to cope. Then there are those who were arrested for major crimes like murder. People hear that, and although those are only a few, they back off."

"Yeah, but as you said, if they did time, they did time. Is your organization willing to take a law that repatriates some but not all?"

"Does that bother you?"

"Well, it's not ideal, but it's also not my place to say, Robert. I'm an American, was born there. I've not been in your shoes, and I'm not prepared to tell you what you should or shouldn't do. I'm also not a vet. I'm here to learn from you," I assured him.

"So, you didn't know that vets were being deported?"

"No, and I don't think most Americans do. I cannot imagine being the immigration agent or judge that does this. Seems like one of those lines I wouldn't be able to cross. I mean Border Patrol, CBP, ICE…they're full of vets. They recruit heavily from there."

We hopped into a taxi and went to the beach for their weekly Sunday prayer service. The east/west highway butted up to the border fence in many areas. I could see the old Clinton and Bush walls right behind the new Trump one, and I thought of how absurd all of it was. Billions and billions on the same walls that brought the same outcomes, no changes except for more deaths.

Tijuana was still TJ. Little had changed even though it had been over a decade since I ventured down there. The smell of open-air mesquite grills mixed with the ocean. Down at the beach, the wall is painted with murals from local artists. There is an upside-down American flag, and all the names of the deported veterans are listed and another part where children had painted butterflies to represent migrants. Paintings by talented artists and those by beginners go as far as the ocean allows. The wall extends into the ocean enough to make even the best swimmer reconsider.

Mother nature does not care for this wall either. It requires constant maintenance as the saltwater eats away the metal. To stand next to it and watch the waves crash on each side, how the same sand swirls in the gusts of wind from one side to the other, to watch the children play on this side just as they do on the other side is to see how nonsensical it all is. The only difference between one side and the other is this metal wall and a man in a green and white truck with an assault rifle. I watched as a seagull flew over and thought it was interesting that the bird had more freedom than humans do.

Catholic services are held every Sunday at the border fence at Friendship Park, a bi-national park first built by First Lady Pat Nixon in 1971 as a place for families from both sides to visit. Passports are expensive and not everyone has the means to travel back and forth across the border. Initially, families separated by the border could sit together, share a meal in the area that was cordoned off. Border Patrol put a stop to that when they claimed that it was a security risk. Then they said that families had to stay behind the wall, but they could touch each other's hands and pray together.

Years later, the Patrol again put more restrictions on gatherings and claimed that drugs were being passed back and forth. This time they lined the wall with a thick grid of wire and made it impossible for families to even touch. From time to time, Border Patrol would get angry about something, accuse families of smuggling this or that, and shut it down. You have to be in decent shape, ambulatory that is, to be able to access the park from the U.S. side, as it is a long walk to the beach, then a fair way south along the beach up to the sandy climb where the park sits on top of a small hill. Seniors and the disabled cannot make the journey. The Mexican side is easily assessable to all.

After services, we served pozole and juice to anyone who needed it, veteran or not. I spoke with as many veterans as I could. Most seemed eager to tell their stories, to be listened to. A few, I could clearly see had mental issues, things I recognized from my days in the spa. Some things I recognized in my own mental health battles. The inability to look at another when speaking, confusion, moments where they froze from memories and flashbacks, ticks, and twitches were prevalent. One vet named Juan told me that he could not go one day without thinking about killing himself. I pulled him aside, closer to the ocean and asked him to tell me about it.

"You won't understand," he said angrily. "How would you know anything about what it feels like to be so lost that you cannot even get out of your fucking bed in the morning?" he cried. "When you can't even remember what it is that you need to do? When you're just lost and it's all too much, even the simplest of tasks?"

"I don't know your story, Juan. I don't, but I know mine." I told him briefly about my traumas, PTSD, my attempt, that I was diagnosed bipolar II. I told him that it meant that I got more depressed than happy, and then I turned my arms over to show him. He ran his finger down my left arm and then my right, turned them over and traced the scars on the tops of my hands, looked me in the eye, and started sobbing.

"Can I hug you?" I asked.

He nodded and cried on my shoulder for what seemed a long time, and I could feel his entire body shake with each breath as he held on tight. This veteran, this man who was my father's age, was broken, absolutely shattered from whatever he had experienced. It didn't matter what his pain was, how traumatic it had been. It was painful to him. I didn't need to know unless he wanted to tell me. I may not have had his experiences, but I knew exactly where he was inside his head, and I understood him better than most at that moment. I understood how hard it could be just to function and make simple decisions when you were lost.

"How do I get to the other side?" he asked.

"Small steps. Get your military assistance settled down so you have some money. That's first and most important. Then you can start looking for mental health help. You may have to visit several places. If you don't feel good about it or safe, then try another. Focus on only those two things for the moment. When your mind wanders to other tasks, remember, just these two for now."

On the ride back to the port, Robert and I hitched a ride with Hector Lopez, the group's director. "If I'm good enough to die for this country, surely I'm good enough to live in the country," he said. He was a giant of a man, and when he spoke, everyone paid attention. There was power and pride in his deep voice.

"I agree. I will do what I can to support your cause. I'm not sure if it will help, but I will do it."

"God put you in that green uniform for a reason, Jenn."

"I don't know about that, Robert. I'm not comfortable thinking like that."

MISSING

Hiram and I went to the beaches in Tijuana one day to take pictures and then go to his favorite taco shop deep within the city. I had been there many a time on a crowded day, when the mariachi music was loud and the tequila was flowing, but never when it was so deserted as that day. I noticed the light poles for the first time that ran along the border wall, standing as tall as the wall itself. All around them were taped notices of missing persons. From the bottom of the pole to as high as one could reach and perhaps farther, I could see pictures of loved ones missing from Tijuana, Mexicali, Guanajuato, Oaxaca, Mexico City, San Luis Potosi, and as far south as Zacatecas. Mentally, I could see them on a map in my old station; the distance that they had to overcome just to reach this stupid wall was amazing.

Crossed July 2016. Last seen October 20, 2019. Said she was crossing in Campo May 10, 2000. My mother, my daughter, my son, my wife, my daddy, my brother. She was a good person. He was not a criminal. Please help us find her. Call if you see him.

"It's terrible, isn't it?" Hiram commented, standing behind me.

"Yeah. That's one word for it."

"What do you think about it?"

"Makes me want to get back into shape and spend my days hiking again. I want to find them. Not all of them would be out there, but I know for a fact many are." We looked at each other and knew the pain we both felt from this border for different reasons and moved on to the next pole.

"I bet these can be found all along the border. In Mexicali, Juarez, Matamoros. Makes it very real. Something more than a number."

"Did you all know the wall was killing migrants back then?"

"Oh yeah, of course. Most of the agents at Campo were pretty unhappy about that in the beginning. It was something we specifically did as part of our duties, finding bodies. Most back then believed no one deserved to die out there for crossing the border illegally. But we were ordered to keep quiet, to not hike in those areas any longer because it was making Operation Gatekeeper look bad. I did exactly what I get angry with agents today for doing, I followed orders."

He looked surprised that any agents would have cared about the deaths of migrants.

"Yeah, but you stopped long ago. You're doing the work to understand that and see the other side of it. Putting yourself out there to experience and listen to people that have been abused by the Border Patrol. What former agent has done that?"

"None? I don't know. Some have, I guess. Doesn't make things go away. Doesn't absolve me of my past. It shouldn't. That guilt is important to me, you know. Whether anyone believes my sincerity in it or not, it's something I gotta do."

More than anyone else at Alliance, Hiram knew me. He knew how I could get lost in the moment with anger and frustration, how it overwhelmed and terrified me to speak out against my former employer, to say it all out loud. He knew that I carried the guilt of not leaving sooner than I had, of how I justified my needs for employment and safety over the abuse and inhumane treatment I witnessed on a daily basis. He knew that much of the hate I had for myself had come from those actions, those times when I denied my core values, those times when I looked the other way and simply said to myself that it was the law.

My anger did not so much come from my childhood any longer. It was not necessarily even aimed at the Patrol, but instead at myself. I had let myself down. I was angrier with me than anyone else.

"The wall was up when you were out there, right?"

"Not at first. Campo station's territory back then extended from the Tecate Port of Entry to Tierra del Sol Road in Boulevard. It was just a barbed wire fence when I first got out there in November of '95. The first wall changed the community a lot though."

"How so?"

"Take Tecate, for example, where they now have that area for the semi-trucks to pull into for inspection in the flat field to the east of the port? Well, that used to be an open field where the Mexican kids would come across to play soccer and swim in the little pond when it was hot."

"What? You had to run them off, I bet."

"No. I never ran them off. I played soccer with them when it was slow. When they swam in the pond, I watched over them, so no one drowned. Their moms would come out on the porch and wave at me, and I yelled down to them it was time for their dinner."

"No way!"

"Yeah. Seriously, and I wasn't the only one who did that. Sometimes they even told me how many groups were in the cemetery next to the mountain, waiting until dark to cross. It was just the way it was. They lived right along the fence and needed somewhere to play. On the east side in Boulevard, the east-west border road on the north side was the only east-west road that the small Mexican village out there had to use. I drove that road slowly, looking for groups crossing as they were using it to go from one house to another. Sometimes their cows got loose, and we helped them rustle them back to the south side. Other times kids ran across, heading north. They waved back at me and yelled that they were going to visit their grandma on the north side."

"What did you do?"

"I told them to be careful and to come back before dark. If any of them got hurt, we didn't care about their citizenship back then, we just got them help any way we could."

"How did it change after the wall was built?"

"I never had a rock thrown at me until that stupid wall came up. Seems counterintuitive but that wall made it more dangerous than if there was no wall at all. We could no longer see on the south side and people who wanted to throw rocks or shoot at us could easily disappear. Kids couldn't come across any longer to play. If they needed medical help, it was their problem. They no longer visited relatives that lived no more than a hundred yards north from their homes in Mexico because they had to apply for a passport and visa, which costs money. It was ridiculous. Don't get me wrong; I'm not saying there didn't need to be some barriers. There were places where carloads of drugs could just drive through. That had to be stopped, but the wall did little to stop foot traffic. They just climbed over it, cut it, or dug tunnels underneath it. What it did was destroy any relationships we may have had with those living right along the border, and of course, push migrants to their deaths. It also created a whole new market for the cartel to become involved in human smuggling. The wall increased prices for smugglers, which in turn made the cartel take over."

"That's amazing."

"Yeah, well, there's a lot that people don't know about the Patrol."

EL PASO

It was the summer of 2019 when I was asked to speak publicly about my time as an agent for the first time.

"We would like to invite you to El Paso, Texas. The great Dr. Reverend Barber intends to visit a shelter in Juarez, Mexico, and would like you to go with him. He's also asking if you wouldn't mind speaking to his congregation, and then joining all the faith leaders at the Repairers of the Breach Moral Mondays protest," Nate Hoffman said. Nate worked with Jose Vargas' immigrant rights organization, Define American.

My letter to current agents about how separating children from their parents would damage their own mental health and their souls had caught the attention of several groups within the immigrant rights community. I was asked to be an ambassador to Jose Vargas' group, which meant that I would speak about the realities of the Border Patrol when they asked me. The reverend's people called Jose's people, looking for me.

To say I was overwhelmed does not adequately describe my feelings. I knew who Dr. Reverend Barber was. I heard him speak of justice, or the lack of it. I often referred to him as the Dr. Reverend Martin Luther King Jr. of our times. The passion and fire with which he spoke gave me chills and inspired me in the way King's speeches had when I watched them replayed on television as a child. The values I believed in the most were what he preached about. I thought he was the bravest man I'd ever seen, willing to call out corrupt and dishonest politicians right to their face, right as they sat behind him on the stage at a community event. He always went to bat for those without rights: the poor, the LGBTQ, those of color, the undocumented.

"What you are doing takes strength, true strength," Dr. Reverend Barber told me in his deep, booming southern accent over the phone. I laid in bed late that night, ruminating on it.

I'd been told before that I was brave for all that I survived: my mother's anger, my father's indifference, the Patrol's rage. To me though, that wasn't what the word *brave* meant. To me, I had just gone along to get along as they said. Now this great man was telling me I was brave to stand up and tell the truth about the Border Patrol, to tell the secrets I knew. I didn't believe that I was all that brave now either. I was just confessing my sins and trying to follow my values.

I believed in Dr. Reverend Barber's words, in his actions. I believed he was doing the work that made life worth living, that it was the work that I wanted to do, the work I needed to do. It didn't matter if he believed in a god and I didn't, because we had the same core values. I felt pulled to El Paso then. To not go would lead to regret. It was an experience that I might never be offered again.

But I did not feel ready to speak.

* * *

El Paso looks like so many other border towns in Texas, like Mexico. That is not a bad thing in my mind, just a different thing. Many of the buildings have the same architectural style found over that monstrosity of a wall. It is the way it should be because it is the way it has always been. Just like the California border I used to work at, El Paso is a unique blend of cultures. The closer to the border, the more billboards you see in Spanish, the more you can find the best Mexican restaurants, the more giant murals are painted on the side of buildings that represent Mexican culture, that represent El Paso.

I noted how the city extended right to the wall in many places. In El Paso, the wall is like an ugly scar winding along the highway, standing tall so that everyone from miles around can see it, so you know that this side is American, and that side is Mexican. Much like San Diego, the closer I got to the border, the more agents I saw, and many more in plain clothes that I knew I didn't see. It felt oppressive, harsh, and cruel which was intentional as the government wants everyone to think that what goes on in border towns is dangerous, that the people must be criminals to need all of this militarization. That is what they want us to think of our border residents and neighbors to the south, but I knew different. Most of our border militarization is a show, a money-making con.

When Dr. Reverend Barber goes places, his people go with him. It was a Sunday when I climbed into a rented, black minivan with his media crew. We crossed into Juarez in the morning, traveled west along the border fence before heading farther south on a dirt road. It seemed so desolate compared to Tijuana. A few young men proudly dressed in their soccer uniforms looked to be heading to play in what I imagined would have been the only greenery in the entire city. We slowed for the occasional dog standing in the middle of the street begging for someone to throw him a bite to eat. It was heartbreaking.

His media team said that they followed Dr. Reverend Barber everywhere. Sometimes they got called in the middle of the night because he decided he needed to go to New Orleans to fight for workers' healthcare rights, or Kentucky to fight for miners' labor rights. It didn't matter where or why; all they knew was that they needed to document his work and be in his presence. As admirable as their dedication was, I did not care to be a part of delivering supplies to a migrant shelter in Juarez just so some famous reverend could get film of himself. I began to question my decision to come in the first place, unsure of our true reason for being there.

I had learned that volunteering was for me and for the people I helped, not for anyone or anything else. It had to be pure, altruistic, or else it felt cheap and smelled of white saviorism, which I could not stand. Questioning my intentions, my motivations for what I do in regard to immigration and migrants is important to me. I always want to consider if my actions will benefit the community or hurt the community. Will my actions take away or step on the work that Latinx activists in the community are doing? This was Dr. Reverend Barber's gig, and suddenly I realized that I failed to consider this and assumed he had, though I did not know for sure.

We pulled into the dirt courtyard of the shelter that consisted of many small, run-down houses. Chickens, pigs, and dogs ran around freely in between the children playing. It was not much different than being raised on a farm in Alabama, just poorer. There was already a crowd of people waiting to see the reverend. As he walked over to the shelter and they crowded around, I noticed others walked up slowly trying to see who this big man dressed in all black was, what he was all about.

"Who is he?" a small voice by my side said in Spanish.

"An important man. He's come to meet you," I said, digging deep for my Spanish.

"Me? Why?"

"Because he loves all people. He is a man of God."

"A priest?"

"Yes."

As he spoke, I stood off to the side with the little boy, away from the cameras and watched. Every few sentences, Dr. Reverend Barber paused for the translator. He commented on the injustices on the U.S. immigration system, on the racism of the Trump Administration, how the land on the other side of the wall had once belonged to these very migrants' ancestors, on how Trump wasn't the only racist in government, on how the Border Patrol was violating people's rights by separating children, on how hypocritical those so-called Christians were.

I looked around and sensed they were confused by who this man was, about why we were there in the first place. Perhaps they thought we'd just come to gawk and have our pictures taken with them, that we had nothing to offer but some supplies and a few kind words, only to leave with the evidence of our good deeds, patting each other on the back, crossing back over that god-forsaken line to our air-conditioned hotel rooms, cable news, and room service.

"May I bless your children?" he asked.

Those with children present shouted, "*Si!*" Others quickly ran off to get their children and desperately called their names, telling the older kids to grab the younger ones. As Dr. Reverend Barber began the blessing, he touched every child on their head. I turned and looked behind us to see little ones unable to keep up; tired from running, they started to cry. I picked one little boy up and felt the intense pain shoot through my arms and hands before passing him to those in front of me so he could bless them. Their parents had tears in their eyes. The thought that this important man would travel so far to lay his hands on their babies and bless them moved them emotionally, spiritually. I felt the sensation pour off everyone around me, and I realized then how large the crowd had become.

"Now I want to ask one of you to pray for us. Can anyone do that?" he asked.

A mother from Honduras came up to him just then. She stood no more than the height of his chest and it made everyone laugh. She had gone to the port of entry that morning with her six-year-old son, who was an American citizen, only to be threatened by CBP officers that they would take her son if she came again.

She started out slowly, quietly, allowing for the interpreters to keep up. With every sentence, Dr. Reverend Barber shouted out an "Amen!" or a "Yes, sister!" or repeated a phrase she had just said but in that southern Black preacher way I loved so much. The momentum built until she cried and yelled her prayer out. The reverend followed along, and the interpreters just let her go because it mattered less what she said and more how she delivered it. I looked around and saw multiple grown men crying when I felt someone slide next to me. A young man in his twenties stood to my right and smiled. He grabbed my hand, and we stood there, soaking it all in together.

I knew in that instant that I had made the right decision to come to Texas. The choice to experience something different, to walk into my discomfort and trust in Dr. Reverend Barber and his people was part of this new journey. It didn't matter how I felt about religion, only how the migrants felt. It was what gave them hope, got them through to the next day, the next week, to try again and again to find safety for their families, to know that most Americans were good people who did not hate them like our president and his followers.

A man like Dr. Reverend Barber, who came to Ciudad Juarez and prayed with asylum seekers and blessed their children was a miracle, an actual blessing even.

* * *

Every seat in the church was filled, and people stood in the aisles. Whenever Dr. Reverend Barber got to his feet, his followers did too. Whenever he shouted, they shouted. You didn't have to be religious to feel the power his presence and his voice summoned. Some said they were filled with the Spirit. Others felt motivated to act. Whatever you called it, whatever it meant to you personally, you had undergone an awakening after listening to him speak.

His people told me that I would speak after two asylum seekers from Guatemala, who were to speak about the brutality that they had fled only to encounter more at the hands of Border Patrol agents. It wasn't until they finally crossed the manmade line in the dirt that is our southern border and flagged down an agent who wore green, that they realized they would not be welcomed. They had been mistaken in thinking that there would be justice and humanity on the other side. Agents had only offered them rotten food, an outdoor cage, and verbal abuse.

I was to tell my story about my time as an agent and the things I had seen, the truth of what it was to be a female agent in the Border Patrol. I took the podium as Dr. Reverend Barber sat directly behind me on a stool. I explained who I was, where I had worked, and why I had joined. I talked about how the agency's motto was "Honor First," but that it was a lie. I heard Barber behind me say, "Oh, this woman can testify," and I paused.

I realized in that moment, following the young asylum seekers, that my story was not needed.

I had never been put in a cage or had all my belongings taken from me. It was true that I migrated across the United States in search of a better life, but it was not the same. I was born an American. Yes, my childhood was traumatic, but I still had food and a roof over my head. I still went to a decent public school. There was a system set in place for people like me when I got to college. No, my parents couldn't have afforded to help me if they'd wanted to, but the government did. And when that ran out, I got a loan from a bank to finish my education. A loan that I only got because my father co-signed for it.

I don't remember exactly what I said. I stumbled through somehow saying that I had witnessed the corruption and cruelty of the agency, and that I believed the young men who had testified before me. Those in attendance clapped as I wrapped up before my time was over and sat back in the choir section, confused about what I had done.

I couldn't sleep that night in the hotel. I felt like a fraud. The church was a space meant for the sharing of experiences of those who suffered at the hands of my former agency. Although I had suffered, it was a different kind of suffering. My suffering had been by choice. I could have left at any time but chose not to. Migrants, asylum seekers, did not have that choice. Their only choice was to flee and seek refuge or die.

I was grateful for the experience, but I needed to do more work and better understand what I was trying to achieve, what I was speaking about, before opening my mouth again.

WITNESSING

"*Vamanos! Vamanos!*" They went as fast as they could. Men and women, most in their early twenties, some a bit older. A little hand usually held in their own. "In one line!" a female agent barked in Spanish.

They lined up as she ordered them to do. The agent was chubby and out of shape like I was now in my many years since I left the Border Patrol. I thought of how easy it would have been for them to overtake her, and I wondered if she ever gave much thought to her safety, if it ever occurred to her that she could be in real danger if her so-called "prisoners" were actual criminals and not asylum-seeking families. That's what the new agents called asylum seekers now: "prisoners" and "invaders." These are the terms they learned from the anti-immigrant hate groups that courted the Border Patrol Union representatives after 9/11.

It was my first day volunteering at the migrant shelter in the middle of San Diego's downtown district. Jewish Family Services had rented an empty city government building to help transition asylum seekers from custody to communities throughout the country. I listed on my application that I was a former agent, but that I had changed my views on immigration. My abilities were limited as my Spanish was based on Border Patrol training and my hands were limited in their strength and function. I added names and numbers from Alliance San Diego for reference so they could determine if I was real, and to confirm that my intentions were genuine.

I watched as fifty or so Central Americans got off the large transport bus marked with the Customs and Border Protection seal on the side. It was a different logo than in my day but might as well have been the same. Trump's Migration Protection Protocol (MPP) that sent asylum seekers back to Mexico to await their asylum hearings in dangerous conditions had not begun yet. The uniformed woman with a badge and a gun called the shots. She pointed and yelled as if she was herding animals just as I had once done. I watched silently as families obeyed her orders, frantically scurrying over here and there as if in some military boot camp.

For the thousands of migrants that I'd arrested in my time as an agent, I had never seen a group so disheveled and ragged. My eyes twitched a bit as I fought off the emotion and watched them stagger in line. Lack of sleep, sickness, dehydration had broken every single one of them. Still, they were the lucky ones because they had survived.

Old habits die hard in me, and I stood there in front of them with my arms folded and my jaw set. My natural expression, the way my mouth naturally falls, is that of a frown, a cop face, a bitch face. My mind flashed back just then, and I saw myself in that green uniform, my gun hung low on my right side and a collapsible steel baton on my left. I saw myself yelling at them to shut up, to sit down. *These people*, *those people*, *the other* as I thought of them, now stood before me with their heads hung low, avoiding my stare like those of long ago.

I had forgotten how intimidating I could be.

When the gate closed and the bus was gone, I could feel their relief. Shoulders began to drop, and their tears began to fall. "*Bienvenidos a* San Diego, California," I exclaimed. A small girl ran up to me and threw her arms around my legs. Her mother cried simply because I did not toss her daughter aside, because I did not yell at her to get away but had instead put by arm around her. "*No hay pinche migra aqui*," I told them. *There are no fucking Border Patrol here.* Little ones peeked out from behind their parents' legs and smiled. Laughter came, likely the first time in weeks.

Those who were sick were ushered down immediately to our volunteer medical staff of doctors and nurses. The rest were seated and given snacks and water while they waited for their medical checks. I helped ensure that every person got new clean socks, underwear, pants, and a shirt. We replaced the laces in their shoes that Border Patrol had taken from them, claiming they could be used to commit suicide. I had never heard of this. Suicides in custody are rare. Extremely rare. The removal of shoelaces is simply to be cruel. Period. Shoes are the most important item a migrant can have. Without them, there is no walking. If they had no shoes or needed new ones, we had those too. Diapers, feminine napkins, bras, baby cloths, hats, coats—whatever they needed, we made sure they got it from our donations.

After a few hours, most had passed through medical and gone up to have a meal in the cafeteria. I stayed behind with a family waiting for a ride to the hospital. Father, mother, son, and daughter. Mom cried quietly, perhaps relieved more than anything to see smiling faces around her children. The little boy played with a toy truck I gave him. His sister couldn't have been more than seven or eight years old and sat next to her mom as dad tried to spoon-feed her some applesauce we provided.

She looked emaciated, like children I'd only seen in pictures from 1940s German concentration camps; sunken eyes with dark circles under them, her head too big for her frail little body. Her hair was tangled and full of lice that she'd contracted from being held outside in a holding pen of sorts in El Paso, Texas, by the Border Patrol. The local press had nicknamed the pen "the dog kennel," because that was what it was. Her face and hands, her clothing were all caked with Texas dirt she'd brought to California when agents shackled them by their hands and feet like terrorists and forced them on a plane. Trump didn't mind spending the money to dump asylum seekers, sick asylum seekers, in a blue state.

When I put my hand to her forehead, I could feel the fever burning her up inside.

Her father said the Border Patrol held them for twelve days. Agents took all their belongings, their clothing, pictures, medicine, documents that proved their asylum case, their food, and threw it all in a dumpster. When it rained, it rained on them, but that was better than when the sun beat down on them, he said. When they asked for water, the agents yelled at them. When the children cried that they were still hungry, the agents told them they shouldn't have come there. Agents told them they were not welcome in America, that they hated them. When they needed to sleep, they had to lay down together in the mud because the cage was overcrowded. People stepped on one another, crawled over each other. It didn't take long for one cough or sneeze to become many.

The agents in green laughed at them and treated them worse than animals, the father told me. They stood outside of their cage, pointed at them and laughed. He held a spoonful of applesauce to his daughter's mouth. Her fever was over 103°, the nurse said. She didn't move, did not open her mouth. I doubt she knew he was even there, or that she even felt the cold, sweet applesauce on her lips. She slumped in her chair and laid her head in her mother's lap. Her eyes stared blankly past me, and I knew she'd given up.

I knew that look well. The one that said it was just all too much. There was no more fight or flight left in this little girl. I never worried too much about the children who cried and were angry. At least they expressed their fear, their emotions. They got things out. I feared for those who sat listless and dazed, dissociated as I once had after being beaten by my mother. She had become one of those kids who could not say if they were hungry or thirsty, one of those babies who no longer cried for their mommas or reached out to be touched.

I knew that feeling, or the lack of feeling, I should say. I knew that it led to dangerous things like trauma that never went away, to building personal walls and attempted suicides such as my own. It was that utterly numb look, the disengaged detachment that preceded an attempt. But it wasn't a natural disaster like a hurricane or earthquake that caused this in her. It was what was done to this little girl, on purpose. This was what those agents in those green uniforms did to her. Her soul was fading away, becoming untethered because it could no longer take the trauma.

Her father collapsed to his knees on the linoleum floor in front of me and held his hands over his face. He sobbed loudly with his entire body like I have never seen a grown man sob before. He wailed for his daughter, for his decision to bring his family to this country, because he thought he was saving them, taking them to safety, to that American dream, to someplace better than where they came from. He heard that American police were honest, brave, and followed the law. He believed that the American government welcomed all those from foreign lands and brought them into the fold. Wasn't there a statue of a crowned lady in New York that carried a torch in her hand to guide all those who sought the solace of her shores?

"What have I done?" he cried. "What have I done?"

I told other volunteers that I would take them, that they should get the girl and the dad to my car in the parking lot while I waited for the doctor's orders. I drove quickly through the crowded streets of San Diego as I watched the dad's face in my rearview mirror. I wanted to tell him he could trust me, that I was not a bad person, but my Spanish failed me in that moment. I could understand more than I could speak.

I did what I should have done years ago, decades ago. I listened, and I believed.

He told me how they had to leave Honduras. That he was a house painter, that he was barely making enough money to get by when the gang stopped him on his walk home one day. They were young, brash, and not afraid of the police because they had paid them off. He was to pay them some amount that I did not catch, each month or they'd hurt his wife. He didn't have the money, hardly had enough to feed his family as it was. So, he took different routes home each day, at different times trying to avoid them. He was not surprised when they eventually found him as they always did, standing outside his little home. They told him that he could give them his wife, or maybe his daughter, and they laughed. Next time they threatened they would take his son and make him one of them.

He said the trip through Mexico was not bad and that people were good to them. Everyone in the group was like them, escaping from the criminals and the corrupt government. They tried to stay together in large groups to protect themselves from the cartels. They paid someone for a ride to the border, not knowing if he was a cartel member or not. The journey was physically hard, he said. They walked for a long time south of the border, and then more once they crossed north.

They would have stayed in Mexico if they thought they could be safe, he said. It would have been easier not to have to learn a second language, and he heard English was difficult. But Mexico was just as dangerous. People took money from the gang who threatened him, offered to take care of him, and bring the others back for a fee. They had to cross. They followed the wall, stayed on the road. He had no intent to hide, wanted only to find the Border Patrol and turn himself in. He begged them for mercy to save his family. He thought they understood because they were likely fathers too and many of the agents had Spanish last names.

"We are good people," he said. "Not criminals. I work hard. I will work hard to be a good American. We will learn English and my children will go to school and be good students."

"I know. There are many good people here. People who will welcome you, help you," I said as I pulled up to the Rady Children's Hospital and turned my hazards on. Luckily, the shelter had called another volunteer to meet us there, one fluent in Spanish.

"You are a good person," he said to me, and my mind flashed on the old man who'd said that to me after I had hit the young man in the shoulder with my flashlight.

If he only knew.

On my return to the shelter, I drove past the part of the hospital I had called home for nearly a month after my suicide attempt. I knew father and daughter were in the best hands possible, that they would be taken care of just as they took care of me. I thought about how much I had learned just by letting go of my fears, by tearing down my walls and allowing people to help me, about how I had no choice, just as this father now had no choice but to accept my helping hand, about how he was forced to trust me, to get into my car and trust that I would take him somewhere to get help, that I wouldn't put him in a cage or send him back to Mexico. I thought of how terrifying that must have been for him, and how terrified I had once been in my inability to trust. He had no reason to believe me after everything they went through. He was at his bottom, and mine was the hand that was extended to him.

I pulled to the side of the road just outside the entrance to the spa and cried with my face in my hands. I didn't cry for my suicide attempt, for fucking up my hands, for being shot at or betrayed by my colleagues, for being raped or the coverup, for being screamed or whipped as a child. I sobbed because I'd chosen to join and stayed in an agency for years that now did this to this poor child, and I wondered what that said about me as a person.

* * *

"Can you spend four hours with a pregnant asylum seeker about to give birth in the hospital tonight? She's only eighteen and alone?" the text from the shelter asked.

Normally, I spent a few days a week, three or four hours at a time, at the shelter. I helped with food service, daycare, welcomed the new arrivals, sorted clothing, hospital runs, and even helped as an airport guide once. Anything that I could do considering my limitations and pain I still endured with my hands, I did. A few hours of volunteering left me in pain for days. I rested, then returned as soon as I could recover, eager for more experiences. Each taught me something new about myself, about my past and my core values. Staying with an expectant mother was a first, though. When they texted back and asked if I could stay all night, I did not hesitate.

She looked barely eighteen and could have been a young girl at one of the local high schools in San Diego. A child having a child, an asylum seeker in a foreign land, dependent on the kindness of strangers. Lourdes' little Jacqueline had come already. The volunteer before me, a mother herself, had already taught her how to nurse, much to my relief. We stood outside the room to talk about what I should expect.

"She's really young. Like, she has no clue how to do this. You have to help her with everything. You're a mom, right?"

"Only to fur babies, dogs."

"Well, you speak Spanish though…"

"Nope. Well, a little. I understand more than I can speak. I'm not worried. We'll get through it. We have to; there's no one else available."

She smiled a worried half-smile. "She's from Honduras. Her mother and father moved here when she was little, leaving her behind with her grandmother, and she has no contact with them. Her husband is still in custody at the port of entry. They would not allow him to come because they could not prove they were married. You have to teach her how to change and feed her. None of the nurses speak Spanish, but the doctor does, though he's never here." She bit her lip, trying to think of anything she may have forgotten.

She gave Lourdes a goodbye kiss and left us to it, and suddenly I became worried. My Spanish was still more limited to what I could remember from the Patrol: orders to shut up, sit down, come here. My verb conjugation was terrible, and I asked if she would please speak slowly for me. She smiled and asked if she could watch television in Spanish like any other teenager would.

I do not make it a habit to ask those I meet while volunteering about their lives. Trauma, in all its ugly forms, is deeply personal. To reveal it to another is the equivalent of standing naked before strangers. If migrants need to share, if they want to, then I listen. It is never about making things right for them, or giving them answers to their problems, but just about listening.

Lourdes slept off and on throughout the night while I maintained my watch. I thought about how I used to spend the same dark hours hunting down people who looked like her, that I would have tracked her like an animal deep into the mountains where few humans ventured, that when I had caught her and she would undoubtedly tell me her sad story, I would tell her to shut up and sit down. I would have put handcuffs on her, shoved her back through the port of entry as fast as possible so that she did not give birth to an American citizen. I would have gone back to the station and told others how I prevented another "anchor baby" from being born.

Only now I chose to spend the night protecting her. Lourdes wasn't a terrorist, a criminal, or a national security threat. She was practically a child herself. She was a stranger in my land, asking for help, needing a hand, a mere twelve hours of my time. I held her baby, showed her how to wipe her and dress her and hold her head; all things I had learned taking care of my sister when I was young. We walked down through the maternity ward and back several times during the long night. We passed a deputy sheriff standing in the hall that made her pull closer to me in her fear. I held her hand. She offered her story to me then, shared it openly, and I listened.

She did it the legal way, she said. They had presented themselves to the San Ysidro Port and requested asylum and then waited for months until her number was called. When her number was finally called, the young couple showed up for their credible fear hearing and were placed in a holding cell while CBP ran their records checks. The cell was crowded, and people stood on top of the benches to get fresher air. The smell of all those people not being able to bathe and sharing one toilet was horrendous. The agents did not seem to care. Lourdes worried for her baby. She felt that she was losing weight on the sparse diet of burritos they gave her. Her husband was with the men in another cell. They had been held for three days before they released her. They didn't let her say goodbye.

When she told the CBP officer that she felt contractions, they quickly loaded her into a truck and drove her a few blocks from the shelter before telling her to get out with her paperwork. The officer pointed up the hill and told her to walk. Fortunately, a shelter employee saw her being dropped off and picked her up. She showered and received new clothing, stayed in an isolated medical room at the shelter for a few days with doctors and nurses monitoring her progress before she went into labor.

It was one thing to walk across several borders over thousands of miles, hitching rides here and there and then crossing into the U.S. That alone was brave, but it was a completely different thing to do while pregnant. Lourdes was as strong a woman as I'd ever seen. Gangs said they'd take her baby when she was born, and so they fled like so many others when the police refused to protect them. She heard the stories of the border, heard that they needed to cross at the port to be considered "legal." They knew that it was difficult to get a number, to be seen by an officer just to have a chance at asylum. Her husband told her that it was important to do it the right way. He did not want to start out in a new country breaking their laws, showing them disrespect.

She did not know how she would find her husband now. She wondered aloud if he would be released like she was or sent back to Mexico. She thought she should go stay with her cousin in Georgia. How far could that be anyhow, she wondered aloud. I did not say, because I did not want her to worry. It would be just her and her baby now. Another brave journey she would be forced to make.

After several feedings and changes, Lourdes finally fell into a deep sleep. I stood at the large window and looked out onto the street, rocking and gently patting Jaqueline's tiny back. Her warm little head against my neck.

My phone said it was a little after three when I heard her behind me ask, "Will they take my baby?" I took in a deep breath and let that question sink in for a second or two. "They said they'd take her in Honduras. Will the United States take her too?"

"No," I lied. "This is the United States. We do not take babies." I turned around from the window and walked over to the crib and laid her back down. "Your baby is a United States citizen. Do you know what that means?" She shook her head. "Because she is a citizen, she has all the rights of a citizen. She can work here, vote, go to school, become a doctor, a teacher, nurse, lawyer. Lourdes, she could be the first president of the United States who is a woman! Whose parents came from Honduras to give her a better life!"

She giggled and smiled; her brown cheeks turned a rosy red. "No!"

I nodded and could see the possibilities and the hope running through her head. I realized that her feelings were something I had never known. The feelings of fear that migrants faced, that type of trauma they endured and what it meant to come out the other side of it alive and have to face even more from a country that claimed it was a country of immigrants was not an experience I had. I could not know the fear she would likely have when agents showed up at her door a couple of years from now. Even though her child was an American, even though she did everything the way they demanded of her, they would still hunt her down like an criminal, likely take her child, and adopt her to some white family.

I did not tell her the truth at that moment. I wanted her to have some time before it came, some rest, some bit of happiness with the thought of what her daughter's future could be.

When mother and daughter fell back asleep, I kept watch over them. *La Migra* would not get them on my watch. Staring blankly at a book I brought, I wondered how many times I had destroyed a migrant's dream. How often did I arrest someone for crossing the border illegally? Someone who was simply looking to feed their family, to find their babies a decent education, a safe place to live. How many times did I ignore their stories, refuse to listen back then? I thought of the times when I told them to shut up about why they were crossing, that it wasn't my problem, that it was the law, that I was just doing my job, just obeying orders. Hundreds? Thousands.

Lourdes was a brave explorer. She was in search of something better, something safe. She'd traveled thousands of miles to an unknown place with an unfamiliar language. She was dependent on the kindness of strangers. She was a refugee of the world that she inhabited, not of her own making. A woman and child thrown out, time and again, when they asked for help. They never gave in, never stopped until someone opened their doors to them. Fed them. Sheltered them. Extended a hand and asked nothing in return.

THE AMERICAN NIGHTMARE

I met Andrea Guerrero, Director of Alliance San Diego, through my work with Christian and Hiram. She once told me a story about running into a Border Patrol agent on a train. It is an important story from which I learned greatly. She gave permission for me to share it so that others may learn from it.

She was on a train going north to Los Angeles and happened to be speaking Spanish on the phone with her father. An agent in green appeared in front of her. The agent probably would have ignored her had she been speaking English simply because she is fair-skinned for a Latina. When he asked her citizenship, she told him she was an American, because she is. Then he asked where she was born.

Andrea told me that at that moment, she felt immense fear. This woman is an immigration lawyer who graduated from Berkeley law school and worked as an attorney with the American Civil Liberties Union in San Diego for years before starting Alliance. She speaks English without an accent because she was raised in Texas. She knows she's a citizen and can prove it beyond a reasonable doubt.

But her experiences in life and with her clients taught her that few agents know the law they are enforcing, and that they often do not believe people who say they are citizens or even when they have documents that allow them to reside in the U.S. She knows that Border Patrol agents will not hesitate to violate her rights. She was well within their patrol area as are two-thirds of Americans who live within one hundred miles of any land or water border. This means that Americans who live nowhere near our borders are within the Border Patrol's enforcement areas.

Would he remove her from the train? Take her to a station where he could legally run records checks on her for hours? Run her fingerprints to see if she was wanted or had a prior conviction? Would she disappear as so many had after encountering the Border Patrol? She told him she was a citizen, and then she waited for his response. Her father listened patiently on the other end of the phone, worried.

It was likely that the agent accepted her statement as true because she is so light-skinned and has no accent. That is just the truth of it. Had she had more melanin in her skin and a thick accent, rolling her "R's" and pronouncing "J's" as "H's," she'd have been screwed. All that fear, that intense trauma, from speaking Spanish on that train to her dad.

This and other stories that I've been fortunate to hear are examples of systemic traumas forced upon specific groups of people simply because of who they are, of where they were born, because of the color of their skin. It does not have to be verbalized to them as children. It is learned culturally, through their parents, from watching television and movies, in the songs sung about migrants and *La Migra*. They see it in the agency's propaganda videos and repeated by the leaders of our government.

I also think of how much more fearful it must have been for Andrea simply because she is a woman. I used to tell myself that the female migrants would not have been put into those positions if they had just not crossed illegally. I now recognize how racist and sexist my thoughts about migrants were. I clearly see this now. I have never crossed the border illegally. I am not a migrant, and yet I was raped by a Border Patrol agent. That I had ever excused sexual violence against anyone simply because they had crossed a manmade line is appalling to me, and yet I did it.

Stories like this helped me to understand how much I didn't understand.

* * *

I sat in the lobby of the Harbor Island Hilton Hotel in San Diego and watched as the waves rhythmically crashed along the rocky banks, almost forgetting why I came down there in the first place. The marbled floors and nice furniture always left me feeling insecure, as if someone would tell me I didn't belong there.

Andrea handled the introductions.

"I'd like you to meet Commissioner Esmeralda Arosemena de Troitino, the IACHR (Inter-American Commissioner on Human Rights) President and Rapporteur on the Rights of Child, Commissioner Luis Ernesto Vargas Silva, the Rapporteur on the Rights of Migrants and Commissioner Margarette May Macaulay, Rapporteur on the Rights of Women and Rapporteur on the Rights of Persons of African Descent and Against Racial Discrimination."

Commissioner Esmeralda Arosemena de Troitino was a Supreme

Court Judge from Panama. Commissioner Luis Ernesto Vargas Silva had served as a judge on Colombia's Constitutional Court. Educated in London and a well-known advocate for women against violence in Jamaica, Commissioner Margarette May Macaulay had also been a judge on the Inter-American Court of Human Rights. Seated with us at the dinner table were various other IACHR executives, translators, and assistants all with various impressive backgrounds.

And then there was me. A girl from Alabama, a long-ago resigned Border Patrol agent who is opinionated, very much overweight, not bilingual, without an advanced degree, who not too long ago was in a mental hospital and has weirdly shaped hands that often do not work and cause me caution in what food I order, lest I be required to ask someone to cut it up for me. I felt like a hillbilly amongst the educated elite.

They were in San Diego to investigate the abuses they'd heard of under the Trump Administration's new immigration policies. Their every waking hour was filled with meetings: CBP, consular offices, immigration courts, the local Otay Mesa immigration detention center run by a private prison company named CoreCivic, local migrant shelters, and as many organizations as they could fit in.

I limited my conversation to those elements in which they took interest, and desperately tried to hide my Alabama mumble. I spoke of how the Border Patrol used to be, that it had always been a racist and an unaccountable agency, but that something even more diabolical had made them worse after the 9/11 terrorist attacks. I talked of how past administrations had been horrible to migrants as well, but that they were nothing like what we were seeing under Trump. I told them how we had built two other walls before and how it only led to more deaths of migrants but did not deter people from coming. I talked about the children and families I regularly saw now in the shelters covered with lice and sick with the flu, about the woman I'd seen with a clearly broken arm that the agents had ignored for weeks. I told them how I'd spoken with Border Patrol agents in El Paso and Campo and how they admitted to me that they were intentionally holding asylum-seeking families for weeks in crowded processing centers, of how they saw this as part of their deterrence strategy and had hoped they would tell others back home not to come.

"They do not have sympathy for these children, these families, because they do not see them as human beings. They believe they are coming here to take what is ours, that migrants are lying about needing asylum," I replied. "Agents are trained with the propaganda that is spread through the anti-immigrant organizations that are dictating policy in this administration. They have close ties to groups like the Federation of Americans for

Immigration Reform and the Center for Immigration Studies and other hate groups through their union."

Throughout the dinner, I answered all their questions regarding the culture and organization of the CBP and Border Patrol. With every answer, I felt more shame because I had worn that uniform. I wanted to get up and run from that table. It would have been so much easier to stop talking about it, to ignore it and just move on as I had tried to do after I left the Patrol, but I knew the deception and the dangers of the easy way. I knew what I was doing had not been done before by an ex-agent. I knew that this more difficult path, the one that made me constantly confess my sins and tell the truth of my former agency, was the only way. I shoved my self-disgust aside and kept answering their questions, because they needed to know the truth.

As I drove home, it occurred to me that I could not know what it was the commissioners were personally experiencing from hearing about the inhumane treatment of fellow Latinx people. I thought of how their faces twisted in disgust, how their brows furrowed, and their mouths dropped at the truths that Andrea and I shared. By their questions and shocked expressions, it seemed they could not wrap their heads around this new America that had quietly always been here in some form or another but was now brandished with extreme delight and labeled heroic and patriotic by those in power.

It was a night of grotesque honesty, one that tore away at the propaganda our country had always spread around the world that I saw now like a virus of self-righteousness and moral fakery. I think it hurt them personally too. I think that they desperately did not want to know about this America, about the depths of our racism as a country. For all its faults and fictions, America was at the very least an idea of equality, of freedom that had constantly been redefined by every generation. One that had never actually been attained, but one that still gave a bit of hope in many a hopeless place. And I wondered if that bit of hope seemed all but gone to them after our dinner.

* * *

Andrea organized the following two days of testimony from various immigrant rights groups, immigration attorneys, volunteers from the shelters on both sides of the border and migrants themselves. Each day, the room overflowed with people desperate to have their stories heard. I sat in the back of the room each day for eight or more hours, simply to be present and listen. It was part of my journey to listen as much as possible.

The Border Patrol agent took my son's birth certificate, tore it up into small pieces in front of me and threw it away saying my son was now unaccompanied. I have not seen him since. Please help me find my son.

My wife and our children were held in a cage outside in the sun and rain for fourteen days in El Paso. The agents called us animals, threw moldy bread and ham at us. They threw all our clothes, pictures, our medicine in the trash. They took our money. They told us we shouldn't have come to their country. Then they put us on a plane to here, San Diego. How am I supposed to get my family back to El Paso in time for my asylum hearing?

I pick up migrants sent through MPP (Migrant Protection Protocols) and sent back to Mexico through the San Ysidro Port of Entry to wait for their immigration hearings. Some wait for six months, others for nine. They are sick from being held in CBP custody, crammed into small cells, one toilet for a hundred people. They have nothing but the clothes on their backs because agents have thrown their belongings into the trash. They have not bathed in weeks or brushed their teeth. Women have menstruated onto their clothes because they are only given one sanitary napkin a day. They have sores in their genitals because they cannot keep themselves clean. Women and young girls keep saying the male agents fondled their privates and breasts while searching them. Sometimes searching them again and again.

My client was told they were taking her children to another room while they interviewed her. She has never seen them again and was not told where they are. That if she didn't want to lose her children, she should have stayed at home.

There are many migrants that do not speak Spanish or English. They do not understand what is going on. Many are from indigenous tribes; others are from other countries.

My client was told he could have his daughter back if he signed a form admitting he committed a crime and took a voluntary deportation. He fled Guatemala because criminal gangs had threatened to kill him and make his daughter a prostitute if he did not pay monthly. The police would not help, he did not have enough money, so he fled.

My client did not want to cross illegally. He tried to present himself and his family at the port, but CBP officers would not allow him to file. Told him to take a number and get in line. He went to where they give out numbers and paid the bribe to get on the list. He's worried though. He cannot find work in Mexico, and he's worried gangs will start looking for him to pay as they have the others. He's also worried that if his number gets called, he won't have enough money to pay the bribe required to get in the van that takes them to the port. MPP has created a system of bribes; a bribe to get a number and a bribe to get through the port when that number is called.

Over and over, hour after hour, the commissioners listened, only pausing for bathroom breaks. Many of the stories were similar but hearing them from the mouths of those who experienced them was the most compelling. It was highly unlikely any would see justice. The vast majority would never receive asylum in the U.S. or even Mexico. Many would become victims to criminal gangs looking for easy marks in Tijuana. Many more would return to their countries likely be killed or lose their children to the criminal gangs and corrupt police. No one would ever know their names, their faces. They were not even a number, a statistic, because it was doubtful that anyone was bothering to count.

But they still wanted to tell their stories.

I listened for those two days and watched as Andrea ran around, getting people ready to testify. It was obvious that not everyone could tell their story; there were far too many and too little time. She organized it so that the accounts would give the commissioners a full picture of the immigration system under Trump. This education had to include how metering at the ports limited the number of migrants allowed to claim asylum each day, how that had created long lines and then a numbering system and a bribery system. They learned how asylum seekers were targeted in Mexico by criminals, how they were then forced to cross illegally in a sort of entrapment style scenario created by CBP. They saw how the Trump immigration policies created a windfall for cartel members as they charged more and more to cross, even charging just to leave the camps when the asylum seekers tried to quit and go home.

The accounts of how agents yelled and cursed, how they sometimes beat and molested the seekers, were horrendous. We listened to the stories of women, men, and children who experienced this brutality while being held in the custody of my former agency. They told all of it: the spoiled food and unsanitary conditions they were forced to endure, how agents had taken their children, their spouses, how the agency did not maintain any way of reuniting parents with children, how they crammed them into small rooms. At times, I thought we were listening to stories about some third-world dictatorship and not my country, not my agency.

In the end, when the last person was heard and only the Alliance staff was left, I watched Andrea's shoulders drop. Deflated like an exhausted balloon, she said that she knew she could not get everyone's voice heard, that some had been disappointed.

THE GAME OF SMILES II

I recognized him immediately as he came up the busy Washington D.C. street that morning to meet me. He was a little slower, a bit more rounded as we all were, but still the same gray-haired man I'd seen in the news. I had admired him from afar for years.

James Tomsheck was the Assistant Commissioner of CBP Internal Affairs from 2006 to 2014, the cop who investigated the CBP for crimes committed by its agents. He had been a Secret Service agent for twenty-three years and former Deputy Assistant Director of the Secret Service Office of Investigations before he was brought in to help clean up the notoriously corrupt ranks of the CBP and the Border Patrol. For his service, CBP and Border Patrol stymied his investigations and falsely accused him of failing to hold its agents accountable. These were the typical Border Patrol tactics that I was accustomed to witnessing when the agency dealt with whistle-blowers or anyone who thought they could change the culture of the agency.

"I'm so honored to meet you," he said as he shook my hand.

"I'm sorry?"

"I know all about you. I know how you stand up and speak the truth about the Border Patrol. That is an honorable thing to do, especially in these times."

I assured him that it was I who was honored to meet him. We were nothing alike except where it mattered, in our core values, in our disgust for agents who committed crimes and those who helped them cover it up. Both of us tried to come forward about the corruption in the agency and were ordered to shut our mouths, look the other way, be a part of the team. We were from different eras, different parts of the country and we held different ranks, but it was essentially the same agency with the same culture, which meant the same reaction from those leading it: shut us up at all costs.

It was well documented at the time in the national press that Tomsheck was ordered by then CBP Commissioner and former Border Patrol Chief David Aguilar to tow the company line, to claim that all use of force incidents, including shootings, were justified. Tomsheck was ordered to lie, claim that the migrants were more aggressive and violent than the agents, that the evidence showed agents were only protecting themselves even when it clearly didn't in many cases. In interview after interview, Tomsheck had stated that Aguilar wanted him to focus on specific corruption such as the taking of bribes and agents who smuggled, not the rapes and assaults and shootings. This method would reduce the number of corrupt agents reported if they did not include certain crimes under the corruption label. It was a numbers game to them, as it had been when I wore the uniform.

The fact that CBP had any say in how internal investigations were conducted within the agency or the Border Patrol was and still is a conflict of interest, an obstruction of justice. When Tomsheck refused and reported Aguilar, he responded by giving Tomsheck a poor evaluation and began a campaign to ruin his career and reputation. Tomsheck was then removed as commissioner because CBP claimed he was not "aggressive" enough in his use of force investigations, even though it was upper management who was the one who did not allow him to investigate in the first place. Ultimately, CBP withdrew its negative evaluation and Tomsheck was forced out. Like me, he became a relentless speaker of truth regarding the corruption and culture of impunity at both the CBP and the Border Patrol. Like me, his life was threatened if he did not leave it alone.

We stopped at a small restaurant for coffee, and before I could slide into the booth, he looked up at me over his glasses and asked quietly, "Have you heard of the Game of Smiles?"

I'd not heard those words uttered by another person in over twenty years. It felt as though I'd seen a ghost. It was that sort of adrenaline rush that comes from fear, that leaves you a bit tingly all over because your nerves are overly stimulated. I realized the waiter was standing next to me, looking at me patiently. "Water, please," was all I could mutter.

The first day Tomsheck walked into his office, there in the middle of his desk like a welcoming present, sat a large file. In the early 2000s, as CBP was formed, a female Border Patrol trainee at the South Carolina academy was invited to a graduation party with male instructors and some graduating trainees. Once drunk, she was forced to play the rape game. After she passed out, they gang-raped her again. Unlike most victims, she filed a complaint and charges.

Months turned into years and as was typical of all internal investigations, the Border Patrol, FBI, OIG, and EEO drug their feet until finally, she gave in and requested to drop the allegations. I imagine the thought of having to relive her trauma over and over was too much. Nothing ever happened to the men involved, as far as I know, as far as Tomsheck knew. They may have served their entire twenty years already and could be retired now, living off that great government pension.

Nobody outside of the agency was to ever know about the horrendous crimes they committed and got away with. I wondered how many other women this had happened to and how many were hidden within the EEO files that no one was ever allowed to look at. EEO is intended to address systemic harassment based on gender, age, and ethnicity. It was intended to level the playing field for those who were not white men. At least that is how it is represented to the American public. The Border Patrol has instead turned it into a warehouse to hide their rape culture and protect its agents who commit crimes against other agents. They use it to wear down victims and silence anything that does not match their "Honor First" image.

They still do this today. The calls I get from current female agents and trainees continue to prove this. They are discouraged from filing criminal charges just as I had been and are instead pushed toward filing complaints with EEO, CBP's Office of Professional Responsibility (Tomsheck's old Internal Affairs Office), or with DHS-OIG. The investigations drag on for years until finally the agency offers a monetary settlement.

Many of the victims incur attorney fees and find they must accept the agency's conditions to move on with their lives. Attorneys are not provided for victims unless they belong to the National Border Patrol Council (union), and even then, the attorney representing them is part of the union attorneys also defending their attackers. Victims rightly do not trust these attorneys and often take on the expense of hiring their own. This then forces them to have to take the payout to pay their bills. It is a legal hush money system.

The agents accused of rape, sexual assault, and sexual harassment are never revealed to the public as the Border Patrol, EEO, OPR, and OIG all follow privacy laws that they claim prevent them from releasing the name of the offenders. Offending agents then can continue to be agents and continue to commit crimes just as those Tomsheck had described. Sometimes, the agency will move the criminal agent to another station or to another sector where he can find new victims to assault.

"Honor First, as they say in the Patrol," I said. "You realize no one ever says those words; no one talks about the game. I mean, I'm sitting with James Tomsheck, former commissioner of CBP Internal Affairs, and then you ask me about the Game of Smiles? This is bizarre!"

He smiled at me and waited for me to digest what I heard.

"I want to come out about my assault. I want to stand up and tell all these women who I know exist and have been victims of Border Patrol agents, whether they are agents or not, that they are not alone," I told him.

Weeks later my personal story came out in *Newsweek*. I refused to allow them to print my attacker's name as I could not prove his actions all these years later. That had never been the point of telling the story. Tomsheck's story was released a few days later by the same writer. Both articles received little attention because the editors released them right before Thanksgiving when most in Congress were busy preparing for the holiday. I doubt anyone in Congress would have paid attention even if it was released at a better time.

I took this personally and frankly regretted having trusted the author. It wasn't that I'd expected to ever find justice for what had happened to me. I knew there would never be any of that. I only wanted to tell the truth, to be heard, for other victims to know they were not alone and that there were many of us, men and women. I wanted to say it out loud so my shame could be released. It was out there, and I suppose that was all that mattered.

From time to time, female agents come across that article and contact me privately. They talk of the sexual assaults and harassment that continue in the agency. Their abusers in green span the ranks from trainees all the way up to assistant chiefs of sectors. Some are still in the EEO complaint system six or more years later, waiting for a response. Meanwhile, their attackers continue to work, unaccountable right alongside other potential new victims. All the while, anyone who comes into contact with these agents has no idea that the person who just apprehended them out in the mountains, the person wearing the uniform of a United States Border Patrol agent, is being or has been investigated for sexual assault or harassment and found guilty.

PEE PEE TAPES

In 2019, I came across a press release by the San Diego U.S. Attorney's Office that I couldn't believe: "U.S. Border Patrol Supervisor Sentenced to 21 Months in Prison for Placing Hidden Camera in Woman's Restroom." It didn't surprise me that an agent had been arrested for such lewd acts. I was shocked because that agent was Armando, my classmate who had been so kind to me, who I believed had been one of the good guys.

According to the release, he was arrested in 2015 for placing a hidden camera in a floor drain aimed at a toilet at the San Diego Sector Headquarters CIT women's bathroom to video women as they used the restroom. The article stated that Armando filmed women for at least eight months before he was caught. He also stored the videos on his computer, edited and named each one, uploaded them to a porn site, and earned money from charging people to view the videos.

When confronted, he lied to his supervisor, then San Diego Sector Chief Rodney Scott, and said that he placed the camera there only because he suspected the one female Border Patrol agent working in the Coverup Incident Team unit at the time was doing drugs. Armando of course had no warrant to do this. Besides, this was not within the scope of the agency's authority to investigate. Even if his accusations were true, Armando's so-called actions to investigate were outside of his authority as a Border Patrol agent.

According to the court testimony of an anonymous female FBI agent caught on camera as she used the restroom, it took three weeks before a subpoena was finally served on Armando's computers, which allowed him plenty of time to delete much of the evidence. The victim further stated that Armando shared the videos with many other agents, including other law enforcement agents from other agencies who routinely worked with the CIT unit on investigations into criminal acts committed by Border Patrol agents, but that this evidence was either erased or ignored. She stated that agents in the FBI, OIG, and San Diego PD who routinely worked with Armando knew all about the videos and were part of the viewing audience. This female FBI agent, the anonymous female Border Patrol agent, and numerous female janitors who were also caught on camera as they used the restroom sued the government, the agency, and Chief Scott for using the CIT unit to obstruct the investigation in addition to failing to supervise his actions and secure the evidence.[2]

This is an important strategy the agency uses when it cannot hide or obstruct the evidence of its rape culture. The silencing of victims is done by settling cases without prejudice, meaning the victims cannot sue the government again for these crimes even if they discover more evidence. The Border Patrol offers them a large sum of money, knowing that the victims will take it because they do not wish to go through the years and years of repeating their personal traumas and pay attorney fees. While I personally understand why victims settle, the result is that their testimonies and much of the evidence never get entered into the court record and therefore never become public. The Border Patrol uses settlement agreements as just one tool to hide its rape culture.

Agents who commit crimes are most often allowed to resign instead of being fired. This is especially true if the agent agrees to resign before they plead guilty. If the guilty plea comes after the resignation, then the Border Patrol can require the press to refer to the criminal agent as a "former" agent in the headlines. This tactic further distances their culpability in the crime in the eyes of the unassuming public. This was done for Armando. When he entered a guilty plea, the media reported it as "a former Border Patrol supervisor pleaded guilty" instead of "a Border Patrol supervisor pleaded guilty" even though he was an agent and used his position as a federal law enforcement agent to commit the crimes. This also allows for the agents to still collect their retirement or pensions.

More importantly, this guilty plea prevents a trial. This is most critical for the Border Patrol because a trial would cause the evidence and the coverups to become documented and open to the media and the public during the discovery process. A guilty plea by Armando kept the details out of the courtroom and prevented the names of his accomplices and the delayed response by the Border Patrol from being documented in court and then reported by the media.

We, the public, do not know how many women were videotaped, which agents engaged in the watching of these tapes, and what agencies they were

[2] See United States District Court for the Southern District of California cases 16-CV-00725-W-BLM, 16-CV-00750-W-BLM, 16-CV-OO374-W-BLM, and 17-CV-00576-W-BLM.

from simply because Armando was allowed to resign and pleaded guilty to voyeurism and making false statements to investigators. He was allowed to retire after serving his twenty years only because he took the entire blame and did not rat on other participants. His guilty plea prevented the details and the names of others involved from being released in court documents since there was no trial. The Border Patrol claimed to have disbanded the San Diego CIT unit in 2015, after Armando was sentenced. In reality, they simply changed the name of the unit to the Evidence Collection Team and put the coverup agents into other sector groups like the Smuggling Interdiction Group (SIG) to hide their activities.

I think about Armando every few weeks. Acknowledging his criminality feels like a personal blow to me because I cared for and trusted him so much. It was painful to see, and difficult to understand simply because I never knew that side of Armando. I often wonder if he'd always been a sexual predator or if the years of being in such a well-organized and structured rape culture led to his crimes. Maybe decades of watching so many other agents get away with such behavior somehow made him cross that line. I just don't know.

For all the wonderful things I could say about him, Armando wound up another disgraced agent like so many others. So many others.

Full Circle

When Andrea called and asked if I would be interested in looking at the San Diego Police Department's investigation files of the Anastacio Hernandez-Rojas murder by over a dozen CBP, ICE, and Border Patrol agents back in 2010, I jumped at the chance. In May 2017, The Inter-American Human Rights Commission (IAHRC) announced it would move forward with the case. It would be the first hearing of an unlawful killing by law enforcement that the IAHRC opened against the U.S. To share such an important case, to ask my thoughts on how it was conducted, made me feel that Andrea trusted me.

I met with Anastacio's widow, Maria Puga, and her attorney, Roxanna Altholz, the esteemed Clinical Professor of Law and Co-Director at the International Human Rights Clinic at Berkeley Law. When Roxanna told Maria who I had been and what she'd asked me to do, I was nervous she would not accept me and turn away. I would not have blamed her if she had. Instead, Maria threw her arms around me and began to cry. "I knew not all of you had to be bad! I knew some of you had to tell the truth!"

My only concern was that I would let her and the family down. Surely the Border Patrol had cleaned up their act from the days when I was an agent. The San Diego Homicide Team had failed to bring charges against any of the agents or the agency, but I did not understand why since the medical examiner had found that his death was a homicide. How a man could die from homicide caught on video, and no one be charged, confounded me.

After the San Diego investigation stalled out, the case was then investigated by the DHS-OIG, who again stated there was not enough evidence to warrant charges against agents. They further claimed that Anastacio had meth in his system and had high blood pressure, making it impossible for them to determine if he would have survived the tasings and beatings if those factors had not been present. Essentially, they argued that the victim's pre-existing medical conditions killed him, and in 2015 the Department of Justice refused to bring any charges.

I sat in my office at home for a couple of months with all the binders from the San Diego Police Department's investigation. There were mounds of evidence to go through: eyewitness statements, affidavits, pictures, autopsy reports, agents' depositions, emails, news articles, dispatch records from Border Patrol and the San Diego Police Department, and videos. I created timelines and charted who was where and when, who was interviewed and by whom, what was said, and where all the evidence ended up. I then sat down months later with Andrea to talk about my findings.

"Do you know what a CIIT or CIT unit is?"

"Not really, but I saw references to them in the reports. It's some sort of liaison the Border Patrol uses with outside agencies that are investigating them, right?"

"Well, that's what they officially say if they are ever asked, but that's not what they are," I said. I had thought long and hard about what I was about to say. Sandi and I had numerous conversations about the repercussions that would surely follow, and we decided that I had to say it. I had to tell the truth. "They are the Border Patrol's cleanup crew or coverup team. They are the guys who make it so that every shooting is a good shoot. Do you understand what I'm saying?"

"I think so but that's a pretty hefty accusation."

"It is. I've never been able to prove it because nothing really exists about them. There's little documentation outside of the agency and the stuff inside is heavily guarded. I learned who CIT is and what they are about when I was an agent. The Patrol likes to brag about every little thing they do, but they don't talk about this because the reality is that the unit's existence is illegal."

I explained how the CIT units are the eyes and ears of the Border Patrol whenever they are investigated for crimes by outside agencies. Looking at dispatch records for the Border Patrol, I could show that the CIT unit was called first to the scene, within the first hour and a half of Anastacio's beating. It took the San Diego PD over fifteen hours before they even heard about the incident, and even then, it was only because a reporter had called inquiring about it. That meant that the CIT unit and the agents who had beaten and tased Anastacio to death had control over the crime scene for over thirteen hours. In other words, the perpetrators of his death had control of all the evidence.

The CIT unit was present at the first meeting the San Diego Homicide

Team had on the case and gave them preliminary false information, stating that Anastacio had fought violently with agents and that they were forced to tase him. At every interview thereafter with agents and even Anastacio's brother who was a witness, the San Diego Homicide team allowed Border Patrol CIT members to sit on the interviews. This was the equivalent of giving the murderers' family access to the evidence and the investigation. It was a conflict of interest, to say the least.

San Diego Homicide never attempted to find the many witnesses crossing the border at the time agents were beating Anastacio. In fact, CBP officers were ordered over the radio as the beating was occurring to usher witnesses along and check their cell phones for any evidence by the same CBP officer who tased Anastacio to death. CBP officers admitted in interviews with the San Diego Homicide team that they had deleted videos and pictures of agents beating and tasing Anastacio and that they ordered witnesses out of the area without getting their names and contact information for investigators. Of the handful of witnesses the homicide team did interview, all had to contact the department themselves and ask to be interviewed.

Additionally, San Diego Homicide investigators noted that there were several cameras at the port that should have recorded the event. They asked the CIT unit to provide them with the camera footage and CIT complied. Only once the investigators reviewed the footage, they saw that it was from an hour before the incident and showed nothing. Investigators repeatedly documented their calls and emails to the CIT unit, to my friend Armando, who happened to be the lead supervisor on the case.

Armando and agents under his and then Acting Chief of San Diego Sector Rodney Scott's command at CIT delayed and did not respond. Sometimes they claimed to be confused and said they thought CBP had the footage even though the cameras were Border Patrol's and it had been the Border Patrol CIT unit who handed over the initial footage taken at the wrong time. As weeks went by, investigators continued to request the videos from CIT and eventually were told that the evidence was forever lost because the system taped over itself every ten to fourteen days. This was a common tactic used back when I was an agent. I was astonished to see that the agency still used systems that allowed the rewriting of footage.

If the homicide team had gotten the correct footage that day, they would have seen clearly what one witness, Ashley Young, had caught on her camera that night. They would have seen how Anastacio was not fighting back, how agents kicked and beat him with their batons while he laid on the asphalt with his hands cuffed behind his back and in the fetal position. They could have seen that agents surrounded Anastacio as he cried out for help and for his mother, that agents kneeled on his back and his neck, that CBP officers joined the Border Patrol and ICE agents in the beating, and tased him not once, not twice, but four times. They could have seen how two of those tasings lasted longer than the training allowed at five seconds and instead lasted for over ten seconds. They would have seen how a Border Patrol agent further humiliated Anastacio by removing his pants, how they laughed at him and circled around him as if he were an animal, and how not even one of them, including four supervisors, ever said they should stop. Unfortunately, the Ashley Young video was not released before the San Diego Homicide team gave up. It was released before DOJ announced its decision not to file charges. Presumably, they either did not view it, or they did not care what it showed.

According to the autopsy report, Anastacio had broken ribs, internal damage to his diaphragm, his neck, face, shins, thighs, stomach, and back. He had teeth knocked loose and black eyes. When paramedics arrived, they pumped many different drugs in him to get his heart started again. At the emergency room, doctors continued to inject him with drugs but ultimately nothing worked. He was pronounced brain dead as CIT agents sat in the first San Diego Homicide meeting, claiming that Anastacio had been the aggressor.

In the fifteen hours it took for the Homicide team to respond, CBP officers and Border Patrol agents had decided that their story would be that Anastacio miraculously leaped through the air with his hands cuffed behind his back after being beaten and then kicked the CBP officer, the one who had tased him, in his shoulder, back, and stomach. Investigators noted that no bruising or redness existed on that officer's body. There was no evidence that Anastacio had hit or kicked anyone, even though that was what the agents claimed.

When the autopsy was conducted, a CIT agent attended even though Border Patrol has no legal authority to investigate homicides. When the medical examiner was finished with his report weeks later, Chief Scott then signed an administrative immigration subpoena to obtain those medical records. When the San Diego Homicide investigators asked CIT for the medical report, Border Patrol refused to turn it over, citing HIPAA privacy laws that did not apply in criminal investigations. This delay, this coordinated obstruction, cost investigators another two weeks before they could obtain the report. There was no legal need for the Border Patrol and Chief Scott to have the report or his medical files. That information was outside of Border Patrol's authority, not to mention that the Border Patrol and CBP were the ones who caused his death. The use of an administrative immigration subpoena to obtain these records was illegal as former CBP

Internal Affairs Commissioner James Tomsheck stated in an affidavit.

Andrea, Roxanna, and Maria never gave up. Over the years, they managed to get affidavits from James Tomsheck and James Wong of CBP Internal Affairs. Under oath, they had stated that they knew about the incident the next day when they walked into their offices in Washington, D.C., that then Deputy Commissioner of CBP and former Border Patrol Chief David Aguilar ordered them and others to state that Anastacio was standing and not handcuffed when he suddenly started assaulting agents. Tomsheck and Wong pointed out that CBP reports did not state this, that it had only been Border Patrol who made this claim. Aguilar did not care and ordered them to lie. Both refused.

Tomsheck and Wong both found themselves and their investigators in San Diego blocked by CBP, Border Patrol, and OIG. They were not allowed to fully investigate Anastacio's murder. Once OIG finished its investigation, Tomsheck and Wong were astonished to see that the file was thin and did not contain an actual investigation by OIG but instead consisted mostly of copies of the San Diego Homicide investigation. The U.S. government never even bothered to do the investigation and just relied on the initial one that had been obstructed and misled by Chief Scott and his Coverup Incident Team unit.

"Think of the CIT team as an evaluator for the Border Patrol bosses at sector and in D.C. Is it a case where the agents without a doubt violated the use of force policy and thus violated the law? Is it a case where there are too many witnesses or other law enforcement is aware of the crime? If it is, they will tell the agent to resign and give the obligatory press statement that this one agent did not represent the fine men and women that make up the Patrol. If it's not, then they will strategize as they did in this instance and come up with a game plan to cover it up or clean it up. There are few incidents in which the CIT unit is not involved, whether the agent is on-duty or off. They report directly to the chief at sector who then reports directly to D.C. There is no oversight into their investigations because Congress does not even know they exist," I told Andrea as I handed over my report.

"Why did they do this to him? Why? Did he see something?"

"Anastacio had lived in San Diego for twenty-five years. He was an American by virtue of living here whether he was documented or not. When Border Patrol arrested him, the agent at the Chula Vista station who searched him, kicked his ankle out. That ankle had a surgical pin because of a previous injury. Anastacio demanded over and over that he wanted to see a doctor. He knew what his rights were and was not afraid to demand them like most migrants are. The agent refused and then brought in his supervisor, who also refused him medical attention. You can clearly see Anastacio giving them a hard time from the processing center's cameras. Look at when they take him out and go to put him in the white car. See how they stop in the hallway, and it takes more agents to get him out the door? See how this female agent runs into the hallway and watches from afar? She doesn't want to get involved. He is passively resisting. He does not want to leave without having that ankle looked at. He knows that if he does, if they take him back to Mexico, he will never get it fixed. They will never pay for it. He is a day laborer and cannot afford this."

"Okay, so they killed him over not wanting to get him medical attention?"

"Have you heard white people say that a Black person is uppity? Usually, it is said as, 'He's an uppity n-word.'"

"Yeah," she said.

"Please pardon me for saying this, but I want you to understand what I believe was going on in their minds as an agent. Anastacio was an uppity t-word. He was not afraid of them. Notice how the agents kept saying he was different than all the other migrants they've encountered, that he wasn't mild and timid like most? They are saying he had an attitude."

"Are you saying they killed him because he demanded medical care?"

"Yes. I'm saying they killed him to teach him a lesson; then they used the CIT unit to obstruct and cover it up. I'm saying it goes all the way to D.C., to the heads of the Border Patrol and CBP, to OIG and the Department of Justice. You have everything you need to prove it in this file. You just didn't know what the CIT unit was. They will say they weren't involved, that they were just assisting investigators, that CIT's only job is to copy reports from the investigating agencies to recommend discipline or to see if their policies were violated, but that's a load of shit. They say their CIT reports are not used for criminal or civil trials, but there's an interesting note from one of the union attorneys that represented the agents in court during the civil trial. See here? Here he states that he has the CIT report and the San Diego Homicide report. If CIT is only used for administrative issues, why are they using their reports to defend their agents in court? It's to protect the agency from civil and criminal liability. The CIT unit has exclusive access to everything the investigators have. They are using that access to defend the agency and its agents against civil and criminal liability and to muck up the investigations. They are investigating a crime that is not under their legal authority and messing with the evidence here so that even if a prosecutor wanted to charge the agents criminally, they cannot because of the evidence tampering and mishandling done by CIT. That's illegal."

On January 27, 2021, Andrea and Roxanna submitted an eighty-one-page brief outlining the obstructions of justice and failures to investigate the murder of Anastacio Hernandez-Rojas to the Inter-American Human Rights Council of which the U.S. is an active member.[3] The family and their representatives are hoping for a hearing sometime in 2022.

* * *

I was riding high on my findings. I'd finally been able to prove that the Border Patrol used an illegal, secret unit to cover up their crimes. It felt as if I had righted some of my past, as if I had made amends. Agents have killed over 130 people since Anastacio was murdered. Not a single one is in jail for any one of those killings. Some of the victims are even U.S. citizens. The statistical odds of every single one of those shootings being justified is unrealistic, improbable even.

Before Roxanna submitted her final complaint, she asked that I review it for any errors or misunderstandings. We talked on the phone off and on for a few weeks, tightening up the arguments and ensuring everything was correct and cited. As I was thumbing through the San Diego Homicide report one last time, I paid special attention to his immigration record. I'd only vaguely looked at it before. Like many undocumented men in California, he had been arrested several times over the years. Back when I was an agent, it was not uncommon for migrants to work and return to Mexico for a while to see family and loved ones. Then they had to make the trek again and cross illegally to get back to their jobs here.

As I flipped through each apprehension, I stopped on one from 1999. The station code on his I-213 or Record of Deportable/Inadmissible Alien was SDC/CAO. That stands for San Diego Sector/Campo Station. It dawned on me that I was still an agent back then. The name he gave was Martineano Hernandez-Rojas, but the picture was clearly him. The left and right index prints came back as belonging to Anastacio. He had been arrested on May 28, 1999, at 2117 hours. This was exactly eleven years to the date and the time that he was murdered.

I shook my head and thought how strange that had been—to be exactly the date and the time that he would die eleven years later. I glanced at the apprehending agent's name, thankful it had not been me. Then I glanced down at the processing agent.

[3] Family Members of Anastacio Hernandez-Rojas v. U.S., case number 14.042, January 27, 2021, Inter-American Human Rights Council, d3n8a8pro7vhmx.cloudfront.net/alliancesandiego/pages/3138/attachments/original/1612382784/210127_Additional_Observations_on_Merits_Case_14042.pdf?1612382784.

It said:
Received: (Subject and Documents) (Report of Interview)
Officer: JENNIFER H. BUDD
On: May 28, 1999 at 2136 (time).

Exactly eleven years before Anastacio's murder by my fellow Border Patrol agents, he had stood before me in the Campo processing center. I entered his biographical data. I took his fingerprints.

I was devastated. I had not beaten Anastacio, but this fact demonstrated to me how my actions, my being an agent, had contributed to the system and institution that did kill him.

I remembered what my mother had told me, about how it took many people to commit the atrocities of the Holocaust and Jim Crow. Anastacio's I-213 is framed and sits on my desk so that I may never forget my actions.

Saving Lives

In May 2021, I climbed into James Cordero's Jeep, and we headed to the high desert mountains in East San Diego County. Both he and his partner, Dr. Jackie Arellano, are well known and respected activists with Border Angels in San Diego County. Both coordinate water and supply drops for migrants in the mountains that I used to work and even farther out in the deserts of Imperial County. James and I had planned to tour my old patrol area to see how it had changed over the decades since I left. I couldn't say no when he offered to let me help drop supplies off on a trail. I was honored to be asked.

James and I rode the bumpy dirt roads that crisscrossed each other in a maze before coming to the bottom of one of the many steep mountains that I had climbed as an agent. He slid his Jeep's transmission into 4x4 easily and we zigzagged back and forth before nearing the top. He stopped and parked on a little embankment as I held my nose and popped my ears to adjust to the altitude.

James backpacked most of the items in. I balanced a crate on my right shoulder, using the only three fingers I had left that worked. It was the lightest milk crate with some cans of beans and tuna and ziplocked packages of hats and clean shirts. My hands have never recovered from my suicide attempt and still do not allow me to carry much. My fingers kept getting caught in the plastic mesh of the crate, threatening to break them if I was not careful. The muscle that protects my bones and nerves was long gone now. This short hike alone would cause me immense pain as any cardio exercise left my fingers purple, cold, and painful. I knew I would spend the next two days recovering from that alone.

When I felt the brush scrape on my forearms, I was instantly transported in my mind to twenty years ago. I remembered how strong I used to feel in my young, fit body and was reminded why I had loved my Red Wing fire boots when I felt my ankles turning in my running shoes on the rocks and roots. Boulders just like the ones that I used to jump off without a care now made me squat and slowly make my way down. I felt old.

On the other side of the boulders was a clearing where a couple of empty milk crates sat. Empty plastic gallon jugs of water, empty cans of tuna and beans, a few items of clothing, a blanket someone had used to lie down, and other trash were scattered about. I stood staring at the mess, lost in memories until James spoke.

"We need to pick up their trash. Border Patrol will say we're littering if we don't. Plus, I don't like leaving trash. It's bad for the environment. They leave clothing because they've been sweating the whole way up and now, they're freezing." He paused. "But I guess you know that."

I nodded and began collecting the empty water bottles and tin cans. We placed them in a pile and then began dating the supplies we brought with black markers. Trash and the clothing they'd left behind went into our milk crates. We took a few minutes to enjoy the view before heading back. As far as we could see, there were mountains. Even with the clouds being low, it was just mountain after mountain. It was beautiful. I had forgotten how beautiful my mountains were.

"Most Americans have no idea what these people are going through, how bad their lives have to be to make this journey," I said.

"No, they don't. Imagine coming all the way from Honduras or Guatemala and now someone tells you to hike through this. It's beautiful unless you're running for your life."

I picked up a soaked sweater left behind and smelled it. It did not smell of the sweat and fear I used to crave, but of soap. A man, I guessed. I pictured him as a young man, thin and fit as he stood looking out as I did now. I imagined he thought of his family that he'd left behind, his children, his wife, his home. As we made our way back up to the Jeep, my head began to pound with the familiar pain of an exertion headache I sometimes got from being out of shape and fat. I sat on a rock and told James I'd be up shortly.

"Take your time."

It was a monumental thing for a former senior patrol agent to leave food and water on the trail for migrants trying to evade the Border Patrol. I wouldn't have been surprised if they tried to arrest me for it, if they said I was aiding and abetting them in their "crimes." That's what they had taught me back then, twenty-six years ago. It was what I believed in. Even though I stopped destroying their stashes of supplies not too long after I arrived, I never once left them water or food. It was considered sacrilege in the Border Patrol.

I thought of what my former colleagues would have said if they knew I was doing this. The simple act of leaving supplies so they would not die on their journey, this act of humanity, would draw criticism, ridicule. They would say that I was never really an agent, never belonged, didn't deserve the badge, that I couldn't hack it, that I was a bad agent. Those insults once cut me like the whips of my father's belt, and I realized that I honestly did not care anymore. They could no longer hurt me or shame me for my beliefs. My value was not based in their approval any longer. They had already said all those things anyhow. They hadn't been true back then, and they weren't true now.

Fact was that I was a great agent. I did all that they asked of me. There were few matters at which I drew the line. I did not have any problem using the racist terms they required, arresting families who were fleeing for their lives and men trying to do anything to make a few dollars to feed their children. I pulled mothers from buses and left their U.S.-born children parentless, deported spouses and partners because my country did not recognize gay relationships. I beat a man with my flashlight when he did not obey my commands. I did it all.

As my headache subsided, I thought of all the times I had rescued migrants. I thought about those on the trains, in wrecked cars, the ones who'd been left behind in the middle of nowhere because they had twisted an ankle or broken an arm, of the car fire I'd help put out that left my forearms singed, and the babies I helped carry to safety. I thought about the ones I'd helped return to their families in a box, and the lost children I took care of before the Mexican Consulate picked them up.

I looked down at my milk crate with empty cans and dirty clothes and realized that this simple act did more to save a life than all the things I'd done in the Patrol. I could clearly see how our immigration laws are unjust, how they are killing people trying to survive.

I had been so wrong.

* * *

When James and I topped the hill heading south towards the Tecate Port of Entry, the new and improved thirty-foot fence stared back at us like an open wound that refused to be ignored. It was grotesque in its ridiculous height. CBP had intentionally chosen that height after running tests to see at what height climbers became dizzy and lost their balance. It was designed with the malicious intent to injure and kill, which it had already done several times over. It was also designed so that everyone could see the border. It was meant as a symbol to say, "This is ours. That is yours. You don't belong over here, and if you try to come across this line in the dirt, we will brutalize you."

"Over there is where I used to play soccer with the kids. I guess they got rid of the pond they used to swim in."

"It's changed a lot, huh?"

"Yeah. Not in a good way though. It's like a war zone."

As we headed east along the border road that I'd once patrolled, memories flooded my mind:

Over there in that arroyo was where I arrested a man who was mentally ill. He liked me and insisted we should marry. I think he was a bit fifty-one fifty or maybe drunk. This canyon was where I found a pregnant woman alone. North of the brickyard was where I saw a rosy boa snake crossing. Here's where someone threw a human head at my truck. That's the mountain where I caught up to a group from Oaxaca who made me laugh so hard I thought I'd pee my pants. Bell Valley was where Mark tripped the sensor one night and then threw a large bullfrog into my windshield when I arrived to check it. Over there was where the Yellow Scraper used to sit; the one all the guys jerked off on.

"Don't be shy. Just jump in there and tell me about this area we are in," James' voice cut through the silence.

"It looks different and yet the same," I said.

We saw the agent headed our way long before he got to us. The cloud of dust he kicked up gave him away. James had stopped and was taking photographs when he pulled his truck up, facing us, passenger to passenger. I noticed his beard and mused how that was not allowed when I was an agent.

"What are y'all doing?" he asked from the safety of his vehicle. If we'd been Brown, he would have jumped out and confronted us. Maybe even with his gun trained on us.

"Just taking pictures of the wall and touring the border," I said.

"Are you with anyone? Media?"

"Nope. Just out sightseeing," James assured him.

"Okay then. Well, be careful," he cautioned.

"Thank you."

With that, he drove away. I knew he would call dispatch and others in the area. He'd tell them that we were tourists, that he'd checked us out though he never came near our vehicle. We could have had people or dope in the car for all he knew. He had no idea why we were there except that we had cameras. We were white people driving a nice Jeep. We were not the enemy, not even suspected of being the enemy.

We continued west until we came upon a tall flagpole that held half of a wind-beaten American flag. It was a memorial, and we noticed a plaque embedded in a boulder at the top and an old, weathered picnic bench sat next to it. I wondered what type of people enjoyed a picnic just twenty yards from this ugly wall.

IN MEMORY OF ROBERT M. BAKER (THE JUDGE)
2/24/1926 – 3/30/2008

HE DIED HERE, "PATRIOTS POINT," SERVING WITH THE MOUNTAIN MINUTEMEN, DOING WHAT OUR GOVERNMENT HAS FAILED TO DO – DEFENDING THIS NATION FROM THE CONTINUOUS "INVASION" OF "ILLEGALS" AND "DRUGS" FROM MEXICO.
HE WAS A "PATRIOT" OF THE HIGHEST ORDER, AND OUR FRIEND.
R.I.P. – BOB (JUDGE)

"Do you know who that is?" James asked.

"Nope, but they were out here when I worked here. At first, we were supposed to stay clear of them. They were mostly old guys. Vietnam vets who liked to call the migrants racist names. I stayed clear of them. I thought it was a matter of time before they killed someone. Somewhere along the way, the agents and management decided it was okay for them to be out here and to associate with them. It's a racist and disgusting comment on our border policies, but then again, our policies are racist and disgusting."

I walked back to the Jeep and got a wad of toilet paper before returning to the picnic table. I dropped my pants and underwear, sat on the bench and peed at the base of the plaque. I felt it was an appropriate response to this monument to racism. Plus, I needed to pee, and I knew I was too out of shape to squat like I used to. I stood and pulled my pants up, turned away from the wall to walk back to our car and waved at the agent who was about three hundred yards away watching me with his binoculars.

We took the old dirt road north from behind my old station and noticed a black Ford Flex station wagon as it passed us heading south. The driver was a Latino male in civilian clothes. His car had no plates.

"Uh-huh," I said to James.

"Yup," he replied.

My old station compound still had the same chain-link fencing with barbed wire on top in the shape of a triangle. A few of the old buildings still existed, but the giant tan processing center was new. Migrants call it an "*hilera*" because agents keep it so cold it feels like an ice box. The sally port where buses pull up is surrounded by chain-link and has a tarp covering most so outsiders cannot see in. As we drove past, we saw a migrant child playing on a toy motorcycle. He was four or five years old, I guessed. An agent stood over him in full uniform with his bullet proof vest, taser, pepper spray, gun, and baton. It was surreal.

"There it is," I said as we circled around to the front of the compound. "Park across the street." We got out and stood on the side of the road in front of the *hielera*.

"What are we looking at?"

"This is 'Budd's crosswalk.' This is where that agent ran me over on purpose. PAIC Dirtycop made them paint a crosswalk here and named it after me. They thought it was funny."

The faint yellow crosswalk paint was still visible. I was reenacting the night for James as he took pictures of me when I caught a glimpse of the same black Ford Flex to my right. He had not expected us to stop at the station and suddenly pulled to the side of the road when he saw us. Without stopping, I asked James if he saw him. He assured me he did. When we were done, we circled back around the station to get in behind the Ford. As we passed, the Latino agent rested his elbow on the windowsill and covered his face with his hand.

"Ha! You'll have to do better than that!" I yelled.

* * *

John Kurc and I were early. We sat in the McDonald's parking lot in Green Valley, Arizona, sipping coffee and eating breakfast sandwiches, which would likely be our only meal until later that evening. I opened the passenger door of my car and poured most of my coffee out, thinking it was wiser to tank up on water. John had joined me to celebrate my fiftieth birthday by driving the border from San Diego to El Paso. I needed help driving such a long distance because of my hands, and it was good to have company. He wanted pictures of my trip as he had quickly become one of the most prolific photographers documenting the environmental destruction that Trump's new border wall had created.

We had been invited to an event called "Flood the Desert," in which multiple Tucson-area samaritan groups spent the day dropping water supplies in the areas where thousands of migrants were known to have died from dehydration. Our hosts, the Green Valley Samaritans, are mostly senior citizens as Green Valley is a retirement community located south of Tucson off Highway 19. With multiple Border Patrol checkpoints surrounding the area, migrants are forced to leave whatever conveyances they are in and hike the surrounding desert to find ways around the checkpoints if they do not wish to be caught. The surrounding areas around Border Patrol checkpoints are graveyards for migrants. From Texas to California, if there is a Border Patrol checkpoint, there are bodies lying in the harsh terrain surrounding it.

Barb Lemmon was our guide for the day. She had been a nurse in New Mexico before retiring to Green Valley. I found myself wondering how much water the seventy-nine-year-old could put out in the treacherous desert before she tapped out. To my surprise, she could do quite a bit. We drove south from Green Valley until we were about twenty-five or thirty miles north of the border.

Many of the water drop sights were not far from the paved access roads surrounding Highway 19. Our first stop was a culvert that allowed for the sudden summer rains that caused flash floods to run under the access road instead of over it. From the road, I could see the evidence that a group had laid up: empty water bottles, torn clothing, empty tuna cans. I slid down the south embankment and looked into the tunnel to find more trash from multiple groups.

"Do you have trash bags?"

"I forgot them," she replied. "I'll come back next week and clean it up. Is it fresh?"

"Yeah. Within a few days. It's a good place to put water," I said as I climbed back up to the road. I popped her hatchback and put a gallon of water in the crook of my left arm, knowing my hand could not hold it. The familiar nerve pain shot from my forearm into my left hand. I grabbed two more gallons using two fingers and the thumb of my right hand that still worked and made my way down the north embankment. I placed them together just inside of the metal tube that was large enough to walk through if you crouched, muttering to myself that I was thankful there were no bodies inside.

"How often do y'all do water drops?" I asked once we were back in the air-conditioned car.

"As much as possible. Two or three times a week."

"Do agents give you a hard time?"

"Every now and then, they'll be an agent that tries to make a point but for the most part, they leave us alone."

Along the way, Barb pointed out the decorated crosses that represented spots where migrant bodies had been found. Alvaro Enciso, an artist, had made it his mission to place a handmade cross at every location a body was found in the Sonoran Desert. To look at a map of the desert with every single body that had been found marked with a red dot in the last twenty-five years since Operation Gatekeeper and its deterrence policies is to look at a sea of red.

It is a genocide.

"It is more difficult for people to understand the amount of death our border policies have caused when riding around my old patrol area in the mountains. You must get out and hike deep into the terrain to find them. Arizona cannot hide their dead as easily," I commented.

"It's easier to see it here because there are so many. That tree there used to be a rape tree," she casually said as she slowed and pointed.

My mind flashed back to when I had been a trainee and first heard that term. I had forgotten all about the rape trees. PTSD flashbacks are part of my work that I must deal with.

"Who told you that was a rape tree?"

"The agents. They said the coyotes bring groups through here and rape the women. They throw their panties in the tree. The whole tree was covered in women's underwear," she replied.

"That's not from coyotes. They lied to you."

"Oh yeah?"

"Yup. Think about it; they're claiming smugglers come north over twenty-five miles and rape women at this specific tree in the middle of nowhere? It's absurd. Those rape trees are actually from agents," I informed her.

"What?"

"Yeah. I had heard of them as a trainee. They are too far north and too deep into the terrain for smugglers to be spending their time raping and creating this trophy tree. Might as well shoot off a flare and tell agents where they are. I'm not saying that smugglers don't rape migrant women. I'm saying they don't hike north twenty miles to a specific tree and decorate it. Plus, when I was a trainee, the guys who thought I filed a sexual assault complaint used to decorate the processing center with panties every time I was assigned there. It's a threat. It was a rape threat that came from agents to me when they did that. They have them all across the southern border. And no, I am not saying all male agents are rapists, but far too many are."

Near the small Arivaca Border Patrol checkpoint, Barb pulled over to a large tan cross decorated with flowers, rosary, candles, and toys. "This is where we found a newborn dead in 2006. It was horrible. He is called Baby Boy Arizaga. The mother was never found."

BORDER PATROL RAPE CULTURE

I often get calls and social media messages from current female agents being targeted by other agents. Male agents are also victims of sexual violence in the Border Patrol, but they are less willing to come forward. They usually start the conversation with all the reasons they do not agree with me.

Most believe that what I am doing, telling my story as an agent, is simply hurting the image of the Patrol. I don't disagree with that. The fact that the Border Patrol has a hearty rape culture is not a secret, but I disagree that the problem is with me bringing it into the light. It is the coverup system that they have developed, the lengths with which they will go to preserve that system and the hypocrisy around "Honor First" that hurts the image of the agency.

Agents who contact me tend to go on and on about my "left-wing" politics. They accuse me of wanting open borders and hating the Patrol, that I am simply seeking revenge for being raped by an agent. When I ask them to point to a specific quote where I said we should have open borders, it is only then that they realize that I have never said that. I have never said that all male agents are rapists, that all migrants are good people, that all agents are corrupt or racist.

It is only through speaking with me that they realize I was once one of them, one of the Fierce Five Percent, a title the agency uses to refer to the few female agents tough enough to make it through the academy while having the extra pressure of sexual assaults or the threats of them. Instead of addressing the sexual assault issues, management decided to spend taxpayer money on trying to brand us as some sort of superhero women. There is something about having endured and come out the other side that binds us as female Border Patrol agents, whether they agree with me or not politically, whether they have yet suffered or not. They know it. I know it. Even the women who pretend that it is not still happening so that they can get their promotions know it.

What I do argue is that statistics have proven that Border Patrol agents engage in corruption at a much higher rate than most other law enforcement agencies. I have argued that walls and deterrence policies have had thirty years to solve our immigration problems and have not. I have stated the fact that thousands of migrants have died because of these policies and compared these deaths to genocide. I have argued that a more humane and robust asylum system is a key component of national security and that using the Border Patrol to handle asylum seekers is not their purpose and must stop.

I argue that secret groups that lack any legal authority like the Border Patrol CIT teams are illegal, that to engage in such actions without congressional authority only harms the reputation of the agency and the agents, that for all the times management has bent the law, obstructed justice, or tampered with evidence in an effort to save the agency's reputation from what they would term a "rogue agent's action," their illegal actions have done more harm than good. Their own actions have done more to harm the agency than anything I have done or said.

And yes, I am the former senior patrol agent who broke the green line and told the truth about the CIT teams. I squealed. I ratted. I dimed the agency out to the Southern Border Communities Coalition, who then demanded congressional hearings that are still yet to come. They may have come and gone by the time anyone reads this book, but it all started on the day I walked into Andrea's office and said the quiet part out loud. It is through my research and others that we discovered how the agency covered up the deaths of Anastacio and many, many others. Those actions are what bring dishonor to the Border Patrol.

Every agency has bad people in it. And sometimes when people cross our borders without inspection, a small percentage are criminals. Not every use of force incident by agents is unwarranted. I have had to use force and was justified in my actions as an agent. I have also used force without justification. I am not so far removed from my time in the Patrol that I have forgotten how difficult and scary patrolling the border alone can be. To use force or not to use it can be a hard decision that is most often made when frightened. Cops are no more perfect than anyone else, especially when they are only listening to the propaganda their agency spews. I most certainly do not hate agents simply for putting on that badge and uniform. I have walked many miles in their shoes. I am not so old that I have forgotten what that feels like.

I do take issue with what the management of the Border Patrol has done to maintain this exterior sense of perfection, this false notion that no agent can do wrong and that migrant lives are not as valuable as agent lives. The lies, the coverups, the political schemes, the racism and sexism, the beatings, Tijuana choke-holds, tasings, rape trees, the Game of Smiles, the secret investigations, CIT coverups, EEO coverups—none of this is "Honor First."

The female agents who call, do so for the same reason family members of victims who have died at the hands of Border Patrol agents wish to speak with me—because they need to tell their stories to someone. They need to be heard. They know that I believe them and that I understand them. Female agents are still harassed and assaulted in the academy. Instructors continue to phone the stations that trainees are assigned to just to target the new female trainees about to arrive. *Did they "play ball?" Did they complain about the male agents? Did they file EEO?*

Female agents tell me that they are still expected to service the men sexually. When they refuse, they are assigned to the most desolate of areas, alone and with no backup just as I had been. They are targeted by management and written up for minor infractions. The male agents still play the betting games of who can get the female agents to have sex with them. The only difference is that they play these betting games on their smart phones using Signal instead of writing it on the bathroom walls and whispering to each other. This harassment will continue as it did for me until they give up and quit.

All these women joined the Border Patrol for the same reasons I did, because they wanted to serve their country, because they wanted to make a difference. While it is true that more is known about the agency today than when I joined, it is just as true that young people joining today still do not know much about the agency. Most are in their twenties, looking to become something, to belong to something bigger than themselves and naïve enough to believe the agency's propaganda just as I had been. They are proud to wear that uniform just as I was. The realization that much of "Honor First" is a smokescreen, a lie wrapped in a flag of patriotism …well, that lesson takes time.

"You don't understand how much I've had to put up with to keep this job, to get through the academy," they often say before stopping themselves because they realize that I do understand. "But everything you describe—the harassment, the lack of backup, the guys getting away with sexual assault—it's true. I see it. It's happening to me," they eventually say.

"I know."

"I just can't quit and let them get away with this. I have gone through so much to just walk away," they say.

"Yeah, I know."

"I want to do what they say, follow my chain of command and file a complaint with my superiors to allow them to do what is right."

"Sure, sure. I hear you. Just know that they will half-ass any investigation and it will get out that you are complaining. They'll start writing you up for every little thing, assign you to dangerous positions and leave you without backup. You'll be passed over for promotions, and if you do get them, they'll say you slept with someone to get it. They'll say you're not one of them, a terrible agent, a conspiracy theorist, that you're a slug, but I know you need to do this and learn for yourself. So, do it and I will be here in a few months when you've had enough."

A few months pass, and they always call back angrier than before because everything I described to them has happened. "Everyone knows that I complained and now they are shunning me. I'm being left out in the middle of nowhere all by myself. Some fucking trainee walked past me and told me I should learn to "play ball" if I want backup in the field."

"Uh-huh. And your female commanders are just shrugging their shoulders, saying this is how it always is, right?"

"Right. Why won't they stand up for junior female agents?"

"Because they got their position by keeping their mouths shut. Rape culture is not just about rape, and women participate just like the guys do. It's about all those other things like harassment and intentionally maintaining under 5 percent female officers and private social media groups that make fun of sexual assault and urging victims to settle crimes through EEO instead of filing charges. It's about keeping the dirty secrets of the Patrol."

"But not all of the male agents are bad," they insist.

"I never said they were. The problem isn't just with those committing these actions. The problem is also with those willing to look the other way. The problem is that management sees nothing wrong with it. The problem is that they do not believe female agents when they come forward, but they always believe the men."

* * *

To say I was astonished feels inadequate, disingenuous. It should have come as no surprise to me when Rodney Scott, Trump's Chief of the U.S. Border Patrol, made a rape threat against me publicly on Twitter. If there's one thing that I have spoken and written about prolifically, it's the agency's rape culture. But even I, someone who has survived that culture and knows it intimately, still question how prevalent it is and whether it extends all the way to the top. This is because I do not want it to be true.

Former Chief Rodney Scott is a highly respected Border Patrol agent.

I did not know him when I was an agent. While he was the chief, I did criticize him and his policies, such as when he ordered the tear-gassing of women and children seeking asylum at the border. Most of the upper management will not engage with me on social media. I do not expect them to. When they do, it is usually through an anonymous account they have created. So, I was surprised when he responded to my reply to one of his own tweets shortly after he had resigned from the Patrol. I normally try not to engage with agents on social media if their comments do not pertain to the Border Patrol, especially if they have resigned. Whatever their personal beliefs are in their private lives is none of my business, but when Chief Scott tweeted about California Governor Gavin Newsom, I felt I had to respond.

Calling CA voters—If U believe in transparency & truth U need to vote YES on the recall. After a ton of pressure, Newsom dedicated 40 whole mins to learn about border security—then he still miss-led U. CA deserves better.

I couldn't care less about what Chief Scott thinks about Governor Newsom. My response was solely regarding his use of the phrase "transparency and truth." This phrase being used by a former chief of the Border Patrol, an agency that knows nothing about such values, got under my skin. Especially, when I know the extent to which he as chief led CIT units in covering up heinous acts such as the killing of Anastacio Hernandez-Rojas.

I replied with a link to an *Intercept* article[4] that detailed the findings of our investigation and the affidavits from other top CBP management officials that proved the coverup and I stated, "You are a traitor to the oath you took."

So what was for breakfast? I investigated all of your allegations. Not a crumb of evidence could be found to support any of them. But I did find out a lot about you. Lean back, close your eyes and just enjoy the show, he replied.

The comment about investigating all my allegations confused me: Was he investigating my rape allegation? If so, why had I not been contacted? Who had he ordered to investigate my rape? CBP-OPR (Office of Professional Responsibility) that is heavily laden with ex-agents? He cannot legally order CBP-OPR to investigate. CBP Intelligence? CIT? Why would Chief Scott think he had the authority to investigate the rape

[4] Devereaux, Ryan. "Border Patrol Beat an Immigrant to Death and Covered It Up," *The Intercept*, February 4, 2021, theintercept.com/2021/02/04/border-patrol-killing-impunity-iachr/.

of a former agent? Did they speak to my rapist? How come I was not notified? Was he referring to my allegations about the Anastacio murder? Is he saying he ordered CIT or CBP-OPR to investigate my allegations that he used CIT to obstruct justice into the case? That's not legal either.

Whatever Chief Scott was saying, the admission that he used CBP resources to investigate me was terrifying and still leaves me frightened. My experience as an agent is that when the Border Patrol states they are investigating allegations, they are in fact only investigating the person making the allegations against them and not the actual allegations that have been made. I have not committed any crimes for them or anyone else to investigate. And if he was in fact referring to the Anastacio case, I considered his comments to be retaliation against me for investigating on behalf of the Hernandez-Rojas family and their attorneys.

But I did find out a lot about you. Lean back, close your eyes and just enjoy the show.

I read this sentence over and over. This comment is a well-known rape threat repeated by mostly right-wing men and women who do not believe sexual assault victims when they come forward. A variety of politicians and famous men have been called out for making comments along this line that if rape is somehow inevitable or unavoidable, victims should just learn to enjoy it.

- Clayton Williams (R-TX) – "Rape is kind of like the weather. If it's inevitable, relax and enjoy it."[5]
- Rick Santorum (R-PA) – "Rape victims should make the best of a bad situation."[6]
- Bob Knight (NCAA men's basketball coach) – "I think that if rape is inevitable, sit back and enjoy it."[7]

I replied to Chief Scott that I could not believe he thought it was okay to threaten anyone in such a manner, especially an ex-agent who is a rape survivor. He is a former chief of a federal law enforcement agency who has over twenty-nine years of law enforcement experience, and I believe he knew that he was threatening me. It hurt me deeply, and scared me to think

[5] Mikkelson, David. "Did Republicans Actually Say These Things about Rape," *Snopes,* February 27, 2014, https://www.snopes.com/fact-check/personal-foul/.
[6] Ibid.
[7] Moran, Malcolm. "Knight Is Criticized Over Rape Remark," *The New York Times,* April 27, 1988, www.nytimes.com/1988/04/27/sports/knight-is-criticized-over-rape-remark.html.

that this man would come at me and twist the knife even deeper into my old wound.

I know it doesn't make sense, but part of that hurt came from the fact that the comment was made by the chief of the Border Patrol, an agency that I had given so much of myself to. All the work that I have done trying to understand my childhood, the Border Patrol, and my actions as an agent still cannot completely break me of my old ways. Their attacks do still hurt me, but I can see why now. I see that pattern in myself that allowed me to forsake my own core values just to try and fit in. I know that I can be the type of person who seeks out acceptance not only at my expense, but also at the expense of others.

Message after message from followers, supporters and even journalists started popping up in response to his threats. I closed my laptop and leaned back in my chair unable to digest it all and stared at the ceiling fan as it slowly spun around. Without warning or requesting permission, images of the night I was raped by a fellow agent at the Border Patrol academy and the aftermath flooded my brain and filled my senses. I could smell him again, feel his stubble against my face, my hair getting stuck on the red brick, the feel of my leather jacket, the inability to protect myself, to control my body.

Chief Scott's public rape threat against me and the fact that Twitter refused to take it down, did more than bring back those memories and feelings of that night. It completely retraumatized me. I spent months unable to sleep, terrified of what he meant. My sensitivity to touch and sound came back, and I started to wonder if I was going to have another mental breakdown. Chief Scott led nearly twenty thousand agents. What if one of them decided to make good on that threat? What if some immigrant-hating Border Patrol fan decided to act on it? I had to take this as a serious threat.

I had spent years hiding my feelings about being raped, then years unraveling those emotions and memories after my suicide attempt. Flashbacks and PTSD are still common for me because I choose to talk about my assault, because I choose to listen and speak with other survivors. That is my choice. I can plan for that. This is what gives me power as a survivor; that I choose how to experience this continuing trauma as opposed to someone else choosing it for me. I decide when and how to talk about my rape, not anyone else. At that moment, Chief Scott's threat took that power away from me.

Whether he had intended the comment to be a rape threat or not, I cannot say. I can only say that I believe it was a rape threat and what my reaction to it was. His response to my allegation that he had threatened me came privately as direct messages and left me even more confused:

Please know that there is no sarcasm, anger or hostility in this message. Just so you know, I really did take your allegations seriously and asked OPR to look into them. I was and continue to be fully committed to Honor First. While still Chief, I wanted to meet with you to hear your perspective firsthand but was advised not to by counsel due to your very public allegations.

The only reason I am sending this today is that I believe you misunderstood my response to your latest attack on me. I want you to know that pushing back was NOT a reference to your previous rape allegation. I was referencing a video interview you did. I realize that it is hard for you to believe but I really do want bad actors held accountable. That goes 10-fold for any bad actors that wear a uniform—especially a BP uniform. Vague allegations don't do anyone any good.

If you have not formed a formal allegation against the individual that did you harm, I encourage you to name him and help hold him accountable.

When I got with OPR they told me they couldn't find any record of you making any formal allegations like the ones you now post regularly. The Patrol, like every organization made up of humans, will always have some bad actors that need to be dealt with. If you want to make a real difference, I ask you seriously consider naming the individual instead of trashing the nearly 20,000 public servants that are doing the best they can to secure our nation with what they have. I realize that somewhere along the line you had a bad experience. Please consider the possibility that you were the exception and not the rule.

As you know, I am retired now and can do and say whatever I want. I would welcome a face-to-face conversation if you are so inclined. Also—if you are willing to provide names, any evidence, witnesses etc. to support your allegations I would be happy to help you hold them accountable.

* * *

On October 7, 2021, I sat outside in the San Diego courthouse hallway, waiting for a judge to evaluate my request for a temporary restraining order against Chief Scott. It was the end of the day, and the clerks' office had closed, although they continued working behind closed doors. Every few minutes, a clerk came out to the lobby to tell an applicant whether their temporary restraining order had been approved or not. When my case was ready, the clerk called me into their closed offices and shut the door.

"The judge wanted me to do this privately. You have a hearing regarding this matter in two weeks on this date. You can have the San Diego Sheriff's Office serve Chief Scott or you can do it yourself. There are private services that you can hire. Make sure he has these papers when he is served. Oh, and the judge denied your request for a temporary restraining order," he calmly added.

I expected as much. Courts protect cops. The fact that my case was treated differently, that I was notified behind closed doors did not surprise me at all. I have seen district attorneys, U.S. attorneys, clerks, judges—the entire system treat cops with kid gloves. Especially when it comes to women accusing male cops of crimes. I thanked the clerk and notified my attorney, much to her dismay.

"Do you still want to go through with it?" my attorney, Michelle Celleri, asked over the phone.

"I don't want to do any of this. I don't want to file a restraining order against the former chief of the Border Patrol. I doubt we will succeed even if we are able to meet the requirements to justify the order because I just don't think a judge will take his weapons away. It's likely this will be an exercise in futility, but I am genuinely afraid. He lives in the same city as I do, and I am concerned about his violent followers, which include trained and armed agents. I've already lived this. I've survived this, and now I must go through this shit again? I can't sit here and preach about how victims must come forward to end this rape culture if I'm not willing to do it myself! No, I don't want to do it, but I will," I assured her.

* * *

The hearing date was set for November 18, 2021, in San Diego Superior Court. I was surprised to see Chief Scott show up. I had wrongly assumed he would just use the Covid precautions and attend virtually. He was alone and intended to represent himself. Michelle and I sat with my wife, Andrea, and two other friends who came to support me. It was early afternoon before we finally got in front of a judge. The new courtroom was empty except for those involved, my support crew, a bailiff, and the court clerk. All statements of the hearing are from court transcripts.

Sitting next to Michelle at the counsel's table, I looked up at the screen showing who all was attending virtually. I noticed Roxanna Altholz, attorney for Anastacio's family, was watching along with several other people I did not recognize. Since Chief Scott had stated he was not referring to my rape in the tweet, I assumed he was talking about my work on the Anastacio case. This in turn begged the question if Chief Scott targeted me and had ordered CBP-OPR to investigate me for advising on the Anastacio case, which is why the family's attorney was interested.

Chief Scott was given the opportunity to provide an opening statement in which he testified under oath to Judge Robert C. Longstreth that he never meant to threaten me with rape, and he denied even knowing that the phrase he used was a classic threat of rape. I thought of the old

Border Patrol motto guys used when they had been accused of sexual assault or threats of sexual assault: deny, deny, deny, counter-allegate, deny.

The following dialogue is taken directly from court transcripts.

"Well, I didn't see that your written statement really addressed the thing to which she had the most concern about," replied Judge Longstreth.

"I assert, sir, that there was no threat," Chief Scott denied.

"I'm just saying that there's one thing that you're not addressing that maybe you want to address. So, just as a heads up. And it's up to you. I've read your comments on that. I'm saying there's one particular comment that you made that she reacted to, and I didn't see anything in your statement about why you made that comment or what you meant by it," the judge warned.

"Okay," Chief Scott replied.

"You know, why given the history of what the Border Patrol has done, you would think that was a clever thing to do. So, you can repeat what you've already said, but that's what I'm really most interested in, and maybe during your testimony, you can address that," the judge continued. "Well, understand that there's a particular statement that she makes that she was particularly concerned about, and if you've addressed that in your statement as to why you said that or what you meant by that, I—you know, that's what I'm looking for, and I'm still not hearing that."

I was called first to the stand and given the option of staying where I was, next to Michelle, or sitting next to the judge on the witness stand. I chose the witness stand so that Chief Scott could see my face as I spoke to him. I did not prepare much, as I wanted my testimony to be raw and real. I had no intentions of anything other than telling the truth, and that requires no rehearsal. As I sat and removed my Covid mask, I noticed for the first time that my hands were shaking. I couldn't believe that after more than twenty years, I was sitting in a courtroom about to talk about my sexual assault and what it did to me.

Michelle asked, "Did anything ever happen to you?"

"I was raped by a classmate in October 1995."

"Can you describe it a little bit more in detail about what happened?"

"Each of the academies have a local bar, and I had gone that evening. It was a weekend evening, and I watched my Auburn Tigers play. I had a burger and a beer and started to walk home, as I usually did, and my classmate walked up beside me and said, 'You know, you shouldn't walk alone. It's dark.' And I kind of laughed and said, 'Well, it's a federal law enforcement academy. If I'm not safe here, I'm not safe anywhere.' And then we talked on the way home. And when we got to the back of my townhome where other female agents resided, that's where he sexually assaulted me."

"And did you report this to anybody?"

"The following day in physical training I was forced to fight my rapist. And they knew about it because I had a black eye and a busted lip and bruised ribs, and so it was visual. And you could tell—I could feel a difference in how people were reacting toward me. And nobody said anything. And I was afraid to say anything because I was afraid I'd lose my job."

"So the next day at training, did you report it to your superiors?"

"I did report it. I reported it to my two physical training instructors, because they forced me to fight my rapist. And I told them that I would fight anybody. I know I couldn't choose who I had to fight. But I wasn't going to fight this guy again. And they told me I had to file EEO. And I said I want to report this to the police. And they said, 'No, you can't. You can only file EEO.' And I said, 'I'm not going to file EEO because every woman in here that files EEO has her training stopped. And I need this job.' So I did report it to my training instructors, and asked to report it to the police, and they said, 'No, your only choice is to file EEO and stop your training.'"

"You stayed with the Border Patrol after that?"

"I did. I stayed for six years."

Then I testified to the rape threat Chief Scott had made and how it affected me, and how his private message claimed to not be about rape, but then seemed like it was. Whether he was referring to my sexual assault or being involved in the Anastacio case, having CBP-OPR investigate me was outside of his authority as the Chief of the Border Patrol and no one ever interviewed me on any of it.

When it was Chief Scott's turn to question me, he asked about my allegations against Dirtycop and why I did not file an official complaint. Once again, I testified that I had but that the San Diego Sector Intelligence PAIC refused to allow it. His argument seemed to be that because I had accused another high-ranking of corruption over twenty years ago and nothing became of it, I was making up his rape threat and wrongly accusing him as well.

And then came the questions from the judge that all rape victims and victims of rape threats must endure: Did I really think that Chief Scott would hurt me or rape me? Did I really think Chief Scott's followers would hurt me or rape me? These questions are always asked by courts and put the victims in charge of determining what the person making the threat actually intended.

My response was that Chief Scott was a member of the infamous 10-15 Facebook group that celebrated the agency's rape culture and did not seem to think the sexual assault memes of Donald Trump playing the Game of Smiles with Representative Ocasio-Cortez was a problem. So yes, I took his threat seriously. Chief Scott claimed that he had not seen that meme or many of the others. The judge asked him if he ever left the group even after the rape memes became public. Chief Scott admitted that he never did leave the group.

Chief Scott testified that he did not know about my involvement with the Anastacio case, and that he was referring to my allegations about Campo station management. He stated that he did not look at the article I referenced from the *Intercept* or at any of the replies that said his comments were considered a rape threat. He was corrected by my attorney and forced to admit that he did see some of the responses describing his comments as a rape threat and had responded to one.

"But I did want to ask you," my attorney pressed, "if you heard that people thought that this was a rape threat or a threat of it—you didn't take it down, did you?"

"I did not. My number one concern was reaching out to Ms. Budd and making sure that she didn't—she knew that was not my reference. And in over twenty-nine years of law enforcement, I've been taught as soon as someone says any type of legal action, you just freeze everything. So, it is what it is," he replied.

"I'm sorry, you freeze on everything except you that you got back to her directly. That's not freezing, right?" asked the judge.

Chief Scott's explanation did not sit well with me. My time in the agency, all the research and talks I've had over the years with agents current and former, from the highest ranks to the lowest, indicated that the Border Patrol still did not teach its agents how to properly handle evidence. The agency was still using its various Coverup Incident Team units, still covering up evidence and tampering with witnesses on every single incident. That included the infamous 10-15 investigation in which agents shut down the entire group and deleted everything before DHS-OIG could collect it. OIG could have subpoenaed the records from Facebook but did not. The investigation was half-assed like always.

"Looking back on it now—maybe you were the one person in the world that's never heard of 'lie back and take it' as referring to rape. I can tell you it's very, very common. And looking back on it now, do you understand where she was coming from?" Judge Longstreth asked Chief Scott.

"So, the short answer is yes now, but I've asked a lot of people, and even I went back and looked at like how many impressions—how many followers Ms. Budd has versus I do, and I asked a lot of people, I read it, and they said they didn't take it that way, and then I said, wait, if you were a rape victim..."

"You need to get out more, sir," the Court interrupted. "You need to get a broader group of people than who you are referring to. You need to, you know, be a little bit more aware, especially in the context of where you knew this was an issue with the Border Patrol."

After he was done denying all my accusations, Chief Scott then made allegations against me just as the motto prescribes. He admitted to personally calling former agents who worked with me to try and dig up dirt on me. He attempted to paint himself and the agency as victims and me as the perpetrator.

"She did not have a good reputation at Campo," he said. "They told me she was a conspiracy theorist and she saw bogeymen, basically behind every door, but whenever people looked into it, they couldn't find any evidence to back up any of the allegations."

In the end, the judge found that we did not meet the legal threshold to obtain the restraining order. Chief Scott insisted that he was merely trying to reach out to me and that I had misunderstood him. The judge responded, "Do you think maybe that if there's all these dozens of people in the Border Patrol that have no idea that using that phrase, you know, suffered rape as a bad thing, and then maybe this is a teaching moment for Border Patrol, you know, maybe—maybe that's something that can happen? And maybe the fact that we can have so many people that you talked to that have no idea that that's an inappropriate thing, including the chief, maybe show us that there is a cultural problem?"

Chief Scott did not address whether he believed the agency had a rape culture or not but replied that every moment was a teaching moment.

* * *

It took Michelle a few minutes to gather her files and things. The judge had decided that we did not meet the requirement of clear and convincing evidence of a threat to warrant a restraining order, which was Chief Scott's argument from the beginning. While the judge recognized the statement as a clear rape threat, Chief Scott's involvement with the 10-15 Facebook group that spread rape memes and that he was questioned about this involvement by Congress before being appointed to the position, he did not find in our favor.

I sat, staring at the empty judge's seat, wondering if he would have decided the same way if Scott hadn't had the title of chief. It's hard to say. I felt thankful that Judge Longstreth had allowed me to speak about my history and that he had called Chief Scott on his bullshit. Still, I could not help but feel like I was the one on trial.

Chief Scott testified under oath that he had me investigated by CBP-OPR for speaking about my rape. He testified that CBP was tracking me. He personally contacted former agents I went to the academy with and that I worked with not to investigate my accusations of being raped, but to find any dirt on me. He sat in the courtroom and claimed he was the victim, that I had "attacked" him. He questioned my work as an agent and suggested that I was probably on drugs or alcohol when I responded to him. He called me paranoid.

And I thought to myself, *this is why victims never come forward.*

It was late afternoon, and the sun was beginning to set when we entered the hallway and met Sandi and our two other friends. Andrea had already left. I saw Chief Scott hovering by the elevators, waiting for me. He asked to speak privately, and I hesitated for a moment before agreeing but only in the presence of my attorney. He stated that everyone could stay and listen.

Chief Scott apologized to me. He reiterated that he was not aware that it was a rape threat and said to me and everyone there that he had already taken down the tweet. I thanked him and told him that I did not believe he did not know. Granted the Border Patrol does not investigate rape, but I still could not accept that he did not know.

"Do you remember Karen Walker from Imperial Beach?"

He paused and thought for a moment. "Yeah, I knew Karen!"

"She was my classmate. She had to screw my law instructor to graduate." Chief Scott's face seemed pained by this.

"I really believe in 'Honor First.' I really do," he said.

"The agency has three agents in Tucson Sector on trial for rape right now. Two of which are high-ranking agents. Two of those are serial rapists."

"Yeah, I know."

"Y'all make us file EEO even when it's a criminal act. You're hiding this culture in those files. You damn well know it."

Looking directly at me, Chief Scott said, "Yeah, that's true. We still do that today."

He wouldn't apologize on the record, but he did in private. He wouldn't admit that the Border Patrol has a rape culture, but he did privately. Admitting that the Border Patrol uses EEO to hide their rape culture made the pain I was enduring worth it. All the sleepless nights, the anxiety, PTSD, flashbacks—it was worth it to hear him, a former chief of the Border Patrol, admit the truth.

The rape threat tweet he had assured Judge Longstreth and privately promised me that he would remove has not been deleted. It is still active.

FINAL THOUGHTS

I began writing simply to work through my personal pain and my suicide attempt. Having spent over a decade with various therapists and psychologists trying to understand my life, writing was a last-ditch effort to save myself. Even after my failed attempt, even though my mind was soft with strong anti-psychotics and painkillers, I still wanted to die. My mind was still swirling with those memories, trying to understand what it was about me that made my mother hate me so much. I wanted desperately to know why my father had abandoned me to her drunken tirades and whippings. I couldn't understand why my rapist was more valuable to the Border Patrol than I was. What was so wrong with me that the agency felt it was better to protect this one man than defend me?

Right or wrong, I was someone who deeply desired to belong. I craved the approval of my mother, the attention of my father, and the backing of my agency. I believed that if I did as they asked, if I studied hard enough and graduated with honors, if I kept my mouth shut and my room clean enough, if I was just physically fit enough, was great at shooting and hiking, if I apprehended enough people, if I spoke their language and repeated their lies enough, maybe they would accept me, maybe I would be a part of their family. It is only through years of writing and rewriting that I discovered this about myself.

This is a difficult revelation for me.

I have always thought of myself as a survivor, as someone who is tougher than most because of what I had endured as a child and as an agent. The internal walls that I built to hide my pain, the dissociation from the physical and emotional pain I had endured is what carried me through those difficult times. It is how I got past the whippings, the punches, and the hateful words that my mother used to call me. It is how I dealt with my father always walking out when I needed him the most. It is the only way I survived being raped and the academy where I had to stand next to my rapist every day. It is how I dealt with the retaliation I faced upon reporting to my duty station. But it was these same walls that I believed protected me that also allowed me to cause trauma to others. Walls have a way of blocking out all feelings. They kept any feelings I might have had about traumatizing migrants away too.

As an agent, this meant that I only listened to the agency. I did not go outside of that green family and listen to any other opinions or experiences. Those rare times when someone managed to scale my walls, like when Pedro questioned my actions that evening when I apprehended him, I quickly used my past pain to knock him off and patch the hole. That is, I used my past traumas to justify my actions, actions that traumatized many migrants I encountered. I had been horribly abused, and then I turned around and became an abuser myself.

Another thing about walls: they are temporary. They cannot last, no matter what material they are made of. Mental walls are no different and require constant repair and rebuilding. Whatever you hide on the other side will eventually find its way through. My problems only seemed to disappear, but pain and trauma cannot be ignored. They live in our bodies and in our souls. My traumatic past is a part of what makes me, me.

My core values have never changed. They remained behind my wall where I left them. If anything, writing about my past enabled me to rediscover them. My actions as an agent required me to hide them. I am ashamed to write that, but it is true. I could not wear that uniform and claim that I put the saving of lives first when I chased migrants down dangerous mountain roads, when I enforced laws and policies that intentionally and knowingly sent families out to the most dangerous terrain to cross. I knew migrants were dying because of our actions, and I did not protest. I could not pin that badge to my chest and claim that I was fighting for justice when I knew about the agency's illegal and secret CIT units that obstructed justice. I have known about the coverups of shootings, beatings, deaths, car crashes, and the like for over two decades and kept silent because of my own self-interest. I have known and understood how the agency has maintained its rape culture since the academy. Perhaps if I had stood up and pushed harder for an investigation after my assault, others would not have been raped too.

This is what I must own.

To heal, to save my life, I had to reclaim my core values which meant I had to confess. I had to tear down my walls and face it all. I had to tell the truth. It also meant that I had to tear down the walls built of Border Patrol propaganda and racism. I had to listen to others who had been victimized by my agency, by me. Seeing and admitting my own prejudices and racism required I go into those uncomfortable moments and listen—and believe. It forced me to be open to new and differing ideas, experiences, and opinions.

I am still learning. It is not easy to undo fifty years of systemic racism and rape culture. Sometimes, I find myself getting a polite ass-chewing from a friend or a social media follower. Sometimes, it's not so polite. My initial reaction of anger has lessened now that my walls are down, but it is still there. If you are white, you know what I mean. It's that uncomfortable feeling, that initial urge to say that you are not a racist and then explain all the reasons why you cannot possibly be prejudiced. This, I have learned, is programmed into us by our culture. It is another internal wall that allows us as white Americans to claim we are not racist or xenophobic even though our entire culture and institutions are designed to give us a hand up while at the same time considering anything that helps those of color or the undocumented a handout.

I have learned to walk into that uncomfortableness and sit with it until I understand why. That is what tearing down walls looks like. It is listening to others even when it is painful, even when it is hard. It is being thankful to have friends of different races and countries willing to help you see your faults and how it hurts them. It is believing them and working to change your ways so that they do not suffer trauma.

* * *

Like most American institutions, especially those involved in law enforcement, the U.S. Border Patrol's roots are deeply rooted in white supremacy. The agency was created by white men who sought to remove anyone of Chinese descent after the railroad system was completed. Our immigration laws were written by racist white men. Many of the first Border Patrol agents came from the Texas Rangers and were members of the Ku Klux Klan. They often engaged in lynching and revenge killings with little oversight and no accountability. (See Kelly Lytle Hernandez' book *Migra!*.)

Today, the Border Patrol refuses to recognize any of this history. This revisionist history is a wall that prevents the agency and its agents from ever being honorable. It is the same wall that they have been building and repairing for nearly a century. Behind it lies a wasteland of atrocities like extrajudicial murders, rapes, kidnappings, and beatings. There are nationwide operations like Operation Wetback that saw hundreds of thousands of Mexican-Americans deported to a country they did not know while losing all of their property and possessions, and Operation Gatekeeper that forced over ten thousand human beings to their painful deaths. There are hundreds of Border Patrol killings covered up by the agency's illegal and secret CIT units, and sexual assault cases that were secreted away into the EEO bowels behind that wall.

The Border Patrol walls they think protect them are overflowing just as mine did.

I cannot understand how agents stay in the Patrol today. How can they be proud of ripping thousands of children from their parents' arms? How can they see videos of children languishing in their processing centers, sitting in their own filth and dirty diapers? How can they ignore a dead child lying on a cell floor for over four hours? How can they knowingly send families back to face kidnapping and violence? How can they throw rotten food at people crammed into their processing facilities? How can they use their leather horse reins to whip at human beings? How can they keep over fifteen thousand human souls under a Texas bridge in the hot sun for months? How can they create a system that purposely sends thousands of human beings to their deaths, while demanding medals and awards for trying to rescue them?

If this is "Honor First," if this is what honor and patriotism looks like, then we don't need it.

What the Border Patrol and its agents do not understand is that there is no honor in abusing people, in treating them inhumanely. There is no honor in racism, xenophobia, propaganda, lies, and deceit. There can never be any honor when they refuse to hold agents accountable for murder, rape, assault, and other crimes. There is no honor in throwing people into the deep end of the pool and then jumping in to save them.

There is no honor without humanity.

When I first began to write this book, I argued that the Border Patrol simply needed to be reformed. I believed it was unfair to describe every agent as racist, cruel, and brutal. I thought that if we could just change the management, get the union under control, have independent hiring, better training, more women and agents of color, if we could have a truth and reconciliation panel, then maybe we could turn it around.

My journey since my attempted suicide has been to listen to those I once policed, those I once brutalized. I did not feel that I could demand accountability and reconciliation from my former agency and its agents without first demanding it of myself. This meant that I had to go to places where the undocumented and asylum seekers were. It was in the shelters on both sides of the border, in listening to the testimonies of those victimized by my agency at hearings, in hospital rooms and cafeterias, in churches and schools, in the homes of those who have lost loved ones to agents that would never be brought to justice that I came to understand my own racism, my own prejudices.

I have had the unique experience of being on both sides of the immigration debate. I have seen the internal workings of the agency and its policies, the results of those policies. I understand their culture, their lingo, and I know many of their secrets and how they hide their corruption and crimes. My critique, my testimony, is a problem for them.

I can no longer tiptoe around this.

If you are an agent today, you are wearing a uniform that has nearly a century of human rights abuses under its belt. You are supporting an agency that lies about its past and its present, that is willing to lie before Congress and the American people. If you pin that badge on your chest, you are saying that you agree with taking babies and children away from their families, that you are not bothered by indigenous children wasting away in Border Patrol processing facilities and eventually dying, that secret and illegal teams covering up crimes committed by agents on and off duty is acceptable, that the thousands of human beings pushed out to our deserts and mountains in search of safety who eventually die is fine by you.

How long do you think you can keep that wall up? Why do you think Border Patrol has the highest suicide rate among any law enforcement agency and reached even higher numbers of agents killing themsleves after four years of Trump? This cruelty, this inhumanity, affects you too. It affects your families, your children.

You are building walls because you are afraid. Afraid of your past, afraid of your failures, afraid everyone will find out what a scam the agency is, afraid that everyone will discover you are not that knight in shining armor. Like that wall on the border, it does not make it all go away. It is a false sense of security that will destroy you and your loved ones, and like that ugly border wall you built, it will come crashing down.

If we are to live up to the core values of a democracy, the United States Border Patrol must be abolished.

No, I'm not suggesting open borders. Although I am currently interested in the open borders concept, I have not been able to reconcile my own experiences as an agent with the idea of having no enforcement. The fact is that we live in a time of global climate change, terrorism, mass poverty, and leaders are currently engaged in creating mass migration to destabilize their enemies. This does not mean that the current militarization or war on our border is the answer either. As with most matters, I believe the solution is somewhere in the middle.

The U.S. Border Patrol must be abolished because it cannot be redeemed. Families who have lost loved ones, documented and undocumented people, even many Americans, see that green uniform as akin to the Stasi or Nazi uniform. The brutality and impunity with which the agency and its agents have operated during its nighty-eight-year history is seared into the consciousness and soul of the borderlands and the people who inhabit it. When I write that seeing this uniform makes children cry, women and men run in fear, I am not being hyperbolic. It literally does. We, as a nation, must accept this truth.

But we must do more than change the name and the uniform. As a nation, to simply forge on without addressing the past atrocities committed by this agency and its agents is to throw those memories over a wall. As a nation, we cannot change the past. We cannot change the genocide of indigenous tribes, slavery, Jim Crow laws, the Chinese Exclusion Acts, the Japanese Internment Camps, the brutality of our LGBTQ laws, the criminalization of asylum seekers, the banning of Muslims, the separating of children, or any other state-sanctioned acts of bigotry and violence. All these shameful moments of our American history and many more not listed here have never been addressed fully. We do not like to think back on them, save for a few small paragraphs in a textbook, a documentary or two. As a culture, we and our government would prefer to move on.

Yet, moving on, throwing these atrocities over our collective wall so we don't have to see them, is what traps us in these moments and prevents either side from ever healing. The many traumas that marginalized groups have endured at the hands of white supremacists and white leaders of this country have not faded. They live deep within the cultures of the victims. Whether the trauma is explicitly taught to younger generations or not, it is passed down from parents to their children. It becomes a part of the culture until one day someone says, "Why are we doing this?" The answer usually is, "Because it has always been this way."

Trauma, when left untreated, is passed from generation to generation, often unknowingly. My mother's trauma was passed onto me through her violence and emotional abuse because she never addressed her past. It became part of my life. It affected the choices I made, and I unknowingly passed my trauma onto those I policed, and to my own family. The only way I stopped this cycle was by tearing down my walls and confronting my past. I couldn't just keep going on as if everything was fine—because it wasn't.

The same is true for the U.S. Border Patrol and the trauma they have intentionally caused. We cannot, as a nation, continue to allow this agency designed and built by known white supremacists to exist. There must be a truth and reconciliation committee that tells the true history of the Border Patrol. This project must tell only the truth and not allow white supremacists masquerading as border experts to contaminate it.

Unpleasant as it will surely feel, we must talk about the lynchings, the dousing of migrants with chemicals, the targeting of Asians, the stealing of

Mexican land to give to whites, the rapes, murders, the intentional running over of migrants, sexual assaults of children, deadly pursuits, the covering up of crimes, the Game of Smiles, the Tijuana chokeholds, the Mexican heart attacks, the mass graves of migrants caused by our own border polices. We must admit that our deterrence policies were designed to kill migrants, that we intentionally funneled them into dangerous terrain where we knew they would drown, fall from a cliff, freeze to death, or die of dehydration.

The agency must release all its records of any investigations conducted by the Coverup Incident Teams/Critical Incident Teams. Every single case must be re-examined by independent teams experienced in police coverups. Each case must be corrected, the agents involved must be prosecuted and the families must be allowed to have their voices heard and given restitution. These units will go down in history as the largest coverup or shadow police unit ever seen in the United States. The shame and guilt we as a nation should feel as the truth is revealed in the next couple of years will rival that of the other great American atrocities.

The federal government must open the Equal Employment Opportunity (EEO) files for investigation and analysis by professionals. We must confront how the agency has, and continues to use, according to former Chief Rodney Scott, the EEO process to hide their rape culture. The truth about agents like former Supervisory Border Patrol Agent John Daly III who was recently discovered through DNA analysis to be an alleged serial rapist for the twenty-plus years as he served in the Tucson Sector must come out. Tucson residents deserve to know how much the Border Patrol knew about Daly. Where there EEO complaints from fellow agents? Did he have complaints against him by migrants? Did the Border Patrol cover up any of his crimes as they did for other agents? The agency must come clean about him, and the hundreds of other agents arrested for violent crimes.

When researchers from the Project On Government Oversight (POGO) called me and asked how to prove the Border Patrol had problems with rape culture and domestic violence, I told them not to bother trying to prove the EEO cases. They cannot be proven unless the government opens the files. Even redacted files could easily prove this, but no government official wants to admit how bad the problem is or that EEO is the place these complaints go to die. Instead, I suggested they look at the recent DHS Office of Inspector General (OIG) report that stated CBP and Border Patrol were not adequately documenting domestic violence within their ranks.

This directly violates the Lautenberg Amendment that requires law enforcement agencies to report domestic violence within their ranks. Officers convicted of a misdemeanor within domestic violence laws are required to have their access to guns and ammunition removed. This, in turn, prevents them from serving as law enforcement officers. The Border Patrol and other agencies get around this law by simply not reporting it, talking to victims and telling them not to file or they will lose financial support for their children if their partners lose their jobs, and by working with prosecutors to reach pleas that are less than the domestic violence charges. I have witnessed these scenarios many times.

On April 14, 2022, POGO published their findings in "Misconduct at CBP Runs Deep, and Congress Must Address this Systemic Problem." Not only did they find that DHS-OIG heavily edited their report to try and make the problem of domestic violence not look as bad as it is within their law enforcement ranks, they discovered exactly what I told them would find; over 10,000 DHS law enforcement employees have suffered sexual harassment or assault at their workplace. In 250 cases where DHS paid settlements for employee sexual misconduct, DHS did not even investigate or take disciplinary action against the perpetrators. This is the rape culture I speak of, and it is alive and flourishing unchecked.

But some progress has been made.

On May 3, 2022, CBP Commissioner Chris Magnus issued a memo ordering the abolishment of Border Patrol Critical Incident Teams. While it is unprecedented to have a federal agency admit the existence of secret coverup units and then abolish them, our work is not done. All CIT reports must be made public. Families who've lost loved ones and subsequently had the evidence destroyed by these teams must be told the truth. Agents involved in the coverups must be brought to justice to set an example, to act as a deterrent for other agents.

It is only when we tear down the Border Patrol's walls that we will see the truth, that victims will have their say, that justice can be done, that people can heal.

* * *

When I think about what type of policing should be on the border, I see an agency that is more like the Bureau of Land Management or the Forestry Service. I believe border agents should not only have a law enforcement function, but a humanitarian one as well. This does not mean a fake humanitarian role where they force migrants to cross in dangerous terrain and then rescue them to claim they are do-gooders. I see agents who look less like soldiers and more like Park Rangers. They will not only be charged with preventing people and goods from entering in between the ports of entry without inspection, they will be required to know about the areas they patrol. What Native lands are they on and what is the history of the area they are working? What animals are native to their locations? What are the state and local laws? They must know the communities they are working in by listening and working together.

Border agents must be required to abide by the U.S. Constitution that states all persons, not only U. S. citizens, have the same unalienable rights. Undocumented people have constitutional rights too, as the Supreme Court has already decided under *Yick Wo v. Hopkins (1886)*, *Wong Wing v. United States (1896)* and *Plyler v. Doe (1982)*. No longer will border residents have to deal with checkpoints that violate their 4th Amendment rights against unreasonable search and seizure simply because they live close to the border. Agents must have probable cause before stopping individuals and warrants before entering buildings located near the border, just as is required for all other police searches. Agents would no longer be able to use racial profiling as a reason to stop vehicles. And if agents decide to pursue a vehicle, they must terminate that pursuit if the vehicle violates any traffic laws, just as many other police agencies do now. The sanctity of human life must come first and above all else.

Congress must ensure that border agents are not investigating themselves. There can be no internal investigations because this is a conflict of interest. In all use-of-force cases, only independent agencies can investigate. Such investigation cannot be conducted jointly or compromised by agents. Agents who do compromise cases or try and coverup evidence must be held accountable. That is, actually held accountable by an external system of discipline. The agency must be transparent with the public by naming the agents involved and allow the investigations to evolve without their influence. Agents accused of sexual assault must be investigated by the appropriate local agencies, and any management found to coverup allegations will be charged with obstruction. Border agents can no longer be allowed to resign or collect their retirement before charges are filed.

Most importantly, Congress must stop allowing agents to resign and then be hired as investigators in the same Office of Inspector General (OIG) or Office of Professional Responsibility (OPR) that is doing investigations into their former employers and coworkers. As it stands now, older Border Patrol agents and CBP officers are encouraged to resign and join these two oversight agencies. This is another conflict of interest. Agents may resign and become investigators with either OIG or OPR if they are not investigating their former agencies.

All of this would require that the federal government create a robust and humane asylum system. An asylum seeker's bill of rights should be penned, stating unequivocally that everyone has the right to seek asylum, that asylum is not a crime, and to criminalize someone for seeking asylum is a crime. These rights must permanently enshrine the right for families to stay together, including extended families and different types of families, such as LGBTQ families. Children may never again be taken from their families without legal cause that demonstrates their safety is in jeopardy. Records checks must be done in a reasonable timeframe and if they cannot be, the cause for delay must be documented. Facilities that hold asylum seekers must be clean, humane, and persons must be allowed to move around relatively freely while they wait for their inspections. Translators of the most common languages needed must be on staff, as well as medical professionals. These facilities must include kitchens with staff, janitorial services, trauma counselors, and employees who can assist in finding transportation for seekers to reach their final destinations.

Across America, I envision detention facilities that hire American guards at low pay with poor benefits replaced by immigration centers that assist asylum seekers with language translation, and help them find housing, employment, schools, and faith communities. These centers will also have immigration advisors that no longer penalize immigrants, but rather assist them in understanding what is required of them in the U.S. They will help asylum seekers find advocacy, legal representation, and assist in making appointments and court dates. The goal is to help immigrants succeed while at the same time creating jobs that will provide good pay and benefits, jobs that will not eat at their souls and make them come home angry at the world. With Americans no longer working at the oppressive detention centers, they will find themselves more accepting of immigrants and see their families thrive.

This is not a pipe dream, a naïve liberal concept. There are countries who have designed and built similar systems and they work quite well. None are perfect, and this would require a great deal of work and expertise, but so did creating the brutal and inhumane punitive system we now have. It is a choice: one or the other. The money we now spend on transporting, detention, food, security, and such would pay for this more humane immigration system easily.

Whether we like it or not, Border Patrol is what we have sewn. Do we want to live up to the ideals of our democracy? Do we really believe that all are created equal? In justice? Are we truly a nation that values immigrants?

If we are, then we must find another way.

ACKNOWLEDGMENTS

I am deeply thankful for the lessons of love I received from Grandma and Pop Budd. I did not realize it then, but they showed me what love was. They taught me the beauty of consistency and that love did not have to be traumatic or come at the end of a leather belt. That love was the simplest of things: the picking of vegetables, folding of clothes, running of errands, naps with dogs, laying in the grass watching the clouds float by, the smell of Guntersville lake and brilliant red poinsettias every Christmas. These are the memories I think more about when reflecting on my childhood now. These are what sustain me.

I recognize every day that the beatings I endured at the hands of my mother thickened my skin. I love her deeply. She made me strong enough to survive. I owe much to my father as well. My profound love of music and sarcastic wit come from him. He taught me so much about justice and equality, of how you can preach it and not live it. His constant abandonment when I needed him the most taught me to rely on only myself and gave me the strength to put myself through school, to step off into the unknown and join the Border Patrol.

And yes, I acknowledge the U.S. Border Patrol. I am not that disgruntled employee who couldn't hack it. I excelled in that agency despite all that they threw at me. I am thankful that PAIC Dirtycop threatened my life and forced me out for whistleblowing. Had that not happened, I would have been present for 9/11 and gone through the changes under DHS and CBP. I might have spent decades continuing to justify my actions and those of the agency. I might have found myself in the streets of Portland, Oregon, throwing teargas at Americans protesting against the very brutality that I engaged in. The Border Patrol taught me who I could become, who I did not want to be.

I am grateful for surviving my suicide attempt. To Dr. Christopher Morache, Dr. Amber, and the staff at Sharp Mesa Vista Hospital, who put me back together and helped with my first steps to healing, I say thank you. Your kindness and patience, your dedication, is what began this journey for me. Likewise, I must thank Dr. Marla Vencil, my therapist. Her no-bullshit type of counseling helped me to take responsibility for my life. I learned that I was not just a victim, but in many ways, a participant in my trauma and that it did not absolve me of my own sins. Thanks to Dr. Kwiatkowski, my psychiatrist, for finding a medicine that finally helped me.

Thank you to Judy Kenyon, Teresa Clark, Rachel Nawrocki, Sheri Usselman and Yolande Trinadad for literally always being there. Thank you to Deb and Helen for your encouragement.

To Christian Ramirez, Andrea Guerrero, Lillian Serrano, Hiram Soto, Erin Tsurumoto Grassi, Vicki Guabeca, Chris Wilson, Tomas Perez, Michelle Celleri, Patricia Mondragon, Miesha Rice, and the whole gang at Alliance San Diego and the Southern Borders Community Coalition, thank you all. The patience with which you all listened to my stories, your willingness to see me as someone who desperately wanted to understand my own racism has brought me to this point of understanding and compassion for others. It was not your responsibility to help me tether my soul, but you all did and continue to walk with me into that trauma and pain so that we may all heal.

I want to thank my literary agent, Jessica Craig, who puts up with my constant changes and ideas. I am not easy to work with. She has been a champion of my work, seeing the bigger picture and how it relates to the conflicts we find ourselves as a nation in today. It was Jessica who saw that my book was not only about immigration policy, but about the #MeToo Movement, white privilege, systemic racism, personal and physical walls and their false sense of security, mental illness, politics, rage, vulnerability, and forgiveness.

I'd like to acknowledge and thank three individuals for helping to get this book across the line and published: Jose Vargas and Adrian Escarate of Define America for the encouragement, advice, lessons and inspiration to keep going. Thank you to Barbara Feinman Todd of Georgetown University School of Journalism for assuring me that I could write and that my story was worth telling. Without you three, I think Jessica and I would have thrown in the towel.

To Shannon Coulter of Grab Your Wallet, thank you for your constructive criticism, and taking time to read my drafts. You once told me that people would come to my side and help me accomplish my goals because what I was doing was important and inspiring. You were right.

I want to thank Heliotrope Books and Naomi Rosenblatt for being brave enough to publish this book.

Of course, I would not have survived without the love of my wife, Sandi. She has always stood by me, watching me as I crashed and burned, only to get up and try again. It is because of her that I had the time to heal, time for my journey, time to write and rest. With her, I have that quiet, peaceful kind of love that I had learned from my grandparents. I am safe.

Thank you to all of those who have helped me along the way: Nicole Ramos, Erika Pinheiro, Al Otro Lado, No More Deaths, Border Angles, James Cordero and Dr. Jacqueline Arellano, Green Valley Samaritans, Armadillos Busquesda y Rescate, Water Stations, James Tomsheck, Alyssa Milano, Representative Joaquin Castro, Pedro Ramos, Unified Deported Veterans, Robert Vivar, Hector Lopez, Yesenia Padilla, Maya Contreras, Karoli Kuns, Marrianna Trevino Wright, Linda Rivas, John Kurc, Diana Martinez, Daisy Gardner, Kathy Griffin, Pastor Kaji Dousa, Reverend Beth Johnson, Dr. Reverend Barber, Otay Mesa Detention Resistance, Pueblo Sin Fronteras, Khadija Gurnah, Nathaniel Hoffman, Define American, Freedom for Immigrants, Amnesty International, Anamaria Vasquez, Tiade Elena, Maria Puga, Roxanna Altholz, Taylor Levy, and so, so many more.

More than anyone, I want to thank the people who have allowed me to sit in their space, to hear their stories. To the mothers and fathers who brought their children hundreds and thousands of miles to our southern border and were brave enough to cross and ask for help, I will be here to help you. To the LGBTQ migrants fleeing sure torture and death, I will fight for you every day. To the deported veterans, I will always listen to you. To the unaccompanied children, I will advocate for you. To those who have lost loved ones to the brutal and inhumane policies of the Border Patrol, I promise to work hard to change them. To the immigration attorneys and activists who fight for them all, you are my heroes.

Taking a break in El Paso, Texas, 2021; Photo by John Kurc

AUTHOR BIO

Jenn Budd was a senior patrol agent with the U.S. Border Patrol in San Diego and an intelligence agent at San Diego Sector Headquarters from 1995 to 2001 when she resigned in protest due to the rampant corruption and brutality she witnessed on a daily basis. Since 2015 she speaks out on national and local news, community panels, podcasts and radio. She regularly is consulted by academics, journalists, humanitarians, and lawmakers. She is often interviewed for outlets such as *The New York Times, Newsweek, The Guardian, Washington Post*, NPR, *Telemundo*, CNN, and many more. She is an ambassador for Define American and the Southern Border Communities Coalition (SBCC). She has more than 40K followers on Twitter (@BuddJenn) and her website is **www.jennbudd.com.**

www.ingramcontent.com/pod-product-compliance
Lightning Source LLC
Chambersburg PA
CBHW021226300125
21126CB00011B/206

* 9 7 8 1 9 4 2 7 6 2 9 3 5 *

"Are you not using protection?"

"I pray."

"You pray? What does that mean?"

"I pray for protection. Look, I prayed with my dad, and I just hope it will be a mistake or something. Can you pray for me?" he seriously asked.

I looked at him like he was crazy and quickly looked back at the road. "I can send you positive thoughts, but no, I won't pray for you. It would be disingenuous."

"What does that mean?"

"It means I'd catch fire. I'm not a Christian. You are the one that took the risks. You are the one that chose to do this without protection with God knows how many women."

"I put my faith in God," he exclaimed. "Plus, men don't normally get it from women. It's more common for men to give it to a woman."

"Wait, are you saying that you knowingly had unprotected sex because you thought men could give it to women but not the other way around?"

As it turned out, Zarkowski's test was a false positive. He spent some time trying to sue the maker of the test and the Red Cross, who had discovered it when he donated blood. He claimed that they had caused him emotional damage. I told him that he was the sole cause of his emotional damage.

For this, he never spoke to me again. He is now an investigator in the Office of Inspector General in the Department of Homeland Security, tasked with investigating crimes committed by Border Patrol agents.

* * *

In my second year as a Border Patrol agent, my parents came to visit me after I begged them. As in college, I almost never heard from my father, and only heard from Mom whenever I made the call. I once tried to see how long it would take for them to notice that they had not heard from me, how long it would take for her to pick up the phone and call me. I made it two months before finally giving in and calling them. They were my parents after all, and I missed them.

I took Dad on a ride-along one day so he could see what I did as an agent. I wanted him to be proud of his little girl, riding in those big trucks, running through the mountains alone, chasing down large groups of men who entered our country illegally. While hiking a trail, we stopped for a break and some water under the hot sun. Though he was skinny, my father was never an athletic man. Even though it was a relatively easy walk, I still worried about him.

As we sat on a boulder to catch our breath, he said, "I think you would do well to forgive your mom and me."

The shock of his words bounced around in my brain. We never really talked about my childhood. I knew that he must have known what Mom did to me all those years ago. The physical and emotional abuse could not have escaped him even if he was away most of the time. I cannot recall her ever whipping me in front of him. Maybe he didn't know the severity of it, maybe he did.

"And what exactly is it that you think I should forgive you for?"

I wanted him to say it out loud.

"You know."

"No, please enlighten me, Dad. What is it that I should forgive you and Mom for? Just say it."

"I read this book that said forgiving is what sets you free. That it helps you to move on and gives you power. I just think it would help you," he said.

"Yeah, but forgive what? How am I supposed to forgive you if you won't even acknowledge it? Or is it that you would rather I forgive you so that you can just move on and not feel guilty about it?"

We walked a bit more down the path until I stopped and clicked my mic attached to my shoulder, "10-15 with thirteen."

"What?"

"You just caught your first group, Dad."

He looked into the brush, around back where we came from through a small valley. "I don't see anyone."

"*Levantense!*" I ordered. My fathered jumped back as the group of men and women stood up from under the brush. I told them he was my father and to not cause any trouble. Some smiled and waved at him as a transport van that had been circling us appeared.

"Wow, Jenn. Are you always alone when you find this many people?" he asked.

"Yes, but usually it's at night and usually way more people."

The transport agent and I patted each person down, checked their bags quickly for drugs or weapons, and loaded them into his van. My father never said if it bothered him that I hunted people for a living. I expect it didn't. We continued working the rest of the day, made the hour-long drive back to my apartment, and ate my mother's lasagna she made for us without ever bringing the conversation back up.

* * *

I was ten years old when she started drinking in the open. She kept the bottles of amber liquor on the open kitchen shelves. She later told me she'd